Ivy Global

SAT Subject Test in Mathematics Level 2

Study Guide and 6 Practice Tests

For automatic scoring and scaling, please visit **cloud.ivyglobal.com**.

SAT Subject Test in Mathematics Level 2: Study Guide and 6 Practice Tests, Edition 1.0

This publication was written and edited by the team at Ivy Global

Editor-in-Chief: Ian Greig

Producers: Lloyd Min and Junho Suh

Contributors: Alex Emond, Mark Mendola, Ward Pettibone, and Nathan Tebokkel

Additional Contributors: Sacha Azor, Thea Bélanger-Polak, Grace Bueler, Alex Dunne, Nathan Létourneau, Geoffrey Morrison, Arden Rogow-Bales, Kristin Rose, and Rebecca Teich

About the Publisher

Ivy Global is a pioneering education company that delivers a wide range of educational services.

E-mail: publishing@ivyglobal.com
Website: http://www.ivyglobal.com

Contents

Practice Test 6

Introduction

Section 1
About This Book

Welcome, students, parents, and teachers! This book is intended to help students prepare for the SAT Subject Test in Mathematics (Level 2), a test created and administered by the College Board.

Many colleges and universities in the United States require the SAT as part of the application process, and some of those schools also require or encourage students to submit SAT Subject Test scores.

Our goal is to provide you with tips, tricks, and plenty of practice to help you do your best on the Math Level 2 test. This book will help you turn a challenging admissions requirement into an opportunity to demonstrate your skills and preparation to colleges.

Here's what's inside:

- A breakdown and detailed review of the format of the exam
- Detailed tables of the mathematical concepts you'll be tested on
- Essential techniques for the skills Math Level 2 frequently tests
- Example questions with solutions that demonstrate these concepts and techniques
- 6 full-length practice tests
- Answer keys and full explanations

The first key to succeeding on an SAT Subject Test is knowing the test, so the rest of this chapter provides details about the structure, format, and timing of the Math Level 2 test, along with key strategies to use on the test. Sections 2-7 delve into the content you will encounter on the test. We recommend working through these chapters, taking the practice exams that follow, and reviewing any material related to questions that you found challenging between exams.

Check out our website for additional resources, including review of foundational concepts, extra practice, answer explanations, and online scoring sheets. You'll also find information about upcoming tests, tutoring services and prep classes, and other tips to help you do your best.

Section 2
About the SAT Subject Test in Mathematics (Level 2)

The SAT Subject Test in Mathematics (Level 2), which we'll also refer to as "the Math Level 2 test," is one of twenty supplemental admissions exams that are used to provide measures of student abilities in more narrowly defined subject areas than the SAT.

In this section, we'll discuss the following topics:

- Format and Timing
- Scoring
- FAQ
- Preparing for Test Day

Format and Timing
Part 1

The format of the Math Level 2 test is straightforward. The test lasts exactly 60 minutes and consists of 50 multiple choice questions, each of which has 5 possible answers. This means you should be spending roughly one minute on each question, on average, which will leave you with 10 minutes at the end to check your work or to work on especially difficult questions. Of course, some questions will take you longer than one minute, but some will also take much less time. In general, the questions are ordered from least to most challenging.

There are six broad topics covered on the Math Level 2 test, and they are outlined in the table below.

Numbers and Operations	5-7 Questions
Algebra and Functions	24-26 Questions
Probability and Data Analysis	4-6 Questions
Trigonometry	6-8 Questions
Coordinate Geometry	5-7 Questions
3D Geometry	2-3 Questions

Some questions on the Math Level 2 test will fall somewhere in between two or more of these categories, so it's important to have a good understanding of how different aspects of math are related to each other and how everything fits together.

Each incorrect answer you give on the Math Level 2 test results in a penalty of −0.25 points toward your raw score. (For more information on how the Math Level 2 test is scored, turn the page.) It can be stressful to think about losing points for incorrect guesses. However, even if you're just guessing at random, the points you lose for unlucky guesses will, on average, cancel out the points you gain for lucky guesses, so you'll break even. Therefore, if you can eliminate even one answer option, or if you have any sort of idea at all which answer might be right, you will tend to gain points by guessing. The best strategy for guessing on the Math Level 2 test is to do your best to eliminate some choices and make the best guess you can.

Scoring
Part 2

SAT score reports include lots of different scores that are based on your performance on different subsets of the whole exam. Subject Test score reports are much simpler. Your score on the Math Level 2 test is expressed in three ways, and there are no subscores.

Raw Scores

You will receive a raw score, which is based directly on how many questions you answered correctly and how many you answered incorrectly. Raw scores are calculated differently on the Math Level 2 test than they are on the SAT. On the SAT, your raw score is just the number of questions you answered correctly. On the Math Level 2 test, your raw score is equal to the number of questions you answered correctly, minus ¼ of the number of questions you answered incorrectly. Subtracting ¼ points can leave you with a raw score that includes a fraction. Fractions in your raw score are rounded to the nearest whole number, and half-points are rounded up. Raw scores are used to calculate other scores, but they are not used on their own as a basis for admissions decisions.

Scaled Scores

Your raw score will be used to determine a scaled score, which is a curved score that is based on how you performed compared to other students. Your scaled score is reported on a scale of 200 to 800. If you look up average test scores at the schools to which you're applying, they'll generally be expressed in terms of scaled scores.

Because the scaled score is curved, on some exams it's possible to get a perfect score of 800 without answering all questions correctly if a small enough number of other students answer all questions correctly. The exact curve is different from one test to another, and tables are provided later in the book for scaling your practice tests.

Percentile Scores

Your scaled score will correspond to a percentile score. This score is a simple ranking that shows the percentage of students that you did better than on the exam. Percentile scores give you the clearest idea of how you did in comparison to other students taking the exam. Just as with scaled scores, percentiles differ from one test to another.

Subject Test in Mathematics FAQ
Part 3

In this section, we're going to address some of the questions that students commonly have about the Math Level 2 test.

How Do I Register to Take a Subject Test?

The easiest way to sign up for the exam is on the College Board website: sat.collegeboard.org. If you've already signed up for the SAT, you can log in to the College Board account that you created to register for that exam. If you haven't already registered for the SAT, you'll need to fill out a personal profile form and upload a recognizable photo, which will be included on your admission ticket.

You can also register by mail. To do this, ask your school counselor for The Student Registration Guide for the SAT and SAT Subject Tests, which includes a registration form and a return envelope. You'll need to enclose a photo with this paper registration form.

When you register, you can sign up for your preferred date and location. However, testing centers often run out of room, so make sure you sign up early in order to reserve your place! There is also a cut-off for registrations a month before the test date, after which you'll need to contact the College Board to see if late registration or standby testing is an option.

When Should I Take the Math Level 2 test?

SAT Subject Tests are administered on standard testing dates at locations worldwide throughout the academic year. These standard dates fall in March, May, June, August, October, November, and December. You can see upcoming test dates in your area on the College Board website: sat.collegeboard.org.

Typically, students take the SAT during 11th grade or the beginning of 12th grade. Most students take subject tests after taking the SAT, so they can prioritize SAT prep over subject test prep. However, you should plan to take the exams when you feel most prepared, keeping in mind when colleges will need your scores.

Most subject tests are closely related to subject areas that you might study in a specific class, so you may be best prepared to take the exam at the end of an academic year in which you've taken a challenging course in the subject area. For the Math Level 2 test, that could be any advanced functions or pre-calculus class.

Almost all schools will accept scores through December of your 12th-grade year. However, you should check the admissions information for the schools to which you are applying. If you are planning to apply for Early Admission to any school, you'll need to take the test by November of 12th grade at the very latest.

Can I Retake Subject Tests?

Yes. Just as with the SAT, you're allowed to retake subject tests if you're not happy with your score. However, we don't recommend taking the exam more than two or three times, because you'll get fatigued and your score will start to plateau—especially if you already have a high score (e.g., 700+) and you're just aiming for that perfect 800. Prepare to do your best each time you take the test, and you shouldn't have to re-take it too many times.

In order to give yourself the option to re-take the test, it is always wise to choose a first testing date that is earlier than you need. That way, if you decide you'd like to re-take the test, you won't miss any deadlines.

How Do I Send My Scores to Colleges?

When you sign up for an SAT Subject Test, you can select which schools you'd like to receive your scores. You can also do this after taking the test by logging into your account on the College Board website. If you have taken an SAT Subject Test more than once, the College Board's "Score Choice" program allows you to choose which test results you would like to report to schools.

However, certain schools don't participate in the "Score Choice" program. These schools request that applicants send their full score histories. Even so, most schools have a policy of only considering your highest scores. You can see how your prospective schools consider your scores by visiting their admissions websites.

Should I Still Take the AP Calculus Test If I Am Taking the SAT Math Level 2 Subject Test (Or Vice-Versa)?

AP tests and Subject Tests are used for different purposes, and many students take both.

SAT subject tests are used in the admissions process to help colleges decide which students to admit to their schools. The most competitive schools generally require students to take one or more subject tests. Some schools or programs may require specific subject tests as part of an application, while others may only indicate a certain number of subject tests. Check the admissions policies of the schools you're applying to if you aren't sure whether you need to take subject tests.

AP tests are intended to be used mainly in the placement process, so that students who have completed advanced coursework in high school can skip ahead to more advanced courses in the first year of college. AP tests are meant to show whether individual students have achieved sufficient proficiency for advanced placement, not to reveal fine distinctions between students. However, the challenging coursework involved in taking AP classes and the skill students demonstrate by attaining high scores can enhance an application, and many competitive schools encourage potential applicants to take AP classes.

What's the Difference Between the Math Level 1 and Math Level 2 Tests?

The Math Level 1 test is another SAT Subject Test administered by the College Board. In general, it contains somewhat easier questions than the Math Level 2 test, although the topics covered are quite similar. The Math Level 2 test contains more advanced questions on trigonometry and functions than the Math Level 1. As well, the Math Level 2 test does not technically cover any plane geometry questions, while the Math Level 1 test does.

Although the Math Level 1 test covers simpler content, this does not mean it is easier to score highly on it than on the Math Level 2. This is because the tests are scaled differently, and you are always compared against the other students who took the same test as you. The Math Level 2 test is significantly more popular than the Math Level 1 test, with over twice as many students writing it each year, and it also tends to have a higher average scaled score. Most schools that require a Math subject test require either the Math Level 1 or Math Level 2 test, but some specifically require the Math Level 2 test.

What's a Good Score on the Math Level 2 Test?

Your scores on SAT subject tests are compared with those of other students applying to the same schools, so there's no single "good" score threshold.

Rather, your individual score goals should depend on your admissions goals. A good score will be one that is above average for the schools to which you are applying. Many schools publish statistics about average test scores for admitted students, which you can check to see what's typical for students who are admitted to the schools you're applying to.

When you score your practice tests, you can also estimate how you're doing compared with other students who take the exam by determining your score percentile.

Why Did I Get a Perfect 800 but Only the 79ᵀʰ Percentile?

The scaled score and percentile differ with every Math Level 2 test, but often attaining the highest scaled score on the Math Level 2 test will result in a percentile ranking around the 80th percentile. Nobody knows the mysterious ways of the College Board and their hallowed scales, but we can guess that because most Math Level 2 test-takers are choosing to take the Math 2 test, they will already be significantly better at it than average. So it could be true that everyone on a given Math Level 2 test who got an 800 "only" got a 79th percentile—this just means that 21% of the test-takers scored an 800.

How Many Questions Can I Omit or Get Wrong and Still Score an 800?

Often, a raw score of 44 is enough to achieve a scaled score of 800. This means that you can omit 6 questions or get 5 questions wrong and still score an 800. However, the scaling varies from test to test and depends on the performance of the other students writing it. On some tests, a raw score of 43 might get you a scaled score of 800, but on other tests, a 45 might be needed.

When Should I Use My Calculator?

The answer to this question depends on how comfortable you are with your calculator. You should buy a graphing calculator well in advance of your Math Level 2 test and familiarize yourself with it by reading its manual and using it on all your practice tests. You should keep track of the questions for which you used and didn't use it, and when using it saved time and stress (or not) relative to not using it. Graphing calculators are often only necessary for one or two questions per test, and sometimes for none at all. However, they are very powerful, and can save you time in certain situations. They can also add time in situations where you know you could have solved a question with mental math and a tiny bit of rough work. You should think about using your calculator when a question requires you to visualize a complicated function or determine properties of its graph that are time-consuming to work out by hand—for example, its intercepts, minima or maxima, end behavior, or general shape. Of course, you should use your calculator for any numeric computation that you can't do instantly in your head—there's no need to waste time doing multiplication or addition by hand.

How Do I Improve My Score?

If you took a subject test before doing any prep, then learning and practicing a few basic test-taking strategies can give you a modest score "bump."

Once you've learned the material tested on the Math Level 2 test, as well as a few basic strategies, the key to raising your score is to adopt a long-term strategy and to diligently evaluate your progress. This book provides extensive practice tailored for the Math Level 2 test, and consistent practice over an extended period of time, plus time allotted for reflection, is key to building your test-taking skills.

Test Day
Part 4

All the prep that you're doing now is in anticipation of test day, so it's very important to make sure that day goes as smoothly as possible. Taking a few minutes to plan a sensible schedule and to go over a simple checklist can be as helpful as hours of studying.

Don't stay up the night before the exam. Try to relax, do something mildly stimulating like solving a crossword puzzle or reading a good book, and get plenty of sleep. The night before you take the exam, make sure to set your alarm and plan a time to leave that allows for delays. You need to be on time, or you can't take the test!

Test Day Checklist

As you plan your test morning, here's a checklist to help you remember what you need to bring:

- ☐ Admission ticket
- ☐ Approved photo ID
- ☐ No. 2 pencils and erasers
- ☐ Approved graphing calculator
- ☐ Non-beeping watch
- ☐ Snack and water bottle
- ☐ Directions to the test center and instructions for finding the entrance

Take a deep breath and remember: you are smart and accomplished! Believe in yourself and you will do well.

Basic Strategies for the Math Level 2 Test

The Math Level 2 test is designed to assess your knowledge and understanding of several mathematical concepts as well as your ability to solve problems. Building your mathematical understanding and experience is key to doing well on the exam.

However, like all standardized tests, the Math Level 2 test is also a measure of how well you handle this particular testing format. This means that, in addition to building your mathematical understanding, you need to build your test-taking skills to perform at your full potential.

We're going to outline a variety of strategies that we think are beneficial for most students. However, all students are different: you shouldn't necessarily do everything that we suggest in this section. Try different strategies out as you practice and figure out what works best for you.

In this section, we'll cover the following topics:

- Test-Taking Tips
- Mental Strategies
- Study Strategies

Test-Taking Tips
Part 1

Because the Math Level 2 test is timed and multiple-choice, strategies that help you make the best use of limited time and narrow down your choices can help you improve your score.

Eliminate Incorrect Answers

When you're dealing with a challenging question and you can't quickly identify the correct answer, you can use the process of elimination: instead of trying to figure out what the correct answer is, start eliminating answers that you can identify as incorrect. When the answer choices are numbers, you can sometimes rule out certain options because they are too high or too low. When they are equations or expressions, you can sometimes rule out ones that don't contain a variable or term that you know must be present in the correct answer, or for other reasons. When they are statements, you can rule out options that you immediately know are false. You may be able to eliminate all of the incorrect choices, leaving only the correct answer. Even if you can't, you can at least narrow down the field.

Mark Up the Test Booklet

Many questions on the Math Level 2 test throw lots of pieces of information at you all at once. It can be helpful to circle or underline details in the question or in a given figure or to write down some notes for yourself beside the question. For example, you can write down the values of certain variables in a way that's easier to refer to than a word problem. You can also write down what variable you're trying to find the value of or circle an important stipulation in the question that you might forget about otherwise.

It can also be helpful to mark up the answer choices. Marking the choices you want to eliminate, for example, means that you don't have to consider every choice again if you skip the question and come back to it later. Circling questions that you weren't sure about makes it easier to find them again if you want to come back to them later. Finally, indicating what answer you choose on your test booklet makes it easy to check that you've bubbled in your answers properly at the end of the test.

Picking and Skipping

Pacing yourself during the Math Level 2 test can be a challenge, especially if you come across difficult content before you get to the end. It's easy to spend so long working through a difficult question that you run out of time and never get to other questions you might have found much easier.

Although the questions on the test are roughly arranged in ascending order of difficulty, you can do them in any order you wish. Often, the order of the questions will not exactly correspond to which ones you personally find the most challenging. If you come across a question that seems complicated or time-consuming, or tests something that you don't know about, simply skip it, move on, and save it for later when you've gone through the rest of the test.

Answering out of order makes it easier to bubble answers into the wrong circles on your answer sheet, which is definitely something that you want to avoid. There are a couple of options to address that kind of error, but they're not ideal.

If you only misplaced a few choices, you can erase them and bubble them in correctly. Be sure to erase completely, because stray marks can confuse the grading computer. If you make a big bubbling mistake, talk to the proctor. They have specific directions for how to handle this kind of error. If you need to speak to the proctor, do it promptly: you will have fewer options if you wait until the test is over.

Practice with and without the pick-and-skip strategy before you use it on test day. If you have trouble getting all of your answers in the right bubbles, if it makes you feel unpleasantly anxious, or if you can reliably finish the test without picking and skipping, don't use this strategy on test day.

Be Prepared

It's important to bring the right tools with you on test day. A full checklist of what you should bring can be found in Part 4 of the previous section of this book. However, it's also important to be mentally prepared for the test. Aside from knowing the material, you should have a good idea of what your pace should be, which types of questions you find easy and which ones you find hard, and where certain questions are likely to occur on the test.

The best way to prepare for these aspects of the test is to take a practice test in a real testing environment. Use the pencils, erasers, and calculator you will use on test day, time yourself, and pay attention to your pacing and the amount of time you spend on different types of questions. Practicing your time management skills will allow you to be more comfortable and feel less rushed on the real test.

Sometimes, the Math Level 2 test asks a complex question about otherwise simple math—for example, a question about the magnitude of a line could be disguised by being graphed on the complex plane. But you should also be prepared for some very difficult questions, perhaps including questions that you have no clue how to do. Don't sweat it! If a question confuses you or seems insurmountable, skip it and return to it later if you have time, and try to think about it a different way, perhaps by rearranging its variables or by using analogies to math you already know how to do. Tell yourself before the test that it's okay to skip questions, or to be unsure how to do questions. If this happens, don't panic, and don't let it get inside your head.

Mental Strategies
Part 2

In the previous part, we talked about strategies that help you get more points by working with the format of the test. In this part, we're going to talk about some strategies that help you do better by improving your mental performance during the exam.

Use Healthy Stress

We've already talked about a few things that you might want to avoid if they stress you out. However, not everything that makes you feel nervous is going to hurt your performance. It's very normal to experience nerves before a big event: even experienced athletes and performers still experience pre-game jitters and stage-fright, so it's natural for even well-prepared students to feel some pre-test nerves.

Pre-test nerves can be good for your performance, especially if you have the right frame of mind about it. Mild stressors are stimulating, which means they can improve your memory and focus so that it's easier for you to sustain attention on the exam. It's important to view that kind of healthy stress as an asset: by focusing on the "rush" that you get from the stress and taking it as a sign that it's "go-time," you can maximize the benefits of improved performance and minimize the unpleasant feelings of unease about the test. In other words, don't tell yourself, "Ugh, I'm getting stressed!" Tell yourself, "Hey, I'm getting excited!"

Manage Excessive Stress

While a healthy level of stress can help you on the exam, you don't want too much of it. Excessive stress can slow you down, distract you, or make it harder for you to make decisions.

First of all, you should try to notice when stress may be getting out of hand. It's surprisingly easy not to notice when a little healthy stress crosses over into unpleasant anxiety, so you may need to look for some common signs of how you're feeling.

You might notice that you're becoming preoccupied with negative thoughts. Alternatively, you might feel like your mind is going blank. Either of those can be a symptom of anxiety, especially if you're also experiencing some physical issues like an upset stomach, sweating, or the feeling of being too hot or cold when the room seems to be at a comfortable temperature. Once you notice that you're feeling a little too anxious, there are a few things that you can do to help yourself calm down.

If stress and anxiety are slowing you down, it makes sense to take a break for a few moments so that you can clear your mind. Take a few deep, slow, regular breaths. If you're not sure what counts as deep, slow, and regular breathing, try inhaling to a mental count of 5 and exhaling to a mental count of 7 to get "slow" and "regular." Practice "deep" breathing by breathing all the way from the bottom of your lungs, so that if you place a hand at the bottom of your ribcage you can feel the top of your belly expanding with your breaths.

Positive self-talk, or mentally "saying" positive things to yourself, can also help. The "I'm excited" example above is a form of positive self-talk that can help you. If you're worrying a lot about how you're going to do, mentally telling yourself, "I've got this" or, "I aced this in practice" can also help.

Doing something physically relaxing can also help. Obviously, you're somewhat limited when you're taking the exam: you can't hop up from your desk for a quick yoga routine or a couple of laps. However, you can do some shoulder or neck rolls, or you can inconspicuously flex and relax your calves or other muscles to relieve tension.

Finally, if test anxiety is consistently a big problem for you, talk to a parent, guardian, or school guidance counselor and let them know so they can help you come up with other strategies for recognizing and managing your anxiety.

Study Strategies
Part 3

In addition to taking a strategic approach to the exam itself, you can arrange your studies in ways that help you get the most out of your time.

Pace Your Studying According to Your Test Schedule

Students sometimes wonder whether it's better to study a little bit at a time for many weeks before an exam, or to study a lot shortly before one. It's actually good to do some of both.

Studying a little each day for a long period of time is a more effective way of learning and remembering things than studying a lot over a short period. Ideally, you should plan a consistent, achievable study schedule that gives you plenty of time to get ready for the exam.

That said, studying more intensively right before you take a test can also be helpful. You should try to spend at least a few days leading up to the Math Level 2 test focusing your studies more narrowly on Math than usual and spending extra time studying if you can. Don't stay up to "cram" the night before the exam, though. In fact, don't stay up at all: spend the evening before the exam doing something fun and mildly stimulating—some light recreational reading, for example—eat a healthy meal, and get to bed at a reasonable hour.

Finally, you should figure out if the times you've picked for regular studying are really working for you, because the time of day can affect how well you learn. Some people find that they retain information best if they study just before bed because they dream about the material that they were studying; other people find that they retain information better if they study earlier in the afternoon because they're not as mentally sharp just before bed. Set aside regular study times that match your needs.

Take Timed Practice Tests

There's been a lot of research into how students can best improve their scores on standardized tests, and one of the most consistent findings is that realistic timed practice has a big impact. There are a lot of reasons this might be true: you get to practice your pacing, you get better at using test-taking strategies to work through the exam, you get more emotionally comfortable with the testing environment, and thinking about the content under test-like conditions makes it easier for you to remember relevant information on test day.

However you schedule your studies, be sure to make time for full, timed practice tests. That means at least one hour of uninterrupted, quiet study time in an environment with limited distractions.

Reflect After Taking Practice Tests

One of the most important skills you can develop during your studying is self-awareness. Know what kind of questions you like, what you don't, what you're good at, what you aren't, and what good and bad habits you have (e.g. getting bored, distracted, sleepy, or careless, twirling your pencil, erasing unnecessarily, or second-guessing yourself). This section will give you some ideas for how you might improve your self-awareness by reflecting after taking practice tests.

When you take a practice test, pay attention to how you feel when completing a question, how long it takes you, how easy it is to remember necessary facts, whether you had to reread the question or draw diagrams or use your calculator, whether you had to erase or scratch out your rough work, and what the outcome of second-guessing yourself or changing your answer was.

After you finish a practice test, compare all of this to the outcome of each question. If there's a mismatch—if you feel confident but answer incorrectly or feel uncertain but answer correctly—then you need to refine your studying habits or test-taking techniques. To determine when to change your answer, for instance, count your changed answers. Everyone regrets changing a right answer to a wrong one, but sometimes we don't even remember changing a wrong answer to a right one. And the frustration you feel from changing one right answer to one wrong one might overwhelm the satisfaction you feel from changing ten wrong answers to ten right ones, so you might incorrectly conclude that you should never change your answer, when really you should! This differs for everyone, though, which is why it's important to evaluate yourself and figure out what works best for you.

Most importantly, after a test, review your answers, the questions, and the answer explanations for questions that you missed or that were "mismatched." Once you've reflected on individual questions, look for patterns. Do you have particular trouble with a certain math topic, or with certain equations or diagrams? Sometimes just being aware of your patterns is enough to improve. Other times, once you've identified a pattern, you can come up with a strategy that might help you overcome it. Make sure this strategy is as specific and concrete as possible. For example, don't say to yourself, "I will pay attention to different units," because you're already trying to pay attention to different units, and that wasn't working. Instead, figure out how you will pay attention to different units, so perhaps say something like, "I will circle each different unit in a question that uses more than one unit."

By paying attention to how you feel during a test and comparing it to your test results, revisiting challenging questions, reflecting on answer explanations, and developing specific strategies, you can use material that you've already worked through to discover new information about your problem-solving process, which will improve your ability to make active choices about how you approach questions.

Math Review

Section 1
Numbers and Operations

The Math Level 2 Subject Test includes roughly 5-8 questions per test on the properties of numbers, particularly integers. These questions test your understanding of complex numbers, basic properties of integers, matrices, sequences, series, and occasionally logic. These topics can be difficult to study together because they are quite different, and they all require different skills. This section will cover what you need to know for each of these topics.

Number Theory

Number Theory is a branch of math that deals with, well, numbers—usually positive integers. Below is a table of the concepts from this branch that you will need to know for the Math Level 2 test.

Term	Definition	Example
Integer	A whole number that can be positive, negative, or 0	4, 0, and –7 are integers, but 2.5 and π are not.
Even Number	An integer that is divisible by 2	2, 4, 6, 0, and –4 are all even. Often, if you know a number is even, it can be helpful to write it as $2k$, where k is an integer.
Odd Number	An integer that is not divisible by 2	1, 3, 5, and –7 are all odd. Often, if you know a number is odd, it can be helpful to write it as $2k + 1$, where k is an integer.
Factor (or Divisor)	A positive integer that divides evenly into another positive integer	The factors of 12 are 1, 2, 3, 4, 6, and 12. Factors come in pairs—in the list above, $1 \times 12 = 12$, $2 \times 6 = 12$, and $3 \times 4 = 12$. Whenever you find a factor of a number, you also find another factor that goes with it to multiply to the number.

Prime Number	A positive integer whose only factors are 1 and itself. Positive integers that are not prime (other than 1) are called composite numbers.	2, 3, 5, and 7 are all prime. 9 is not prime because 3 is a factor of 9. 1 is not considered a prime number. 2 is the only even prime number, because every other even number is divisible by 2 (as well as 1 and itself).
Prime Factorization	A representation of a positive integer as a product of prime numbers	Every positive integer can be broken down into prime factors. For example, $60 = 2 \times 2 \times 3 \times 5$. To find the prime factorization of a number, you can start by finding any factor, and writing the number as a product of that factor and another number. Then you can continue breaking these numbers down, until you are only left with prime numbers. For example, you could start by writing $60 = 6 \times 10$, and then rewrite 6 as 2×3 and rewrite 10 as 2×5. You would end up with $60 = 2 \times 2 \times 3 \times 5$, the prime factorization.
Remainder	The amount left over after performing division	When 13 is divided by 5, the remainder is 3, because 5 goes into 13 twice and 3 is left over.

Example Question	Solution
183 cars are parked in rows so that each row contains the same number of cars, except for the last row, which contains only 3 cars. Which of the following could NOT be the number of cars in each row? A) 10 B) 12 C) 15 D) 20 E) 24	To answer this question, you should realize that 183 must have a remainder of 3 when divided by the number of cars in each row, because you are told there are 3 cars left over. If you ignore the last row of cars, there are 180 of them arranged in a grid. Therefore, the number of cars in each row must be a factor of 180. Of the numbers listed, only 24 is not a factor of 180, so there could not be 24 cars in each row.

Essential Technique: Logic

This section is tangentially related to number theory, because numbers and logic are intimately linked. Occasionally, the Math Level 2 test will ask you to make inferences about statements of the form "If P, then Q." There are four related statements to know: first, the "If" statement, "If P, then Q." P and Q are sub-statements. To test whether an "If" statement is true, assume that P is true and then decide whether Q must also be true. If so, the statement is true; otherwise, it's false.

The "If" statement is logically equivalent to its contrapositive, which takes the form "If not-Q, then not-P." This means that if an "If" statement is true, its **contrapositive** is also true, and if an "If" statement is false, its contrapositive is also false.

The "If" statement is not logically equivalent to its **converse**, which takes the form "If Q, then P," nor to its **inverse**, which takes the form "If not-P, then not-Q." This means that the truth or falsity of an "If" statement cannot tell you anything about the truth or falsity of its converse nor of its inverse. Let's see what all these Ps and Qs look like in an actual example.

Example Question	Solution

Which of the following are true?
 	
   I.   If $x = y$ then $x^2 = y^2$.
   II. If $x^2 = y^2$ then $x = y$.
   III. If $x \neq y$ then $x^2 \neq y^2$.
 	
A) I only
B) III only
C) I and III only
D) II and III only
E) I, II, and III
	The correct answer is (A). You can tell that (I) is true by assuming that $x = y$ and realizing that x^2 must also equal y^2. To test (II), start by assuming that $x^2 = y^2$ and ask yourself whether x must equal y. The answer is no, since x could equal $-y$ instead (for example, $5^2 = (-5)^2$, but $5 \neq -5$). It looks a little harder to evaluate (III), but you can do it quickly if you realize that it's the contrapositive of statement (II). Since (II) is false, you know its contrapositive must also be false, so (I) is the only true statement.
	
	You could have evaluated statement (III) on its own, but being able to recognize patterns in the structure of logical statements can save you time on the test.

Complex Numbers

Term	Definition	Example
Imaginary Number	The square root of -1 (written as i), or multiples of it, which do not exist in the set of real numbers	$i = \sqrt{-1}$
Complex Number	The sum of a real number and an imaginary number, which has the form $a + bi$, where a and b are real numbers	$3 + 2i$ $5 - 10i$
Pattern of Powers	$i^1 = i$ $i^2 = -1$ $i^3 = -i$ $i^4 = 1$	$i^5 = i^1 = i$ $i^{5055} = i^3 = -i$

| Complex Plane | A system of graphing complex numbers in which the horizontal axis is used for the "real" part of the number and the vertical axis is used for the "imaginary" part. Every complex number is represented by a point in this plane. | 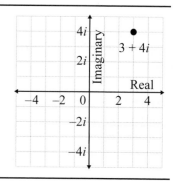 |

Essential Technique: Simplifying Complex Numbers

When working with complex numbers, it helps to know how to use differences of squares and FOIL to simplify expressions—both techniques help transform expressions involving i into expressions involving i^2, which can be replaced by –1. These techniques are shown in the example question below.

Example Question	Solution
If $i = \sqrt{-1}$, what is the value of $\dfrac{1}{2+i}$? A) $-\dfrac{i}{2}$ B) $-\dfrac{2-i}{5}$ C) 1 D) $\dfrac{2-i}{5}$ E) $\dfrac{2+i}{5}$	The correct answer is (D). When a complex number appears in the denominator of a fraction, you can simplify it by multiplying by an expression that will result in a difference of squares. Since you know that $i = \sqrt{-1}$ and therefore that $i^2 = -1$, this difference of squares will allow you to substitute –1 for i2 : $$\frac{1}{2+i} \times \frac{(2-i)}{(2-i)}$$ $$= \frac{2-i}{4-i^2}$$ $$= \frac{2-i}{4-(-1)}$$ $$= \frac{2-i}{5}$$

Matrices

Although matrices generally account for no more than one question per Math Level 2 test, it will help you to know how to add and multiply them.

Term	Definition	Example
Matrix	A rectangular array of numbers. An $m \times n$ matrix has m rows and n columns.	$\begin{bmatrix} 3 & 0 & -1 \\ -2 & 8 & 3 \end{bmatrix}$ This is a 2×3 matrix.
Matrix Addition	To add or subtract two matrices of the same dimensions, add or subtract each component separately. Matrices with different dimensions cannot be added or subtracted.	$\begin{bmatrix} 2 & 7 \\ -4 & 5 \\ 0 & -1 \end{bmatrix} + \begin{bmatrix} 3 & 4 \\ -2 & 0 \\ 6 & 1 \end{bmatrix} = \begin{bmatrix} 5 & 11 \\ -6 & 5 \\ 6 & 0 \end{bmatrix}$
Multiplying a Matrix by a Scalar	To multiply a matrix by a scalar, multiply every number in the matrix by that scalar.	$3 \begin{bmatrix} 0 & -2 \\ 3 & 2 \end{bmatrix} = \begin{bmatrix} 0 & -6 \\ 9 & 6 \end{bmatrix}$
Matrix Multiplication	Two matrices can be multiplied together if the number of columns of the first matrix is equal to the number of rows of the second. For example, you could multiply a 2×1 matrix by a 1×2 matrix. The result would be a 2×2 matrix.	$\begin{bmatrix} 1 \\ 2 \end{bmatrix} \times [0 \; -4] = \begin{bmatrix} 0 & -4 \\ 0 & -8 \end{bmatrix}$

Essential Technique: Matrix Multiplication

Matrix multiplication is only defined when the number of **columns** of the first matrix is equal to the number of **rows** of the second. In general, if you multiply an $m \times n$ matrix by an $n \times p$ matrix, the result will be an $m \times p$ matrix. You can think of crossing out the two "n"s and being left with "$m \times p$." Let's work through an example and see how to carry out this multiplication.

1. Let's say you want to multiply the following two matrices: $\begin{bmatrix} 2 & 3 & -1 \\ 0 & -2 & 4 \end{bmatrix} \times \begin{bmatrix} -3 & 1 & 0 & 4 \\ -2 & -2 & 5 & 0 \\ -1 & 3 & 3 & 1 \end{bmatrix}$

Before doing anything else, you should ask yourself whether these two matrices can even be multiplied together. In this case, the first has 3 columns, and the second has 3 rows, so they can be multiplied. Since you're multiplying a 2×3 matrix by a 3×4 matrix, the result will be a 2×4 matrix. You can write down an empty 2×4 matrix and fill in the cells one by one.

$$\begin{bmatrix} \square & \square & \square & \square \\ \square & \square & \square & \square \end{bmatrix}$$

2. Let's start by finding the entry in the first row and the first column of our solution. Look at the first row of the first matrix and the first column of the second matrix. These are lists of numbers.

$$\begin{bmatrix} 2 & 3 & -1 \end{bmatrix} \text{ and } \begin{bmatrix} -3 \\ -2 \\ -1 \end{bmatrix}$$

3. Multiply the first number in each list, the second number in each list, and the third number in each list—and then add those three results. The answer is the entry in the first row and the first column.

$$\begin{bmatrix} -11 & \square & \square & \square \\ \square & \square & \square & \square \end{bmatrix}$$

$$[2 \times (-3)] + [3 \times (-2)] + [(-1) \times (-1)]$$
$$= -6 - 6 + 1$$
$$= -11$$

4. Now, you need to repeat this process for the next entry. To find the entry in the **first** row and the **second** column, take the **first** row of the first matrix and the **second** column of the second matrix, and perform the same operation.

In this case, you get the lists $\begin{bmatrix} 2 & 3 & -1 \end{bmatrix}$ and $\begin{bmatrix} 1 & -2 & 3 \end{bmatrix}$, so the result will be:

$$\begin{bmatrix} -11 & -7 & \square & \square \\ \square & \square & \square & \square \end{bmatrix}$$

$$[2 \times 1] + [3 \times (-2)] + [(-1) \times 3]$$
$$= 2 - 6 - 3$$
$$= -7$$

5. Continue performing this operation for every cell in your solution matrix.

Remember: to find the entry in the jth row and the kth column of your solution, look at the jth row of the first matrix being multiplied, and the kth column of the second. Eventually, you will fill in all the cells of your solution. You have your answer!

$$\begin{bmatrix} -11 & -7 & 12 & 7 \\ 0 & 16 & 2 & 4 \end{bmatrix}$$

If $A = \begin{bmatrix} 2 & 3 \\ 0 & -1 \end{bmatrix}$ and $B = \begin{bmatrix} 1 & 7 & -3 \\ -2 & 0 & 2 \end{bmatrix}$,

what is the product AB?

A) $\begin{bmatrix} -4 & 14 & 0 \\ 2 & 0 & -2 \end{bmatrix}$

B) $\begin{bmatrix} -4 & 2 \\ 14 & 0 \\ 0 & -2 \end{bmatrix}$

C) $\begin{bmatrix} 2 & 21 & -3 \\ 0 & 0 & 2 \end{bmatrix}$

D) $\begin{bmatrix} 2 & 5 \\ 14 & 21 \\ -6 & -11 \end{bmatrix}$

E) $\begin{bmatrix} 2 & 21 \\ 0 & 0 \end{bmatrix}$

The correct answer is (A). Since A is a 2×2 matrix and B is a 2×3 matrix, the product AB exists and will have dimensions 2×3 (note that the product BA does not exist)! Using the formula for matrix multiplication, the product AB is equal to.

$$\begin{bmatrix} 2 \times 1 + 3 \times (-2) & 2 \times 7 + 3 \times 0 & 2 \times (-3) + 3 \times 2 \\ 0 \times 1 + (-1) \times (-2) & 0 \times 7 + (-1) \times 0 & 0 \times (-3) + (-1) \times 2 \end{bmatrix}$$

$$= \begin{bmatrix} -4 & 14 & 0 \\ 2 & 0 & -2 \end{bmatrix}$$

Sequences and Series Matrices

Term	Definition	Example
Sequence	An ordered list of numbers. In general, "sequence" refers to an infinite sequence. Sequences can be defined by a formula or simply by listing the numbers in some pattern.	$2, 3, 6, 11, 18, 27, 38, 51, 66, \ldots$ $x_n = n^2 + 2$ where $n = 0, 1, 2, \ldots$ These are two different ways of writing the same sequence. The first way shows the first few terms of the sequence, while the second provides a general rule.
Arithmetic Sequence	A sequence in which the difference between any two consecutive terms is a constant. This constant is called the **common difference**, often denoted d. The general rule for a term of an arithmetic sequence is $x_n = a + dn$, where a is the first term in the sequence, and $n = 0, 1, 2, \ldots$	$x_n = 2 + 3n$ $2, 5, 8, 11, 14, 17, 20, \ldots$
Geometric Sequence	A sequence in which the ratio between any two consecutive terms is a constant. This constant is called the common ratio, often denoted r. The general rule for a term of a geometric sequence is $x_n = ar^n$, where a is the first term in the sequence, and $n = 0, 1, 2, \ldots$	$x_n = (-2)^n$ $1, -2, 4, -8, 16, -32, 64, -128, \ldots$
Recursive Sequence	A sequence that is defined in terms of previous terms in the sequence. Often, sequences defined recursively do not have an explicit formula for their nth term, unlike arithmetic and geometric sequences.	$x_0 = 1$ $x_1 = 1$ $x_n = x_{n-1} + x_{n-2}$ This recursive definition defines the Fibonacci sequence $1, 1, 2, 3, 5, 8, 13, \ldots$ It says that any term (x_n) can be found by adding the previous two terms (x_{n-1} and x_{n-2}) together.

Series	The sum of all the elements in a sequence. In general, "series" refers to an infinite series. For many sequences, trying to add up all their terms does not make sense, since the numbers keep growing and so their sum will tend toward infinity (or negative infinity). However, certain geometric series have a well-defined sum.	The series made from the sequence 1, 2, 3, 4, 5, 6, … does not have a sum because the sum will grow to infinity. The series made from the sequence $1, \frac{1}{2}, \frac{1}{4}, \frac{1}{8}, \frac{1}{16}, \frac{1}{32}, \ldots$ has a sum equal to 2. Imagine having a full pie, then having half of a second pie, then a quarter of that pie, then an eighth of that pie, and so on—you would never finish your second pie!
Geometric Series	A series made from a geometric sequence. If $\lvert r \rvert < 1$, the series will have a finite sum, which is given by the formula $$S = \frac{a}{1-r}$$ where a is the first term in the sequence.	$$2, -\frac{2}{3}, \frac{2}{9}, -\frac{2}{27}, \frac{2}{81}, \ldots$$ This sequence has a common ratio of $-\frac{1}{3}$, so its series will have a finite sum. That sum is equal to $$\frac{a}{1-r}$$ $$= \frac{2}{1-\left(-\frac{1}{3}\right)}$$ $$= \frac{2}{\left(\frac{4}{3}\right)}$$ $$= \frac{3}{2}$$

Section 2
Algebra and Functions

Algebra and Functions is the broadest and most common question category on the Math Level 2 test, making up 24-26 questions—roughly half the test! These questions test your understanding of various types of functions and expressions, the different ways they can be represented, the ways their equations relate to their graphs, and the ways their equations can be manipulated, as well as the idea of a function as an abstract concept.

Many simpler concepts, such as solving linear and quadratic equations, factoring, and manipulating rational, radical, and exponential expressions, are not covered in this book. For more information on these concepts, please refer to Ivy Global's SAT 6 Practice tests book.

What Is A Function?

You can think of a function as a machine that contains a rule for transforming an input number into an output number. The set of all possible input numbers is called the function's **domain**. The set of all possible output numbers is called its **range**.

Often, functions you will encounter on the Math Level 2 test have some sort of algebraic rule for determining what their output is. For example, consider the function that, when you input a number x, outputs the number $x^2 + 3$. So, if you input the number 4, it will calculate $4^2 + 3 = 19$, and output 19. If this function is called f, we write its equation as $f(x) = x^2 + 3$. We calculated above that $f(4) = 19$. Sometimes, functions will be presented in a table, graph, or some other way, instead of as an equation. Sometimes, functions can take more than one input at a time. For example, the function $f(x, y) = x^2 + y$ takes an ordered pair of real numbers as an input and returns a real number as an output. For example, $f(3, 5) = 3^2 + 5 = 14$, and $f(5, 3) = 5^2 + 3 = 28$.

Term	Definition	Example
Function	A relationship between sets that associates each number in the input set (the domain) with one number in the output set (the range)	$f(x) = 2x + 3$ $g(x) = 4x^2 - 7x + 1$ $h(x) = 5$

Domain	The set of all possible numbers that a function can take as its input. On the Math Level 2 test, you can assume that all functions have a domain equal to all real numbers, unless there is a reason to conclude otherwise.	The function $f(x) = 2x + 3$ can take any real number as its input. The function $g(x) = \dfrac{3}{x}$ can take any real number except 0 as its input, because dividing by 0 is not defined.
Range	The set of all possible numbers that a function can output	The function $f(x) = 2x + 3$ can output any real number. The function $g(x) = x^2$ can only output nonnegative real numbers, since no negative number is the square of any real number.
One-to-one Function	A function in which no two inputs produce the same output	The function $f(x) = 2x + 3$ is one-to-one. The function $g(x) = x^2 + 3$ is not one-to-one because, for example, $x = 4$ and $x = -4$ produce the same output.
Inverse Function	The inverse of a function is the function that "reverses" the direction of the original function. That is, if a function f has $f(a) = b$, then the function f^{-1} ("f inverse") has $f^{-1}(b) = a$. To find the inverse of a function algebraically, replace x with $f^{-1}(x)$ and $f(x)$ with x, and then solve to isolate $f^{-1}(x)$. Only one-to-one functions have inverses.	If $f(x) = 3x + 2$, then $f^{-1}(x) = \dfrac{x-2}{3}$. If $g(x) = x^3 - 8$, then $g^{-1}(x) = \sqrt[3]{x+8}$ If $\sin^{-1} x = \sin x$, then $h^{-1}(x) = \sin^{-1} x$. (Note that $\sin^{-1} x$ has a domain of $-1 \le x \le 1$, and a range of $-\dfrac{\pi}{2} < h(x) < \dfrac{\pi}{2}$). If $f(x) = 2^x$, then $f^{-1}(x) = \log_2 x$.
Graph	A representation of a function on the xy-plane. The points that lie on the graph of the function are all of the form $(x, f(x))$.	This is the graph of all points satisfying the function $f(x) = x^2 + 3$.

Even Function	A function for which $f(x) = f(-x)$ for all values of x. Even functions are symmetric when reflected across the y-axis.	$f(x) = \cos x$ $g(x) = 3x^2 + 7$
Odd Function	A function for which $f(x) = -f(-x)$ for all values of x. Odd functions are symmetric when rotated $180°$ around the origin.	$f(x) = \sin x$ $f(x) = 4x^3$
Argument	The number or variable that a function takes as its input. This is the term that goes inside the brackets of a function.	The argument of $f(x)$ is x. When you write $f(3)$, you are evaluating the function f with the argument 3.

Types of Functions

There are several common types of functions that you will encounter on the Math Level 2 test. The table below outlines what they are and what their graphs look like.

Term	Standard Equation	Constants	Graph
Linear	$f(x) = mx + b$	m is the **slope** b is the *y*-**intercept** For more information on equations and graphs of lines, refer to Chapter 2 Section 5, Coordinate Geometry.	$f(x) = -4x + 9$ 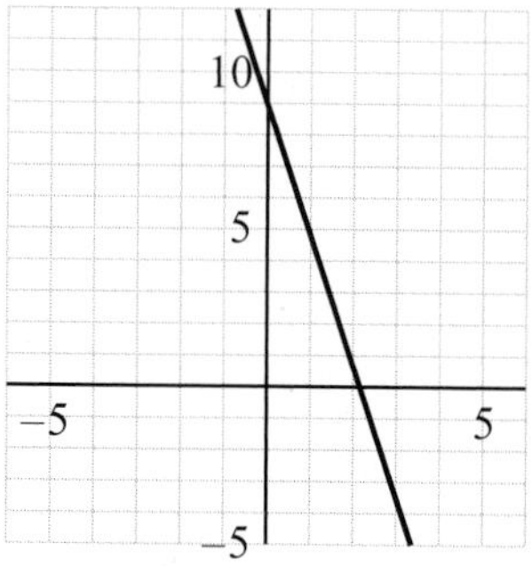
Quadratic	$f(x) = a(x - h)^2 + k$	a is the **stretch factor** (h, k) is the **vertex** The shape formed by a quadratic function is called a **parabola**. It will open upward if a is positive and downward if a is negative. To convert a quadratic function or equation into the form shown here, you may need to complete the square. This is described in Chapter 2 Section 5, Coordinate Geometry.	$f(x) = 2(x - 3)^2 + 1$ 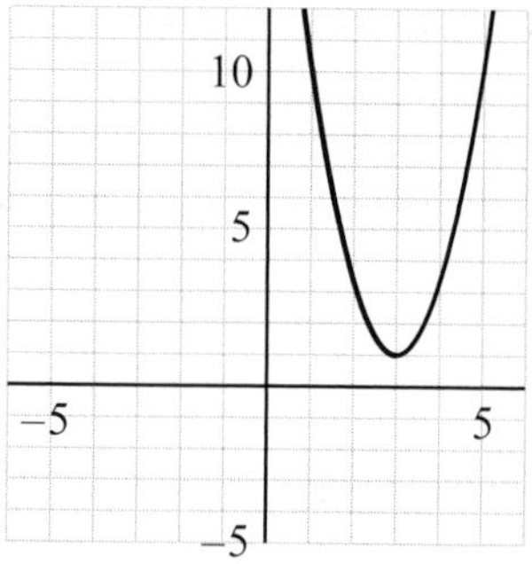

Polynomial	$f(x) = a_n x^n + a_{n-1}$ $x^{n-1} + \cdots + a_1 x + a_0$	n is the **degree** of the polynomial A polynomial function of degree n can have as many as $(n-1)$ points at which it changes direction, and can have as many as n x-intercepts. Polynomial functions of an even degree either go upward or downward toward both the left and right of their graphs. Polynomial functions of an odd degree go upward toward one direction and downward toward the other.	$f(x) = 3x^7 - 4x^6 + 9x^4 + x$
Rational	$f(x) = \dfrac{P(x)}{Q(x)}$ where P and Q are polynomials.	See the section below for more detailed information on rational functions.	$f(x) = \dfrac{1}{2x}$
Radical	$f(x) = \sqrt[n]{x}$	When n is even, the domain of the function will only include values of x that make the expression under the root nonnegative. When n is odd, the domain will be all real numbers. Remember that $\sqrt[n]{x}$ is the same as $x^{\frac{1}{n}}$ —this can be helpful when manipulating expressions involving radicals.	$f(x) = \sqrt{x-1}$

Exponential	$f(x) = ar^{tx}$	When modeling exponential growth or decay of a quantity, a is the **initial quantity** r is the **growth factor** t is the number of times the quantity changes by the growth factor per unit of time, x	A bacterial colony starts with 10 cells and triples in number every 5 hours: $f(x) = 10(3)^{0.2x}$
Logarithmic	$f(x) = \log_a x$	The domain of a logarithmic function will only include values of x that make the expression inside the logarithm positive.	$f(x) = 2 \log_7 x$
Trigonometric	$f(x) = \sin x$ $g(x) = \cos x$ $h(x) = \tan x$	For more information on trigonometric functions, refer to Chapter 2 Section 4, Trigonometry.	$f(x) = \cos x$

Essential Technique: Synthetic Division

Sometimes, you will be required to divide a higher-degree polynomial by a lower-degree polynomial, usually a linear polynomial, as a step in factoring it, to determine whether it has removable discontinuities or asymptotes, or to otherwise understand its behaviour. The easiest way to do this is through synthetic division. Let's say you're dividing $x^4 + 3x^3 - 11x^2 - 3x + 10$ by $x - 2$. Set up the synthetic division by writing the coefficients of the polynomial you are dividing in the top row in order, starting with the highest term. If you are dividing by $(x - a)$, write a in the bottom left. In this case, $a = 2$.

$$2 \quad \begin{array}{|ccccc} 1 & 3 & -11 & -3 & 10 \\ \hline \end{array}$$

The first step is easy: just bring down the first coefficient to below the horizontal line. Next, multiply the number below the line by the number on the left, and write that number below the second coefficient. Add the numbers vertically, write the sum below them, and repeat the process as you work your way to the right.

$$
\begin{array}{r|rrrrr}
2 & 1 & 3 & -11 & -3 & 10 \\
  &   & 2 & 10 & -2 & -10 \\
\hline
  & 1 & 5 & -1 & -5 & 0 \\
\end{array}
$$

If the polynomial expression is divisible by the linear expression, the rightmost number below the line will be 0. If you don't end with a 0, then you are left with a remainder and you know that the polynomial is not divisible by the linear expression. The numbers below the line simply give the coefficients for the solution: $x^3 + 5x^2 - x - 5$. This means that

$$
\frac{x^4 + 3x^3 - 11x^2 - 3x + 10}{x - 2} = x^3 + 5x^2 - x - 5.
$$

Because you are dividing, the degree of the resulting polynomial will always be one less than you started with. If you start with a 4th degree polynomial, the solution starts with an x^3 term instead of an x^4 term.

Rational Functions

Rational functions consist of a polynomial (possibly a quadratic, linear, or constant function) divided by another polynomial. They often include some sort of discontinuity at values of x for which the denominator is equal to 0. Here is the graph of the simplest rational function, $f(x) = \frac{1}{x}$.

You can see that this graph has two disconnected pieces—one when $x > 0$ and one when $x < 0$. Often, rational functions have domains that are not equal to all real numbers, since they are not defined at x-values that make their denominator equal to 0.

Term	Definition	Example
Vertical Asymptote	A vertical line (a certain x-value) that the function approaches but never reaches. In rational functions, this occurs at an x-value that makes the denominator 0 but the numerator non-zero.	The function $f(x) = \frac{1}{x-2}$ has a vertical asymptote at $x = 2$.
Horizontal Asymptote	A horizontal line (a certain y-value) that the function approaches but never reaches. The y-value of this line depends on how the function behaves as x gets infinitely positive or infinitely negative.	The function $f(x) = \frac{7x+4}{x-1000}$ has a horizontal asymptote at $y = 7$. This is because, as x grows to infinity, the constant terms have an increasingly small impact on the value of the numerator and denominator, and all that is relevant is the ratio $\frac{7x}{x} = 7$.

Removable Discontinuity (or "Hole")	An x-value at which a rational function is undefined but near which it does not behave erratically (unlike an asymptote). This occurs at an x-value that makes both the numerator and denominator equal to 0.	The function $\dfrac{x^2 - 5x + 6}{x - 2}$ has a removable discontinuity at $x = 2$ because, here, both the numerator and denominator are equal to 0, so the function is undefined.
Oblique Asymptote	An asymptote that is neither vertical nor horizontal.	The function $\dfrac{3x^2 + 2}{x - 1}$ has an oblique asymptote alone the line $y = 3x + 3$.

Essential Technique: Finding Oblique Asymptotes

Oblique asymptotes, which run diagonally instead of vertically or horizontally, occur in rational functions in which the degree of the numerator is exactly one more than the degree of the denominator. The figure on the right shows an example of a rational function with an oblique asymptote. The first step to finding an oblique asymptote of a function is to rewrite the function using synthetic division, which is explained above. This process is similar to rewriting an improper fraction as a mixed number. Let's take a look at an example. Here's how to find the oblique asymptote of the function $f(x) = \dfrac{3x^2 + x - 2}{2x + 6}$.

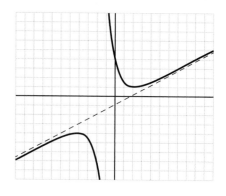

Start by using synthetic division (or polynomial long division) to divide the numerator by the denominator. This gives you a result of $\dfrac{3}{2}x - 4$ with a remainder of 22. This means that you can rewrite the function as $f(x) = \dfrac{3}{2}x - 4 + \dfrac{22}{2x + 6}$. This is like a mixed number—the "$\dfrac{3}{2}x - 4$" part is like the "whole" part of the number (the part that was divided out cleanly), and the "$\dfrac{22}{2x + 6}$" part is like the "fraction" part of the number (the part that was left over and is kept as a fraction). Now, we can think about what happens to the behaviour of this function as x grows to infinity. The term $\dfrac{22}{2x + 6}$ will get smaller and approach 0, since the denominator will continually grow larger. So, as x grows to infinity, we can ignore that term, and the function will approach the line $\dfrac{3}{2}x - 4$. Therefore, this function has an oblique asymptote along the line $y = \dfrac{3}{2}x - 4$.

Example Question	Solution

What is the y-intercept of the oblique asymptote of the function $f(x) = f(x) = \dfrac{4x^2 + x}{x + 5}$?

(A) $(0, 19)$
(B) $(0, 6)$
(C) $(0, 0)$
(D) $(0, -6)$
(E) $(0, -19)$

The correct answer is (E). Perform synthetic division on the function $f(x)$ to find its oblique asymptote:

$$
\begin{array}{r|rrr}
 & 4 & 1 & 0 \\
-5 & & -20 & 95 \\
\hline
 & 4 & -19 & 95
\end{array}
$$

Therefore, the oblique asymptote is $y = 4x - 19$, and its y-intercept is $(0, -19)$. If you chose (C), you found the y-intercept of the function $f(x)$.

Logarithms and Logarithmic Functions

Logarithms are essentially the inverses of exponents. If $x = a^b$, then $\log_a x = b$. In this equation, a is called the base of the logarithm. The base of the logarithm is the same as the base of the exponent—this can help you remember which variable goes where when converting between an exponential equation and a logarithmic equation.

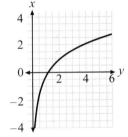

If you see an expression like $\log x$, without a base, the base is assumed to be 10 (and this is what the "log" button on your calculator does). The notation $\ln x$, where "ln" stands for "natural logarithm," indicates that the base of the log is the number e. Considering logarithms of negative numbers leads to some major problems, so on the Math Level 2 test, both the base (a) and the argument (x) of the logarithm will always be positive.

Below is a table of tricks you can use to manipulate expressions with logarithms—often called "Log Laws".

Log Law	Equation
Logarithm of a reciprocal	$\log_a x = -\log_a\left(\dfrac{1}{x}\right)$
Logarithm of a product	$\log_a(xy) = \log_a x + \log_a y$
Logarithm of a quotient	$\log_a\left(\dfrac{x}{y}\right) = \log_a x - \log_a y$
Logarithm of an exponent	$\log_a(x^y) = y\log_a x$
Change of base	$\log_a b = \dfrac{\log_c b}{\log_c a}$

Log Laws are, in a way, their own essential technique, because they can help you on many other logarithm and exponent questions. Below is an example that demonstrates how to use them.

Example Question	Solution
If $\log a = x$ and $\log b = y$, then which of the following expressions is equivalent to $\log\left(\frac{a}{b}\right)^3$? (A) $x - y$ (B) $3x - y$ (C) $3(x - y)$ (D) $\frac{x}{y}$ (E) $\frac{3x}{y}$	The correct answer is (C). First, use the logarithm of an exponent law to transform $\log\left(\frac{a}{b}\right)^3$ into $3\log\frac{a}{b}$. Next, use the logarithm of a quotient law to transform $3\log\frac{a}{b}$ into $3(\log a - \log b)$, and substitute x and y for $\log a$ and $\log b$ to get $3(x - y)$.

Transformations of Functions

An important part of the Algebra and Functions section of the Math Level 2 test is relating algebraic representations of functions to their graphical representations. The table below summarizes how changes in the equations of functions change their graphs.

Graphical Transformation	Algebraic Transformation	Examples
Vertical shift by b units	Add b to the equation for the function: $f(x) \to f(x) + b$	$x^2 \to x^2 + b$ $\frac{x+1}{x-6} \to \frac{x+1}{x-6} + b$ $3e^x \to 3e^x + b$
Horizontal shift by a units	Subtract a from the argument of the function: $f(x) \to f(x - a)$	$x^2 \to (x - a)^2$ $\frac{x+1}{x-6} \to \frac{(x-a)+1}{(x-a)-6}$ $3e^x \to 3e^{x-a}$
Vertical stretch by a factor of k	Multiply the entire function by k: $f(x) \to kf(x)$	$x^2 \to kx^2$ $\frac{x+1}{x-6} \to k\left(\frac{x+1}{x-6}\right)$ $3e^x \to 3ke^x$
Horizontal stretch by a factor of h	Divide the argument of the function by h: $f(x) \to f\left(\frac{x}{h}\right)$	$x^2 \to \left(\frac{x}{h}\right)^2$ $\frac{x+1}{x-6} \to \frac{\frac{x}{h}+1}{\frac{x}{h}-6}$ $3e^x \to 3e^{\frac{x}{h}}$

Reflection across the x-axis	Multiply the entire function by –1: $f(x) \rightarrow -f(x)$	$x^2 \rightarrow -x^2$ $\dfrac{x+1}{x-6} \rightarrow \dfrac{-x-1}{x-6}$ $3e^x \rightarrow -3e^x$
Reflection across the y-axis	Multiply the argument of the function by –1: $f(x) \rightarrow f(-x)$	$x^2 \rightarrow (-x)^2 = x^2$ $\dfrac{x+1}{x-6} \rightarrow \dfrac{-x+1}{-x-6}$ $3e^x \rightarrow 3e^{-x}$

Essential Technique: Changing Words to Numbers

It can be tricky to translate words and phrases into their equivalent graphical representations, especially when you have more than one transformation to compute. The table above gives you a good place to start: the phrase in the "graphical transformation" column corresponds exactly to the math in the "algebraic transformation." The other important thing to remember is to break a multiple transformation down into its component parts. It can help to separate the horizontal transformations from the vertical transformations, since the former affect the "argument" and the latter affect the "whole function." The example question below demonstrates this.

Example Question	Solution
If the function $f(x) = (x + 1)^3$ is stretched vertically by a factor of 3, reflected across the x-axis, and shifted two units to the right to form the function $g(x)$, then which of the following equations represents $g(x)$? (A) $g(x) = -2(x - 2)^3$ (B) $g(x) = -3(x - 1)^3$ (C) $g(x) = -3(x + 3)^3$ (D) $g(x) = 3(-x - 1)^3$ (E) $g(x) = 3(-x + 3)^3$	The correct answer is (B). First, apply the vertical stretch by a factor of 3, which means multiply the function by 3: $3(x + 1)^3$. Next, reflect it across the x-axis, which means multiply the function by –1: $-3(x - 1)^3$. Finally, shift the function 2 units to the right, which means subtract 2 from the argument: $-3(x + 1 - 2)^3 = -3(x - 1)^3$.

Operations with Functions

You can also perform operations with functions, like addition, subtraction, multiplication, division, and composition. The table below may seem a little confusing at first glance, so we'll go through an example here.

If f and g are functions (with the same domain), you can add them to create a new function, $(f + g)$. But what is this mysterious new function? To tell you what it is, we have to tell you what rule $(f + g)$ follows to transform an input into an output. The rule is this: $(f + g)(x) = f(x) + g(x)$. That is, when you input a number x into the function $(f + g)$, the machine calculates $f(x)$ and $g(x)$ separately and then adds them together.

Operation	Definition	Conditions
Addition	$(f+g)(x) = f(x) + g(x)$	Defined wherever f and g are both defined.
Subtraction	$(f-g)(x) = f(x) - g(x)$	Defined wherever f and g are both defined.
Multiplication	$(f \times g)(x) = f(x) \times g(x)$	Defined wherever f and g are both defined.
Division	$\left(\dfrac{f}{g}\right)(x) = \dfrac{f(x)}{g(x)}$	Defined wherever f and g are both defined, and $g(x) \neq 0$
Composition	$(f \circ g)(x) = f(g(x))$	Defined wherever g is defined, and $g(x)$ is in the domain of f. On the Math Level 2 test, you will rarely see the "o" symbol used for composition. Instead, you will simply see "$f(g(x))$". Both mean that you evaluate $g(x)$ first, and then plug the result into f.

Example Question	Solution

x	$f(x)$
0	4
1	2
2	2
3	1
4	3

The table above defines the function f, which has domain $\{0, 1, 2, 3, 4\}$. What is the value of $f(f(0))$?

(A) 0
(B) 1
(C) 3
(D) 4
(E) Cannot be determined from the given information

The correct answer is (C). To find $f(f(0))$, you first need to find $f(0)$. To find the output when f is given the input $x = 0$, look at the first row of the table. When $x = 0$, $f(x) = 4$. This is another way of saying that $f(0) = 4$. Now that you know $f(0) = 4$, you know that $f(f(0)) = f(4)$. To find $f(4)$, look at the last row of the table to find that $f(4) = 3$. Therefore, $f(f(0)) = 3$.

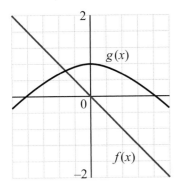

The graphs of *f* and *g* are shown in the figure to the left. Which of the following is the graph of *fg*?

The correct answer is (B). You can see from the figure that $f(0) = 0$, since $f(x)$ passes through the point $(0, 0)$. Since $(f \times g)(0) = f(0) \times g(0)$, and $f(0) = 0$, you know that this product will also equal 0. So, right away, you can eliminate (A) and (D), since those graphs do not pass through $(0, 0)$. Now, you can think about when the product function $(fg)(x)$ will be positive or negative. Since both $f(x)$ and $g(x)$ are positive to the left of 0 (until just to the right of –2), you know that $(fg)(x)$ will also be positive on this interval. Similarly, you know that $(fg)(x)$ will be negative to the right of 0 (until just to the left of 2), since $f(x)$ and $g(x)$ have opposite signs on that interval. The only graph that fits this description is (B).

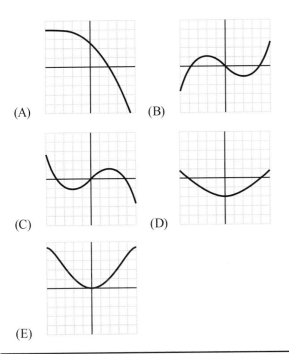

(A) (B) (C) (D) (E)

Piecewise Functions

In all the examples above, the equation for a function did not depend on the input value. However, some functions follow different rules depending on what the input is. For example, a function might follow the rule $f(x) = 3x^2 - 2$ when x is negative, but follow a completely different rule (for example, $f(x) = \sin 5x$) when x is positive or equal to 0. Functions whose equation depends on their input are called piecewise functions. The function above would be written like this:

$$f(x) = \begin{cases} 3x^2 - 2, x < 0 \\ \sin 5x, x \geq 0 \end{cases}$$

This says that the value of $f(x)$ is equal to $3x^2 - 2$ *if* $x < 0$, and is equal to $\sin 5x$ IF $x \geq 0$. To the right is the graph of this piecewise function.

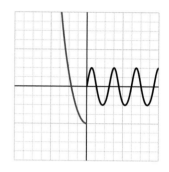

This piecewise function has two pieces, but they can have even more. When finding the output of a piecewise function for a certain input, remember to always check the domain first—find the correct expression to use to evaluate the function and then plug the number in as usual.

Parametric Equations

In most functions, two variables (often x and y) are related by an equation. However, some relationships are easier to express when both x and y are defined in terms of a third variable, often t. Let's look at a very simple example:

$$x = 2t$$
$$y = 4t + 3$$

At first glance, it's not easy to tell what is going on in this set of parametric equations. However, with some algebra, you can substitute $x = 2t$ into the equation for y to find a more familiar form of the equation: $y = 2x + 3$. So, you know that these parametric equations represent a line with a slope of 2 and a y-intercept of 3. This isn't a particularly helpful use of parametric equations, since it is easier to write and understand the line in its standard form. However, this should give you an idea of how parametric equations are written and how you can substitute to simplify them.

More often, parametric equations are used to graph relations (which are not necessarily functions, since each x-value may correspond to more than one y-value). Here are some common examples.

Shape	Equation	Parametric Equations	Graph
Circle	$x^2 + y^2 = 1$	$x = \cos t$ $y = \sin t$	$x = \cos t$ $y = \sin t$

Ellipse	$\dfrac{x^2}{a^2} + \dfrac{y^2}{b^2} = 1$	$x = a \cos t$ $y = b \sin t$	equation $x = 2 \cos t$ $y = 5 \sin t$ 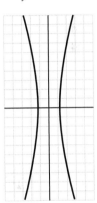
Hyperbola	$\dfrac{x^2}{a^2} - \dfrac{y^2}{b^2} = 1$	$x = a \sec t$ $y = b \tan t$	$x = \sec t$ $y = 3 \tan t$ 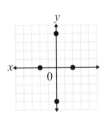

Essential Technique: Understanding Parametric Equations

When you first see a set of parametric equations, it can be very difficult to know how to visualize or conceptualize them. There are two basic techniques for interpreting parametric equations.

First, perhaps the easiest and most straightforward way you can interpret them is by choosing values for t, plugging them in, and plotting the resulting pair (x, y). Doing this a few times can give you a good idea of what the graph looks like. For example, given the parametric equations $x = \cos t$ and $y = 2 \sin t$, you can plug in some easy values like $t = 0, \dfrac{\pi}{2}, \pi,$ and $\dfrac{3\pi}{2}$ to get the following coordinate pairs: $(1, 0), (0, 2), (-1, 0),$ and $(0, -2)$. A quick graph of these points, shown here, suggests that you might be dealing with an ellipse—and, if you look at the table above, you can see that you are.

Second, you can attempt to eliminate the parameter, t, to find a function only in terms of x and y. This way of understanding parametric equations can be more computation-heavy, so it's a good idea to try the plug and plot method above first, especially if there are complicated functions involved (though trigonometric identities, detailed in Chapter 2 Section 4, Trigonmetry, might help!). For example, given the parametric equations $x = t^2$ and $y = t + 4$, you can rearrange both equations to isolate t, then set them equal to each other to eliminate t:

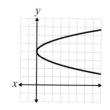

$t = \pm\sqrt{x}$ and $t = y - 4$, so $y - 4 = \pm\sqrt{x}$, which ought to be written as two equations: $y = \sqrt{x} + 4$ and $y = -\sqrt{x} + 4$. This looks like a sideways parabola, as seen on the right.

Example Question	Solution

$$x = (\sin t)\,(1 - \cos t)$$
$$y = (\cos t)\,(1 - \cos t)$$

Which of the following curves could be represented by the parametric equations above?

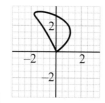

(A)

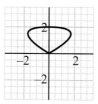

(B)

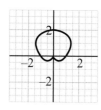

(C)

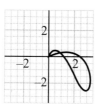

(D)

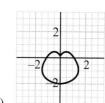

(E)

The correct answer is (E). At first glance, these just look like a bunch of curves you've never seen before—how could you possibly know which one goes with the given equations? The answer is: you can plug in values for t, as described above, and use process of elimination to find the correct answer. This method might be better than trying to eliminate t because that could take a while with all those trigonometric functions.

It makes sense to start with some easy values of t, like $t = 0$. Since $\cos 0 = 1$, plugging in $t = 0$ gives you $x = 0$ and $y = 0$, which tells you that $(0, 0)$ is on the curve. Unfortunately, this doesn't help you eliminate anything just yet. Next, you can try another easy value of t, like $t = \dfrac{\pi}{2}$. Since $\cos \dfrac{\pi}{2} = 0$ and $\sin \dfrac{\pi}{2} = 1$, this produces the point $(1, 0)$. Similarly, plugging in $t = -\dfrac{\pi}{2}$ produces the point $(-1, 0)$. So, you can eliminate (A), (B), and (D), because these curves do not pass through those points.

Next, you can try to distinguish between (C) and (E) by plugging in $t = \pi$. Since $\cos \pi = -1$ and $\sin \pi = 0$, this produces the point $(0, -2)$, which is only included in the graph of (E). Therefore, you know that (E) must be the correct answer.

Section 3
Data Analysis and Probability

The Math Level 2 test contains roughly 4-6 questions on data analysis, statistics, and probability, so it is important to have a good grasp of these concepts.

Data Analysis
Part 1

Measures of Center and Spread

Measurements such as **mean**, **median**, and **mode** are all measures of the center of a data set: they try to find a typical or representative value for the data set. Measurements such as **range** and **standard deviation** are measures of the spread of a data set: they try to measure how spread out or clustered together the values in a data set are.

Some questions may ask you to simply compute one of these values. Most questions, however, are more complex. For example, you may need to add or remove a value from a data set and then calculate the effect of this change on a measure of center or spread of the set. The chart below defines various measures of center and spread and shows how they are calculated on an example data set.

Term	Definition	Example
Data Set	A collection of values, often presented in a list, table, or graph	1, 3, 4, 6, 7, 7, 10
(Arithmetic) Mean	The sum of all the elements of a data set divided by the number of elements. This is often simply called the "average".	$\dfrac{1+3+4+6+7+7+10}{7} = 5.4$
Geometric Mean	The product of all the elements raised to the power of $\frac{1}{n}$, where n is the number of elements	$\sqrt[7]{1 \times 3 \times 4 \times 6 \times 7 \times 7 \times 10} = 4.5$
Median	When the elements of a data set are arranged in ascending order, the value that occurs in the middle of the list. If there is an even number of elements, the median is the mean of the two middle elements.	~~1, 3,~~ 4, 6, ~~7, 7, 10~~ The median is 6.
Mode	The value that occurs most frequently in a data set. A data set can have multiple modes if some values occur the same number of times.	Since 7 occurs twice and every other element occurs only once, the mode of this data set is 7.
Range	The difference between the largest and smallest values in a data set	$10 - 1 = 9$

Standard Deviation	A measure of how spread out the values in a data set are from the mean. On the Math Level 2 test, you will not need to actually calculate standard deviation, but you should understand that a lower standard deviation means the elements in the data set are more clustered around the mean.	
Percentile	The value at the nth percentile is the value which is above $n\%$ of the data set. Percentiles are often only used in larger data sets. The 50th percentile is the median.	
Interquartile Range	The difference between the 75th and 25th percentiles of a data set	

Graph and Plots

Data visualizations are a core component of the Math Level 2 Subject test. You should always take the time to examine any graphic closely and make note of the axes and labels. Below are some examples of common types of graphs or plots you might see on the Math Level 2 test.

Graph type	Description	Example
Pie Chart	Represents data as sections of a circle adding up to a whole.	Favorite Ice Cream Flavor 10%, 20%, 40%, 30% ■ Chocolate ■ Vanilla ■ Strawberry ■ Other
Bar Graph	Represents data as bars of different heights or widths. The size of the bar indicates the number of items or elements in the corresponding category.	Hair Color of Students 12, 8, 4, 0 Brown Black Blonde Red Other

Line Graph	Represents data as lines tracking the value of a quantity in terms of some other quantity, usually time.	**Stock Price ($)**

Stock Price ($)

6

4

2

0

2001 2002 2003 2004 2005 2006 2007 2008 2009 2010

Scatterplot

Represents data in two variables plotted against each other, with one variable along each axis. A scatterplot can be used when elements of a data set are ordered pairs instead of simply numbers.

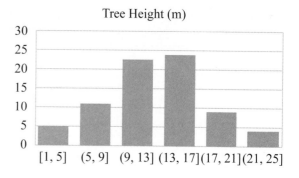

Heights and Weights of Soccer Players

Histogram

Shows how frequently certain values occur in a data set. They look similar to bar charts, but they are used to represent continuous data (data that can fall anywhere in a range) instead of discrete data. For example, the histogram shown here tells you that there are 24 trees with heights between 13 and 17 m tall.

Tree Height (m)

30
25
20
15
10
5
0

[1, 5] (5, 9] (9, 13] (13, 17] (17, 21] (21, 25]

Box Plot

Displays data with lines at the minimum and maximum values, a box with edges at the 25th and 75th percentiles, and a line at the median value.

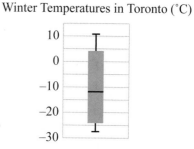

Winter Temperatures in Toronto (°C)

Frequency Table	Shows how frequently values occur in a data set in table form.	Pet	Number of Students
		Dog	8
		Cat	6
		Lizard	2
		Bird	1
		Other	4

Stem and Leaf Plot	Displays numerical data separated by the leftmost digit(s) of the numbers. For example, the stem and leaf plot shown here tells you that the teachers at this school are aged 24, 24, 26, 28, 29, 32, 33, and so on.	Age of Teachers at a Local School	
		2	4, 4, 6, 8, 9
		3	2, 3, 5, 7, 7, 7, 9
		4	2, 4, 9
		5	0, 1, 5, 5, 8, 8
		6	3, 5, 9
		7	0, 1

Essential Techniques: Extrapolation

The line of best fit or trend line is a line that approximates the data in a scatterplot, like the one shown below, which shows the heights and weights of the 12 players on a high school soccer team.

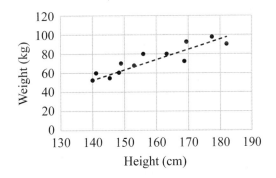

It is possible to **extrapolate** from a line of best fit to determine what other element or elements are likely to come from the same data set. You should think of the line of best fit as a predictor of the approximate region where data points that have not yet been collected are likely to lie on the graph.

To extrapolate or predict accurately, it's important to estimate a good trend line. Pay attention to how far apart the points are and where their "average" might lie, how quickly they look like they increase or decrease (the line might not be a line at all, but exponential or some other function), and any outliers or anomalies.

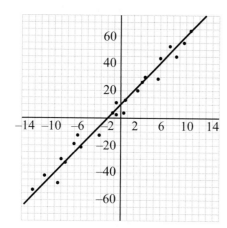

The correct answer is (B). Although any of the points might have come from the given data set, choice (B) is quite far from the trend line compared to the other points, and so is least likely to have come from the same data set.

Given the scatterplot above, which of the following data points is NOT likely to come from the same data set?

(A) (–1, 5.2)

(B) (0, 0.5)

(C) (1, 15.3)

(D) (2, 18.8)

(E) (3, 22.5)

Probability

Part 2

Probability is perhaps the most commonly tested topic under the Data Analysis umbrella. Probability is a measure of how likely an event is to happen. While in the real world, probabilities are often computed on large data sets, you will only be expected to perform basic computations on the test.

Fundamentals of Probability

Term	Definition	Example	Formula
Probability	The probability of an event is the likelihood of the event occurring, between 0 (impossible to occur) and 1 (guaranteed to occur). The probability of an event A is denoted $P(A)$.	If you flip a coin, the probability of getting heads is 0.5. If you roll a 6-sided die, the probability of rolling a 3 is $\frac{1}{6}$, or around 0.17.	$\dfrac{\text{\# of desirable outcomes}}{\text{\# of total outcomes}}$
Independent Events	Two events are independent if the outcome of one does not affect the outcome of the other.	If you flip a coin twice, the outcome of the first flip will not affect the outcome of the second flip.	If events A and B are independent, then $P(A \text{ and } B) = P(A) \times P(B)$.
Dependent Events	Two events are dependent if the outcome of one is affected by the outcome of the other.	If you randomly draw a King from a deck of cards, the next card you draw is less likely to be a King (and more likely to be any other card).	If events A and B are dependent, there is often no easy way to calculate $P(A \text{ and } B)$. It can be helpful to remember that $P(A \text{ and } B) = P(A) \times P(B \mid A)$, where $P(B \mid A)$ is the probability of B occurring given that A has occurred.

Complementary Events	Two events are complementary if exactly one of them, but not both, must occur.	If you roll a die, you must either roll an even number or an odd number. Therefore, rolling an even number and rolling an odd number are complementary events.	If events A and B are complementary, then $P(A) + P(B) = 1$ and $P(A \text{ and } B) = 0$. Every event A is complementary with the event not-A, meaning that $P(A) = 1 - P(\text{not-}A)$.

Example Question	Solution

A bag contains 7 red marbles, 5 blue marbles, and 3 green marbles. If a child pulls two marbles out of the bag, one after the other, what is the probability that both marbles will be blue?

A) 9.5%

B) 11.1%

C) 33.3%

D) 57.1%

E) 66.7%

The correct answer is (A). The probability that the first marble pulled out will be blue is $\dfrac{\# \text{ blue marbles}}{\# \text{ total marbles}} = \dfrac{5}{15} = \dfrac{1}{3}$. Once one blue marble is pulled out, there will be 14 total marbles in the bag, 4 of which are blue. The probability of drawing a second blue marble, then, is $\dfrac{4}{14} = \dfrac{2}{7}$. Finally, we can multiply these probabilities together to get $\dfrac{1}{3} \times \dfrac{2}{7} = 9.5\%$.

In questions like this, it is important to know whether the drawn marbles are put back in the bag or not, because it affects the probabilities of future draws. In this case, because the first marble drawn is not returned to the bag, the probability of drawing a blue marble changes when any marble is drawn.

Example Question	Solution

Computer A uses a hard drive that has a 1 in 1000 chance of failing on any given day. Computer B uses two hard drives that each have a 1 in 500 chance of failing on any given day. What is the probability that all three hard drives fail on the same day?

(A) 5×10^{-4}

(B) 1×10^{-6}

(C) 2×10^{-6}

(D) 4×10^{-9}

(E) 2×10^{-10}

The correct answer is (D). Because nothing in the problem indicates that any of these events are dependent, you can simply multiply the probabilities: $1/1000 \times 1/500 \times 1/500 = 1/250{,}000{,}000$ or 4×10^{-9}.

Essential Techniques: Factorials and Counting

You are unlikely to encounter a question that only asks you to compute a factorial by itself. You are more likely to be asked to calculate how many ways there are of doing something (such as *how many ways* 5 people can line up). For these sorts of questions, it is important to understand the difference between a combination and a permutation.

The **factorial** of a number n is written as $n!$, and it is equal to the product of all positive integers less than or equal to n. For example, $6! = 1 \times 2 \times 3 \times 4 \times 5 \times 6 = 720$. By convention, $0! = 1$.

A **combination** is a selection of items from a set in which order does not matter. If a set contains n elements, the number of ways to choose k of them is written as $\binom{n}{k}$, is pronounced "n choose k", and is equal to $\frac{n!}{k!(n-k)!}$.

A **permutation** is a selection of items from a set in which order matters. If a set contains n elements, the number of ways to choose k of them (in order) is equal to $\frac{n!}{(n-k)!}$.

Example Question	Solution
A research council with 8 members needs to select 3 of its members to attend a conference. How many different groups of attendees are possible? (A) 3 (B) 8 (C) 56 (D) 336 (E) 512	The correct answer is (C). Because the order in which you select the group of attendees does not matter, this is a combinations question. The number of ways to select 3 people from a group of 8 is $\binom{8}{3} = \frac{8!}{3!(8-3)!} = \frac{6 \times 7 \times 8}{3 \times 2 \times 1} = 56$.
A talent show needs to award first, second, and third prize to 3 of its 10 participants. How many different ways are there to award the prizes? A) 3 B) 10 C) 120 D) 720 E) 1,000	The correct answer is (D). Because the order in which you select the winners matters, this is a permutations question. For any values of n and k, there will be more permutations than combinations. The number of ways to select 3 people, in order, from a group of 10 is $\frac{10!}{(10-3)!} = 10 \times 9 \times 8 = 720$.

Section 4
Trigonometry

Trigonometry accounts for approximately 6-8 questions on the Math Level 2 Subject test. These questions cover topics like the Pythagorean theorem, trigonometric ratios, and identities. The test also contains approximately 2 questions on trigonometric functions, which cover topics like amplitudes, periods, and maxima.

You will need to know the different types of angles (acute, right, obtuse, straight, and reflex), and the relationships between angles (complementary, supplementary, and congruent). You will also need to know how to convert between degrees and radians: $180° = \pi$ radians. This information can be found in more detail in our SAT 6PT Book or online.

Triangles

Term	Definition	Example	Formula
Right Triangle	A triangle that contains a right angle		
Isosceles Triangle	A triangle with two equal sides (and therefore two equal angles). Bisecting the non-congruent angle produces two right triangles.		

Area	The space bounded by a triangle	$\text{Area} = \frac{1}{2} \times \text{base} \times \text{height}$	The area of this triangle is $\frac{1}{2}(4)(7) = 14\,\text{cm}^2$
Angle Sum Theorem	The sum of the interior angles of a triangle is always $180°$, or π radians.		The measure of angle c is $180° - 30° - 37° = 113°$.
Triangle Inequality Theorem	The sum of the lengths of any two sides of a triangle must be greater than the length of the third side.	$A + B > C$ $B + C > A$ $A + C > B$	If a triangle has two sides measuring 5 and 8, then its third side could have any length between 3 and 13.
Pythagorean Theorem	In a right triangle, the square of the hypotenuse is equal to the sum of the squares of the legs.	$c^2 = a^2 + b^2$	A right triangle with a hypotenuse of length 20 and one leg of length 4 has another leg measuring $\sqrt{20^2 - 4^2} = \sqrt{384} \cong 19.6$.
Angle-side Relationship	The shortest side of a triangle is always opposite the smallest angle, and the longest side is always opposite the largest angle.		

Similar Triangles	Triangles that have congruent angles and proportionate sides	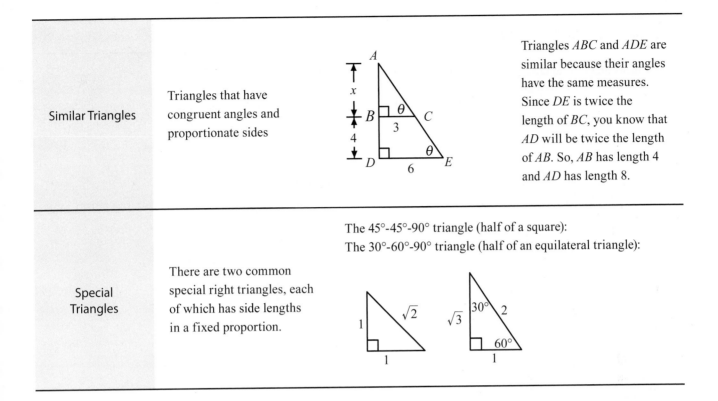	Triangles *ABC* and *ADE* are similar because their angles have the same measures. Since *DE* is twice the length of *BC*, you know that *AD* will be twice the length of *AB*. So, *AB* has length 4 and *AD* has length 8.
Special Triangles	There are two common special right triangles, each of which has side lengths in a fixed proportion.		The 45°-45°-90° triangle (half of a square): The 30°-60°-90° triangle (half of an equilateral triangle):

Essential Technique: Composite Shapes

Often, the Math 2 Subject test will present you with shapes that are composed of several smaller shapes. It will help to separate these composite shapes into their components so that you can address each simple shape separately. This method of analysis means that you need to have a good grasp of your plane geometry fundamentals (e.g. the interior angles of polygons, area and perimeter formulae), which can be found in our 6PT book.

When you have broken a complex shape into simpler parts, you may be able to apply some of the definitions and theorems above (e.g. complementary angles, similar triangles, special triangles, or Sine Law). Memorizing these will let you answer questions much more quickly. For example, a regular hexagon can be divided into 6 equilateral triangles or 12 special 30-60-90 triangles.

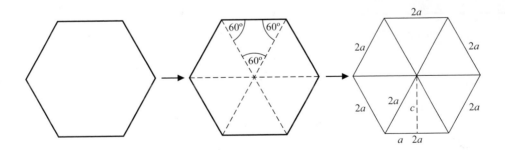

The measure of the angle between the two congruent sides of an isosceles triangle is 18°, and the measure of the side opposite that angle is 7 meters. What is the perimeter of the triangle?

(A) 22.37 m
(B) 22.65 m
(C) 51.75 m
(D) 52.30 m
(E) 96.49 m

The correct answer is (C). One way to solve this problem involves using the Angle Sum Theorem to find the measures of the other two angles in the triangle, and then using the Sine Law. However, it may be easier to transform this isosceles triangle into two right triangles (it may help to draw a diagram) and then use a simple sine ratio to determine the missing lengths. Each right triangle has a base of 3.5 m, a top angle of 9°, and a hypotenuse of a, so $\sin 9° = \dfrac{3.5}{a}$, and $a = 22.37$ m. Because the question asks for the perimeter of the triangle, multiply a by 2 and add 7 to get 51.75 m.

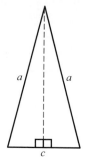

Trigonometric Ratios

A **trigonometric ratio** is a ratio between the lengths of two sides of a right triangle that depends on the measure of the triangle's other angles. For example, the **sine** of a certain angle θ is the ratio of the length of the side opposite θ to the length of the hypotenuse, when θ is an angle in a right triangle. There are six common trigonometric ratios, and they are listed in the table below. The easiest way to remember which ratios are which is to remember "SOH-CAH-TOA": SOH means that <u>s</u>ine is <u>o</u>pposite over <u>h</u>ypotenuse; CAH means that <u>c</u>osine is <u>a</u>djacent over <u>h</u>ypotenuse; and TOA means that <u>t</u>angent is <u>o</u>pposite over <u>a</u>djacent.

Term	Definition	Formula	Example
Sine	The ratio of the side opposite an angle to the hypotenuse	$\sin x = \dfrac{opp}{hyp}$	Hypotenuse (H) 5, 3 Opposite (O), 4 Adjacent (A)
Cosine	The ratio of the side adjacent to an angle to the hypotenuse	$\cos x = \dfrac{adj}{hyp}$	$\sin x = \dfrac{3}{5}$
Tangent	The ratio of the side opposite an angle to the side adjacent to the angle	$\tan x = \dfrac{opp}{adj}$	$\cos x = \dfrac{4}{5}$ $\tan x = \dfrac{3}{4}$

Cosecant	The reciprocal of sine	$\csc x = \dfrac{1}{\sin x} = \dfrac{hyp}{opp}$	
Secant	The reciprocal of cosine	$\sec x = \dfrac{1}{\cos x} = \dfrac{hyp}{adj}$	
Cotangent	The reciprocal of tangent	$\cot x = \dfrac{1}{\tan x} = \dfrac{opp}{adj}$	

Hypotenuse (H)
5

3
Opposite (O)

4
Adjacent (A)

$$\csc x = \frac{5}{3}$$

$$\sec x = \frac{5}{4}$$

$$\cot x = \frac{4}{3}$$

Quadrants	Four quarters of the xy-plane	

Quadrant II | Quadrant I

0   x

Quadrant III | Quadrant IV

CAST Rule	Based on the quadrant in which an angle is located, this rule reminds you which trigonometric ratios are positive.	

S (sine is positive) | A (all are positive)

0   x

T (Tangent is positive) | C (Cosine is postive)

For example, the angle $\theta = 125°$ is found in Quadrant II (because $90° < 125° < 180°$), so $\sin\theta$ is positive and $\cos\theta$ and $\tan\theta$ are negative

Essential Technique: Sine Law and Cosine Law

Sine Law and Cosine Law are two rules that can help you solve for unknown side lengths or angle measures in a triangle. Remember that the side labeled a is always opposite from the angle labeled A, and so on.

Law	Equation	Purpose
Sine Law	$$\frac{\sin A}{a} = \frac{\sin B}{b} = \frac{\sin C}{c}$$ $$or$$ $$\frac{a}{\sin A} = \frac{b}{\sin B} = \frac{c}{\sin C}$$	Use Sine Law to solve a triangle when you know 2 angles and a side, or two sides and an angle opposite one of them.
Cosine Law	$$a^2 = b^2 + c^2 - 2bc\cos A$$	Use Cosine Law to solve a triangle when you know 2 sides and the angle between them, or all 3 sides.

Example Question	Solution

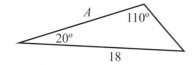

What is the length of side A in the triangle above ?

(A) 6.6
(B) 8.0
(C) 14.7
(D) 18.0
(E) 22.1

The correct answer is (C). Because you are given two angles and a side, you can use Sine Law to find the other angle and sides of the triangle. Since you are trying to find the length of side A, you will first need to find the measure of the angle opposite it. This angle is equal to $180° - 20° - 110° = 50°$. Now, you can set up the Sine Law equation, using the other pair of an opposite side and angle that you know:

$$\frac{A}{\sin 50°} = \frac{18}{\sin 110°}$$

$$A = \frac{18 \sin 50°}{\sin 110°} = 14.7$$

Example Question	Solution

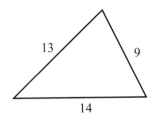

In the triangle above, what is the measure of the angle between the sides of length 13 and 14?

(A) 25.4°

(B) 38.7°

(C) 64.6°

(D) 76.7°

(E) 87.2°

The correct answer is (B). Because you are given the measures of three sides but no angles, you should use Cosine Law. Since the angle you are trying to find will be A in the Cosine Law equation, the side opposite it (the one with length 9) should be a. You can set up your equation like this:

$$9^2 = 13^2 + 14^2 - 2(13)(14)\cos A$$
$$-284 = -2(13)(14)\cos A$$
$$\cos A = 0.78022$$
$$A = \cos^{-1} 0.78022$$
$$A = 38.7°$$

Trigonometric Identities

Trigonometric identities are equalities between trigonometric functions that are true for every value of the functions' arguments. It is useful to remember one "base identity" from which a host of other identities can be derived. Often, on the Math Level 2 test, you won't have to derive any other identities—the "base identity" will work just fine.

Term	Base Identity	Derivable Identities
Cofunctions	$\sin\left(\frac{\pi}{2} - \theta\right) = \cos\theta$	$\cos\left(\frac{\pi}{2} - \theta\right) = \sin\theta$ $\tan\left(\frac{\pi}{2} - \theta\right) = \cot\theta$ $\cot\left(\frac{\pi}{2} - \theta\right) = \tan\theta$ $\sec\left(\frac{\pi}{2} - \theta\right) = \csc\theta$ $\csc\left(\frac{\pi}{2} - \theta\right) = \sec\theta$
Quotients	$\tan\theta = \frac{\sin\theta}{\cos\theta}$	$\tan\theta = \frac{\sec\theta}{\csc\theta}$ $\cot\theta = \frac{\cos\theta}{\sin\theta}$ $\cot\theta = \frac{\csc\theta}{\sec\theta}$

Pythagorean	$\sin^2\theta + \cos^2\theta = 1$	$\sin^2\theta = 1 - \cos^2\theta$ $\cos^2\theta = 1 - \sin^2\theta$ $\sec^2\theta - \tan^2\theta = 1$ $\sec^2\theta = 1 + \tan^2\theta$ $\tan^2\theta = \sec^2\theta - 1$ $\csc^2\theta - \cot^2\theta = 1$ $\csc^2\theta = 1 + \cot^2\theta$ $\cot^2\theta = \csc^2\theta - 1$
Even/odd	$\sin(-\theta) = -\sin\theta \text{ (odd)}$ $\cos(-\theta) = \cos\theta \text{ (even)}$ $\tan(-\theta) = -\tan\theta \text{ (odd)}$	$\csc(-\theta) = -\csc\theta \text{ (odd)}$ $\sec(-\theta) = \sec\theta \text{ (even)}$ $\cot(-\theta) = -\cot\theta \text{ (odd)}$
Double-angle	$\sin 2\theta = 2\sin\theta\cos\theta$ $\cos 2\theta = \cos^2\theta - \sin^2\theta$	$\tan 2\theta = \dfrac{2\tan\theta}{1 - \tan^2\theta}$

Trigonometric Identities are, in a way, their own essential technique, because they can help you on many other trigonometry questions. Below is an example that demonstrates how to use them.

Example Question	Solution
Which of the following could be a value of θ if $\sec\theta = \cot\theta$? (A) 19° (B) 38° (C) 45° (D) 67° (E) 90°	Take the reciprocals of the given functions and solve: $$\sec\theta = \cot\theta$$ $$\frac{1}{\cos\theta} = \frac{\cos\theta}{\sin\theta}$$ $$\cos\theta = \frac{\sin\theta}{\cos\theta}$$ $$\sin\theta = \cos^2\theta$$ Substitute this result into the Pythagorean Identity, $\sin^2\theta + \cos^2\theta = 1$, to get $\sin^2\theta + \sin\theta = 1$. Rearrange the identity so you have a quadratic equation: $\sin^2\theta + \sin\theta - 1 = 0$. Because using "$\sin\theta$" as a variable in a quadratic equation would be difficult, replace it with x. Now, your equation becomes $x^2 + x - 1 = 0$, which is easier to solve. Use the quadratic formula, but note that a and b equal 1, and c equals –1: $$x = \frac{(-b \pm \sqrt{(b^2 - 4ac)})}{2a} = \frac{(-1 \pm \sqrt{1^2 - 4(1)(-1)})}{2(1)} = \frac{(-1 \pm \sqrt{5})}{2},$$ so $x = 0.6180$ or $x = -1.680$. Now translate x back to $\sin\theta$. The second answer above is impossible, because $-1 \le \sin\theta \le 1$. Therefore, $\sin\theta = 0.6180$, so $\theta = \sin^{-1} 0.6180 = 38°$.

Trigonometric Functions

The table below gives some general equations for trigonometric functions and their features. The cosecant, secant and tangent functions are not included below because they are rarely tested, but because they are reciprocals of the basic functions, it is important to know that their graphs include vertical asymptotes—for example, whenever $\sin x = 0$, the function $\csc x$ has an asymptote.

Trigonometric functions are often used to model periodic phenomena—that is, phenomena that repeat after a certain amount of time. Examples of periodic phenomena include the height of a pendulum, tides, and waves (sound, light, or water).

Term	Definition / Formula	Example Graph
Sine	$f(x) = A \sin (Bx - C) + D$	
Cosine	$f(x) = A \cos (Bx - C) + D$	
Tangent	$f(x) = A \tan (Bx - C) + D$	

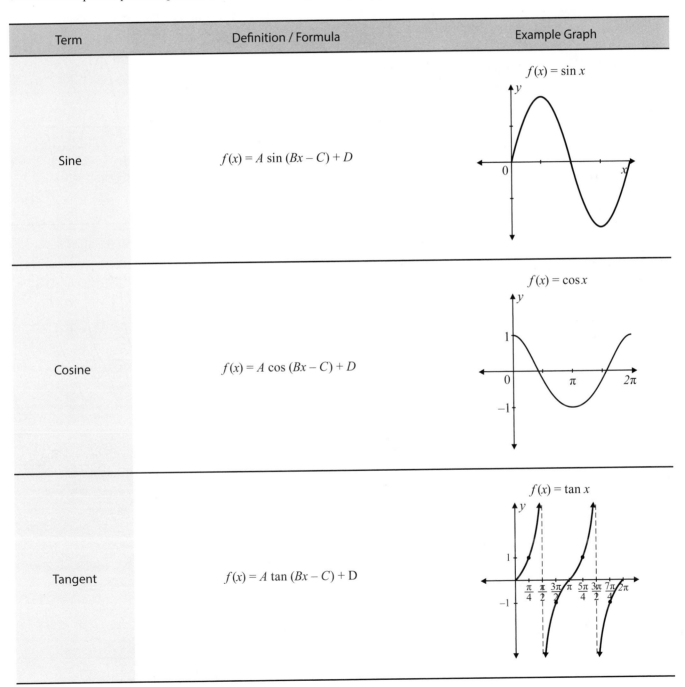

Period	The horizontal distance a function takes to complete one full cycle	$\omega = \dfrac{2\pi}{B}$	The period of the function $f(x) = \cos 4x$ is $\omega = \dfrac{2\pi}{4} = \dfrac{\pi}{2}$.
Amplitude	The magnitude of the vertical stretch or compression, or the maximum distance the function is from the midline. (Note: tangent functions do not have an amplitude.)	$a = \lvert A \rvert$	The amplitude of the function $f(x) = 3 \sin 2x$ is $a = 3$.
Phase Shift	The horizontal translation of the function. A negative value is a shift to the left, while a positive value is a shift to the right.	$\varphi = \dfrac{C}{B}$	The phase shift of the function $y = \tan(2x - 5)$ is $\varphi = \dfrac{5}{2}$ to the right.
Vertical Shift	The vertical translation of the function. This indicates the midline, which, when graphed, can make it easier to determine the amplitude, maxima, and minima. For basic functions, like $f(x) = \sin x$, the midline is the x-axis ($y = 0$).	$\vartheta = D$	For the function $y = \sin x + 4$, the vertical shift is 4, and the midline is at $y = 4$.

Essential Technique: Multiple Variables

Trigonometry problems will often present you with multiple variables (e.g. when using Sine or Cosine Law, transforming a trigonometric function, or converting between trigonometric identities). They can also require you to create your own variables as replacements for values in more complicated functions or to model word problems in mathematical terms. In some questions, it can be difficult and time-consuming to keep track of which variable refers to which value. In general, when you create variables, use letters that are intuitive, like "w" for "weight" (rather than x or y). When you're given variables, jot down a key that decodes them, especially if there's more than one. You could also draw a diagram with them or add them to an existing diagram.

Example Question	Solution

Fishing boats require a depth of at least 3 meters to safely maneuver. High tide in a certain harbor occurs at 3:00 a.m. and again at 7:00 p.m., when the water is 4.41 meters deep. Low tide occurs at 11:00 a.m., when the water is 0.45 meters deep. If the level of the tide can be modeled by a trigonometric function, what is the latest time before noon at which fishing boats can safely enter the harbor?

(A) 3:49 a.m.

(B) 4:12 a.m.

(C) 6:04 a.m.

(D) 6:05 a.m.

(E) 6:08 a.m.

The correct answer is (C). You can model the tides using a trigonometric function, because the tides repeat after a certain period of time (the question tells you that high tide occurs at 3 a.m. and again at 7 p.m.). Although you could also use the sine functions, cosine is the easiest function to use because it is at its maximum at $t = 0$.

Let $d(t)$ represent the depth of the water at a certain time t, where t is "number of hours after 3:00 a.m.," because the basic cosine function, $\cos t$, is at its peak when $t = 0$. Therefore, the function will look like this: $d(t) = A\cos(Bt + C) + D$. Because the maximum depth is 4.41 m and the minimum is 0.45, you can calculate the vertical shift: $D = \dfrac{4.41 + 0.45}{2} = 2.23$ You can find the amplitude by subtracting the vertical shift from the maximum: $A = 4.41 - 2.23 = 2.18$.

Next, recall that the basic cosine function, $\cos t$, reaches its minimum at $t = \pi$ and has a period of 2π. This function reaches its minimum at 11:00 a.m., or $t = 8$, because 11:00 a.m. is 8 hours after 3:00 a.m., and it reaches its maximum again at 7 p.m. or $t = 16$. Therefore, it has a period of 16. Recall that $\omega = \dfrac{2\pi}{B}$. Since the period (ω) here is 16 hours, you can solve for B: $16 = \dfrac{2\pi}{B}$, so $B = \dfrac{2\pi}{16} = \dfrac{\pi}{8}$. Because this period transformation means that the basic cosine maxima and minima are transformed exactly into these tidal maxima and minima, there is no phase shift necessary (no change in C above).

The function is $d(t) = 2.18\cos\left(\dfrac{\pi}{8}t\right) + 2.23$. Set $d(t)$ equal to 3, the minimum safe depth for the fishing boats, and solve for t:

$$d(t) = 2.18\cos\left(\tfrac{\pi}{8}t\right) + 2.23$$

$$3 = 2.18\cos\left(\tfrac{\pi}{8}t\right) + 2.23$$

$$0.3532 = \cos\left(\tfrac{\pi}{8}t\right)$$

$$\cos^{-1}0.3532 = \tfrac{\pi}{8}t$$

$$t = 3.0807$$

Because t = hours after 3 a.m., your answer is "3.0807 hours." To determine how many minutes this is, multiply $0.0807 \times 60 = 4.842$ minutes. Therefore, a fishing boat can safely enter the harbor until 6:04 a.m., or (C). A fishing boat could not enter the harbor at 6:05 a.m. because the water would already be too shallow. Alternately, once you determined the function, you could graph it on your graphing calculator.

Section 5
Coordinate Geometry

The Math Level 2 SAT Subject test often asks about the relationships between equations and their geometric representations on the Cartesian plane, as well as ways they can be manipulated. These questions make up approximately 5-7 questions of the test. In this section, we'll go over some key concepts to remember when tackling coordinate geometry questions.

The Cartesian Plane and Linear Graphs

Term	Definition	Example Graph
Cartesian Plane	A 2-dimensional, flat surface that extends in all directions. The x-axis (horizontal) and y-axis (vertical) provide a coordinate system that is used to describe any point in the plane with the ordered pair (x, y), where x is the point's coordinate along the x-axis and y is the point's coordinate along the y-axis.	

Standard Line Equation	$y = mx + b$ Slope: m y-intercept: b	 $y = 2x - 1$
Slope	The slope of a line tells you how steep the line is. Slope is calculated as: $$m = \frac{y_2 - y_1}{x_2 - x_1}$$ where (x_1, y_1) and (x_2, y_2) are any two points on the line. • Vertical lines have undefined slopes. If m is undefined, the line is vertical. • A slope is positive if the line goes up from left to right. If $m > 0$, the line goes up from left to right. • If $m < 0$, the line goes down from left to right.	 $$m = \frac{4 - 2}{6 - 2} = \frac{1}{2}$$
Parallel Lines	Two lines whose slopes are equal. Parallel lines run in the same direction and never intersect.	

Perpendicular Lines	Two lines whose slopes are the negative reciprocals of each other, which means the product of their slopes is –1. Perpendicular lines intersect at a 90° angle.	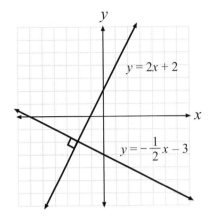
Distance Between Points	To find the distance between two points (x_1, y_1) and (x_2, y_2), you can use the formula: $$d = \sqrt{(x_1 - x_2)^2 + (y_1 - y_2)^2}$$	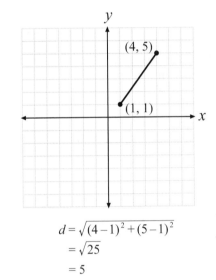 $$d = \sqrt{(4-1)^2 + (5-1)^2}$$ $$= \sqrt{25}$$ $$= 5$$

Essential Technique: Polar Coordinates

The polar coordinate system is an alternative to the standard Cartesian system for describing where points are in the plane. In this system, points are labeled by their distance from a fixed reference point and their angle away from a fixed reference direction. Any point is represented by the ordered pair (r, θ), where r is the distance of the point from the origin, and θ is the angle between the positive x-axis and the line that the point makes with the origin.

It might be helpful to think about rectangular coordinates (the (x, y) pairs that you're used to) as being the legs of a triangle that make up a point, while (r, θ) are the hypotenuse and angle. Use the same kind of thinking you do when working with the unit circle: remember that an angle can go through multiple quadrants, go in a negative direction, or be greater than 360°. Similarly, x and y coordinates can be negative depending on which quadrant they fall in.

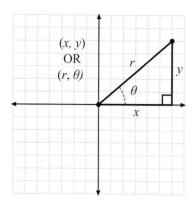

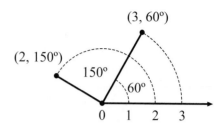

To switch from cartesian to polar coordinates, you can apply the Pythagorean Theorem as well as some trigonometry: $r = \sqrt{(x^2 + y^2)}$ and $\theta = \tan^{-1}\left(\dfrac{y}{x}\right)$. To switch from polar to cartesian coordinates, use the following: $x = r\cos\theta$ and $y = r\sin\theta$.

Example Question	Solution

The point (8, 240°) in polar coordinates represents what point in standard Cartesian coordinates?

(A) $(4, 4\sqrt{3})$

(B) $(-4, -4\sqrt{3})$

(C) $(-4\sqrt{3}, -4)$

(D) $(-2, -2\sqrt{3})$

(E) $(-8\sqrt{3}, -8)$

The correct answer is (B). It might help you to draw a diagram, as shown below.

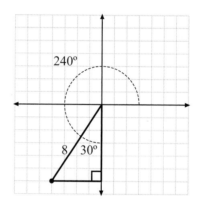

Since the angle in the given point is 240°, which is between 180° and 270°, you know the point lies in the third quadrant. You know that the upper angle of this triangle (at the origin) measures 270° − 240° = 30°, and you know the hypotenuse has length 8. Because this is a special 30° − 60° − 90° triangle, the vertical side has length $4\sqrt{3}$ and the horizontal side has length 4, since the sides are in a $1 : \sqrt{3} : 2$ ratio. Therefore, since these measurements are negative on both axes, the coordinates of this point are $(-4, -4\sqrt{3})$.

Conic Sections

Conic sections are shapes that can be formed by the intersection of a plane and a cone. You can find a handy diagram of them in the 3D Geometry Chapter 2 Section 6 of this book. There are four types of conic sections—circles, parabolas, ellipses, and hyperbolas—and each can be represented in the Cartesian plane as a graph with a corresponding equation. By looking at the equation, you can determine many things about the graph.

Conic Section	Equation	Interpretation	Example
Parabola	$y = a(x-h)^2 + k$	Vertex: (h, k) Stretch factor: a Axis of symmetry: $x = h$	 $y = (x-2)^2 - 3$
Circle	$(x-h)^2 + (y-k)^2 = r^2$	Radius: r Center: (h, k)	 $(x-1)^2 + y^2 = 9$

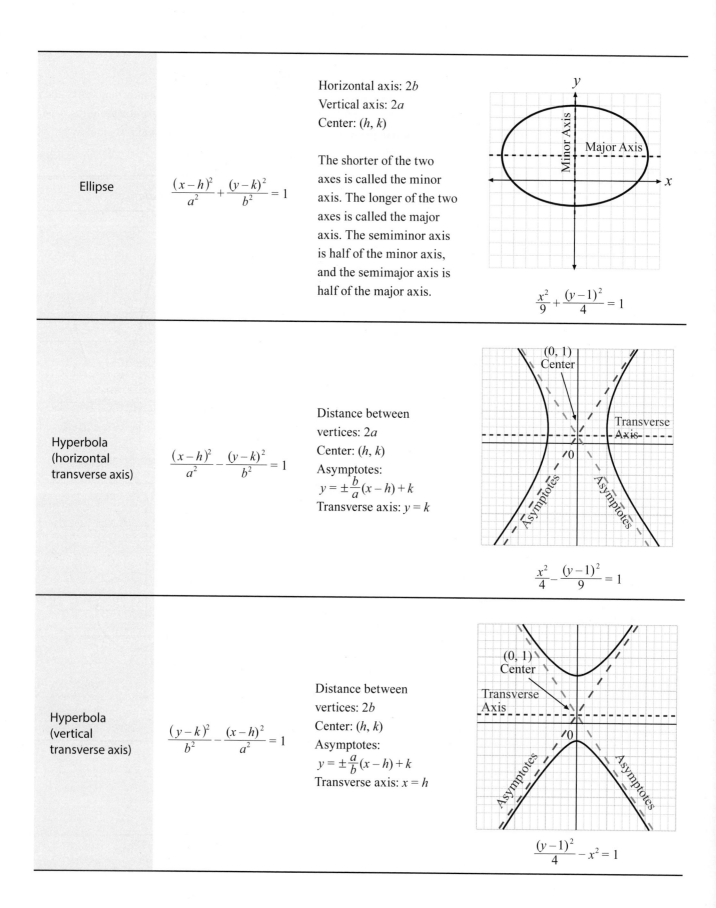

Ellipse	$$\frac{(x-h)^2}{a^2}+\frac{(y-k)^2}{b^2}=1$$	Horizontal axis: $2b$ Vertical axis: $2a$ Center: (h, k) The shorter of the two axes is called the minor axis. The longer of the two axes is called the major axis. The semiminor axis is half of the minor axis, and the semimajor axis is half of the major axis.
Hyperbola (horizontal transverse axis)	$$\frac{(x-h)^2}{a^2}-\frac{(y-k)^2}{b^2}=1$$	Distance between vertices: $2a$ Center: (h, k) Asymptotes: $y=\pm\frac{b}{a}(x-h)+k$ Transverse axis: $y=k$
Hyperbola (vertical transverse axis)	$$\frac{(y-k)^2}{b^2}-\frac{(x-h)^2}{a^2}=1$$	Distance between vertices: $2b$ Center: (h, k) Asymptotes: $y=\pm\frac{a}{b}(x-h)+k$ Transverse axis: $x=h$

$$\frac{x^2}{9}+\frac{(y-1)^2}{4}=1$$

$$\frac{x^2}{4}-\frac{(y-1)^2}{9}=1$$

$$\frac{(y-1)^2}{4}-x^2=1$$

Term	Definition	Interpretation	Example
Focus	A point of reference used to define conic sections, particularly ellipses and hyperbolas.	An ellipse is the set of points for which the sum of the distance from each point to both foci is a constant, and a hyperbola is the set of points for which the difference of the distance from each point to both foci is a constant.	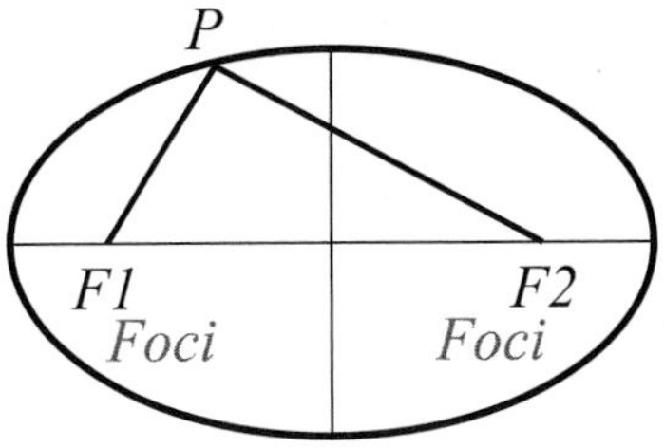

Essential Technique: Completing the Square

You'll often need to use a process called completing the square to simplify equations of conic sections, to eliminate linear terms (terms that aren't raised to any exponent), or to make your equation look like one of the standard forms of a conic section shown in the chart above.

For example, you are given the equation of a circle, $x^2 + 6x + y^2 - 4y = 3$ and asked to find it's radius. At first glance, this equation may not even look like a circle — but you can convert it to that form by completing the square.

1: Group the x and the y terms together.	$(x^2 + 6x) + (y^2 - 4y) = 3$
2: For each bracket, take the coefficient of the linear term, divide it by two, square the result, and then add and subtract this number in each bracket.	$(x^2 + 6x + 9 - 9) + (y^2 - 4y + 4 - 4) = 3$
3: Move the subtracted numbers to the other side of the equation.	$(x^2 + 6x + 9) + (y^2 - 4y + 4) = 16$
4: Factor each bracket as a perfect square trinomial.	$(x + 3)^2 + (y - 2)^2 = 16$

You're done! This equation is now in the standard form for the equation of a circle. You can see that the center of the circle is $(-3, 2)$ and the radius is $\sqrt{16} = 4$.

Example Question	Solution

What is the length of the semimajor axis of the ellipse with the equation $25x^2 - 50x + 4y^2 + 16y = 59$?

(A) 2
(B) 4
(C) 5
(D) 8
(E) 10

The correct answer is (C). This equation doesn't look much like the usual equation of an ellipse, but you can complete the square to write it in the usual form. Use the same process as the example shown above, and remember to factor the coefficient in front of the quadratic term out of each bracket before beginning to complete the square.

$$25(x^2 - 2x) + 4(y^2 + 4y) = 59$$
$$25(x^2 - 2x + 1 - 1) + 4(y^2 + 4y + 4 - 4) = 59$$
$$25(x^2 - 2x + 1) - 25 + 4(y^2 + 4y + 4) - 16 = 59$$
$$25(x - 1)^2 + 4(y + 2)^2 = 100$$
$$\frac{(x-1)^2}{4} + \frac{(y+2)^2}{25} = 1$$

The equation is now in the usual form for an ellipse, where $a^2 = 4$ and $b^2 = 25$, so $a = 2$ and $b = 5$. This means that the semimajor axis has length 5, and the semiminor axis has length 2 (since $5 > 2$).

Reflections, Rotations, and other Transformations

The Math Level 2 test sometimes asks questions about transforming shapes or points in the plane, or about transforming the plane itself. The table below indicates how the coordinates of a point change when it is subjected to various transformations.

Geometric Transformation	Change in Coordinates
Reflection across the x-axis	$(x, y) \rightarrow (x, -y)$
Reflection across the y-axis	$(x, y) \rightarrow (-x, y)$
Reflection across the line $y = x$	$(x, y) \rightarrow (y, x)$
180° rotation around the origin	$(x, y) \rightarrow (-x, -y)$
Translation k units to the right	$(x, y) \rightarrow (x + k, y)$
Translation k units to the left	$(x, y) \rightarrow (x - k, y)$
Translation k units up	$(x, y) \rightarrow (x, y + k)$
Translation k units down	$(x, y) \rightarrow (x, y - k)$

Geometric transformations are, in a way, their own essential technique, because they can help you on many other coordinate and 3D geometry questions. Below is an example that demonstrates how to use them.

Example Question	Solution

The quadrilateral with vertices (2, 3), (5, 2), (–2, 0), and (–1, –1) is translated 1 unit down and then reflected across the x-axis. Which of the following is NOT a vertex of the new quadrilateral?

(A) (2, –2)
(B) (–1, 2)
(C) (2, –1)
(D) (–2, 1)
(E) (5, –1)

The correct answer is (C). Apply the transformations to each point to find the vertices of the resulting quadrilateral. Translating each vertex down one unit changes them into (2, 2), (5, 1), (–2, –1), and (–1, –2). Next, reflecting them across the x-axis changes the sign of their y-coordinates, so the vertices become (2, –2), (5, –1), (–2, 1), and (–1, 2). Therefore, the answer option (2,–1) is not a vertex of the new quadrilateral.

Example Question	Solution

If $f: (x, y) \rightarrow (x, y - x)$ for every pair (x, y) in the plane, for what points (x, y) is it true that $f: (x, y) \rightarrow (x, y)$?

(A) The set of points (x, y) such that $x = 0$
(B) The set of points (x, y) such that $y = 0$
(C) The set of points (x, y) such that $x = y$
(D) The set of points (x, y) such that $x = -y$
(E) (0,0) only

The correct answer is (A). You may be unfamiliar with this notation, but the question is telling you that some function or transformation, called f, transforms every point (x, y) in the plane into the point $(x, y - x)$. For example, f sends the point (5, 3) to (5, –2). The question is asking you to describe all the points (x, y) that do not change under the transformation f. Once you are able to think of this question algebraically, it becomes much easier. You can simply ask yourself for what points (x, y) is it true that $(x, y) = (x, y - x)$, or in other words, $y = y - x$ (since $x = x$ is always true). For y to equal $y - x$, x must equal 0. If $x = 0$, then f will transform (x, y) into (x, y), so this is the condition you are looking for, and the answer is (A).

Section 6
3D Geometry

Three-dimensional geometry only makes up about 2-3 questions on the Math Level 2 test. However, these questions can be challenging, so it's worth brushing up on the concepts they cover! For the definitions of more fundamental terms like solid, surface area, volume, face, edge, and vertex, check out our website or our New SAT 6 Practice Tests book. 3D Geometry questions also frequently test material covered in the Coordinate Geometry and Trigonometry sections.

3D Coordinates

Term	Definition	Examples
Point (3D)	A point in 3D space represented as an ordered triplet (x, y, z).	$(4, 3, -1)$
Distance (3D)	The distance between the points (x_1, y_1, z_1) and (x_2, y_2, z_2) is given by the formula $\sqrt{(x_1 - x_2)^2 + (y_1 - y_2)^2 + (z_1 - z_2)^2}$. This is the same as the distance formula in two dimensions, except with a third pair of coordinates.	The distance between the points $(3, -5, 2)$ and $(-2, 4, 4)$ is $d = \sqrt{(3-(-2))^2 + (-5-4)^2 + (2-4)^2}$ $= \sqrt{110} \cong 10.5.$

Vector (3D)	A line segment that also has a direction, usually represented as an arrow. Often, vectors are written in the form $\langle a,b,c \rangle$, which indicates a vector pointing from the origin to the point (a, b, c), The magnitude, or length, of the vector $\langle a,b,c \rangle$ is equal to $\sqrt{a^2+b^2+c^2}$. Vectors are often denoted by an italicised letter with an arrow above it ($\vec{v}$) or by a bolded letter (**v**).	The magnitude of the vector $\langle 1, 3, -4 \rangle$ is $\sqrt{1^2+3^2+(-4)^2} = \sqrt{26} \cong 5.1$.
Plane	A flat, two-dimensional surface that extends forever in both dimensions. Planes can be defined by two intersecting or parallel lines, a line and a non-collinear point, three non-collinear points, or an equation of the form $ax + by + cz = d$, where a, b, c, and d are constants.	$9x + 7y + 6z = 1$ 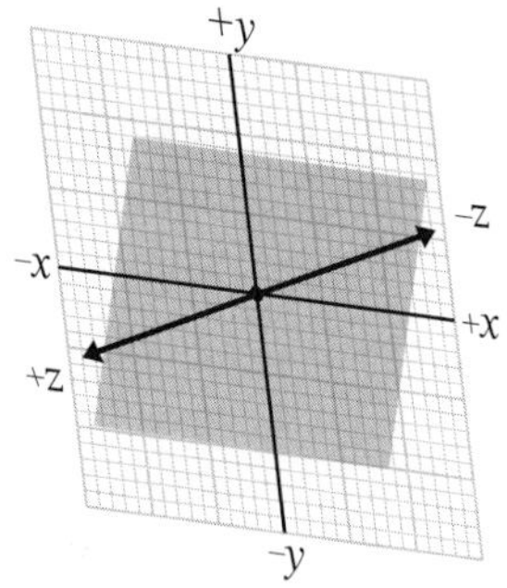

Essential Technique: Vector Operations

Vectors can be added, subtracted, or multiplied by constants. Generally, you will be asked to perform these operations when vectors are written in the form $\langle a,b \rangle$ or $\langle a,b,c \rangle$. On the Math Level 2 Subject test, vectors will have either 2 or 3 coordinates.

To add or subtract two vectors, just add or subtract the numbers "component-wise." In other words, the first coordinate of the solution will be the sum of the first coordinates of each of the two vectors, and so on. For example:

$$\langle 7,2,1 \rangle + \langle -2,0,1 \rangle = \langle (7+(-2)),\ (2+0),\ (1+1) \rangle = \langle 5,2,2 \rangle$$
$$\langle 4,3,-2 \rangle - \langle 1,5,2 \rangle = \langle (4-1),\ (3-5),\ (-2-2) \rangle = \langle 3,-2,-4 \rangle$$

To multiply a vector by a constant, multiply each entry by the constant:

$$3 \langle 0,-2,3 \rangle = \langle (3\times 0),\ (3\times(-2)),\ (3\times 3) \rangle = \langle 0,-6,9 \rangle$$

On the Math Level 2 test, you will not be asked to multiply a vector by another vector.

Adding two vectors together can be interpreted geometrically as placing them "tip-to-tail" adjacent to each other, as shown in the figure to the right. Multiplying a vector by a constant can be interpreted as stretching the vector by that constant, and reversing the direction if the constant is negative. For example, multiplying a vector by –2 will double its magnitude and reverse its direction, whereas multiplying a vector by –1 will reverse the direction without changing the magnitude.

Example Question	Solution
If $\mathbf{u} = \langle 2,3,1 \rangle$ and $\mathbf{v} = \langle 2,1,-2 \rangle$, then what is $3\mathbf{u} - 2\mathbf{v}$? (A) $\langle 2,7,7 \rangle$ (B) $\langle 2,-3,-8 \rangle$ (C) $\langle -2,3,8 \rangle$ (D) $\langle 10,11,-1 \rangle$ (E) $\langle 2,7,-1 \rangle$	The correct answer is (A). To answer this question, you should first multiply $\mathbf{u}$ by 3, then multiply $\mathbf{v}$ by 2, and then subtract. $$3\mathbf{u} = 3 \times \langle 2,3,1 \rangle = \langle 6,9,3 \rangle$$ $$2\mathbf{v} = 2 \times \langle 2,1,-2 \rangle = \langle 4,2,-4 \rangle$$ $$3\mathbf{u} - 2\mathbf{v} = \langle 6,9,3 \rangle - \langle 4,2,-4 \rangle = \langle 2,7,7 \rangle$$

Basic 3D Shapes

Term	Definition	Equations	Examples
Cube	A solid formed by six congruent square faces meeting at twelve congruent edges.	$Volume = a^3$ $Surface\ Area = 6a^2$	
Prism	A solid formed by two congruent polygonal faces at opposite ends, with the bases connected by rectangles.	$B = Area\ of\ base$ $Volume = Bh$	
(Rectangular-based) Pyramid	A solid formed by connecting the vertices of a rectangular base to a single point.	$Volume = \frac{1}{3}lwh$ $Surface\ area = lw + ls + ws$	

Example Question	Solution

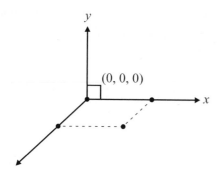

The base of a right pyramid with edges measuring 4 units is plotted on a graph as shown above. Which of the following could NOT be one of the pyramid's vertices?

(A) $(4, 0, 0)$

(B) $(0, 4, 0)$

(C) $(4, 0, 4)$

(D) $(2, \sqrt{8}, 2)$

(E) $(2, -\sqrt{8}, 2)$

The correct answer is (B). Since you know that the edges of the base of the pyramid have length 4, you know the four points indicated in the figure are $(0, 0, 0)$, $(4, 0, 0)$, $(4, 0, 4)$, and $(0, 0, 4)$. Therefore, you can already rule out (A) and (C). Since the pyramid is right, the apex of it must be directly above (or below) the center of the square base, which is at $(2, 0, 2)$. This means that the remaining vertex of the pyramid could be at any point of the form $(2, y, 2)$, where $y \neq 0$. However, it could not be at $(0, 4, 0)$, since this point lies on the y-axis and not above the center of the pyramid's base.

Essential Technique: Visualization

The process of converting between numbers or equations and mental images or diagrams is called visualization, and it can make questions significantly easier. When you can form a mental image of a solid, you can manipulate it by rotating, stretching, segmenting, shrinking, and so on. These manipulations correspond to algebraic and graphical transformations. You can visualize in a few ways:

- Imagine a real object similar to a solid in a question (e.g. a baseball as a sphere or a shoebox as a rectangular prism), which you can then manipulate in your mind just as you would manipulate that object in your hand.

- Sketch some two-dimensional faces of the 3D solid and connect them with parallel lines:

- Sketch the two-dimensional front, top, or side view of the 3D solid and fill them out in different planes:

- Sketch the xy-plane, then add a diagonal z axis, and plot a 3D point by tracing up, down, and along each axis. Each pair of axes forms its own plane: the familiar xy-plane, the xz-plane, and the yz-plane.

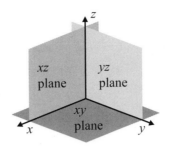

- Draw nets of shapes (two-dimensional layouts that can be "folded" back into three- dimensional shapes) to understand their faces, edges, and vertices, their volumes, and their surface areas:

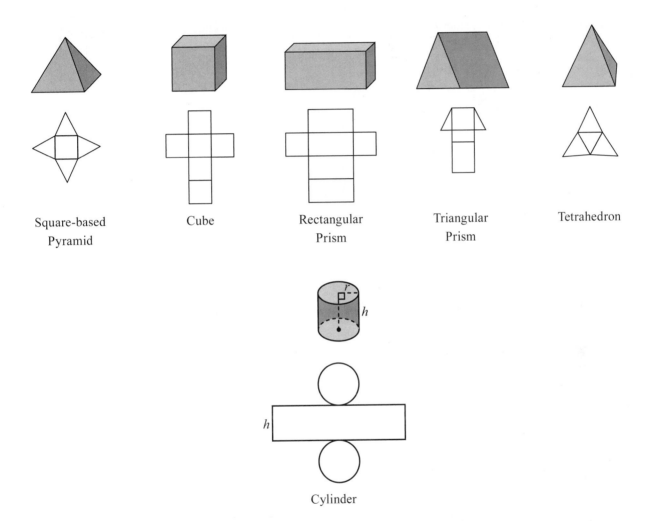

| Square-based Pyramid | Cube | Rectangular Prism | Triangular Prism | Tetrahedron |

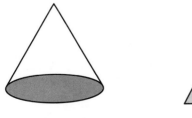

Cylinder

- Rotate a 3D shape in your mind and look at it from different angles:

Perspective View   Side   Top   Bottom

- Keep one variable constant and change the others—for example, keep the height of a cylinder the same, change the radius, and see what happens to the surface area and volume:

All this talk about visualization might not sound sufficiently "mathy," but many important mathematical discoveries, from Euclid's elements to Mandelbrot's fractals, were made through visualization. The best way to improve your visualization skills is with practice!

Visualization can help you figure out what shape will be produced by the intersection of a plane with a solid. Imagine you are cutting the solid with a knife and looking at the resulting face. Perhaps the most well-known intersections are those of planes with cones, shown below. Though you don't have to memorize these shapes, they can help you with visualizing coordinate geometry questions about conic sections. For more information on these conic sections, turn to Chapter 2 Section 5 in the Coordinate Geometry section of this book.

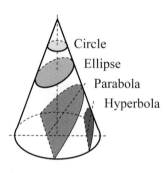

Example Question	Solution
Which of the following CANNOT be produced from the intersection of a cube and a plane?	The correct answer is (E). You could make a square by slicing parallel to one of the existing faces, and you could make a triangle by slicing off one corner of the cube. It's a little harder to imagine how you could make a pentagon or hexagon, but the pictures below illustrate them:

Which of the following CANNOT be produced from the intersection of a cube and a plane?

(A) A triangle
(B) A square
(C) A pentagon
(D) A hexagon
(E) A heptagon

The correct answer is (E). You could make a square by slicing parallel to one of the existing faces, and you could make a triangle by slicing off one corner of the cube. It's a little harder to imagine how you could make a pentagon or hexagon, but the pictures below illustrate them:

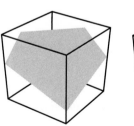 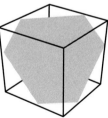

However, there is no way to make a heptagon by intersecting a plane with a cube.

Term	Definition	Equations	Examples
Cone	A solid formed by connecting every point on the circumference of a circle to a single point above it. You can think of a cone as a pyramid with a circular base. *Note: you will not be asked to calculate the surface area of a cone.*	$Volume = \frac{1}{3}\pi r^2 h$	
Cylinder	A prism with circular bases connected by a rounded rectangular surface.	$Volume = \pi r^2 h$ $Surface\ Area = 2\pi r^2 + 2\pi rh$	
Sphere	A round solid whose surface points are equidistant from its center.	$Volume = \frac{4}{3}\pi r^3$ $Surface\ Area = 4\pi r^2$	

Essential Technique: Proportionality

The test may also ask you to determine what happens to one quantity when another quantity in relation to it is changed. For these questions, it's a good idea to think about the proportionalities between the different quantities, the way that a change in one of them affects the other, so that you don't get distracted by variables that aren't being discussed or by constants. In a cylinder, for example, volume is proportional to the square of the radius and to the height, and the constant of proportionality is π. Proportionality is represented by an operator that looks like the Greek letter alpha ($\propto$):

$$V = \pi r^2 h$$
$$V \propto r^2$$
$$V \propto h$$

The relationship $V \propto r^2$ tells you that if the height of the cylinder stays the same, but the radius doubles, the volume must increase by a factor of $2^2 = 4$.

If a spherical watermelon growing in a field triples in surface area, by what factor does its volume increase?

(A) 1.4142

(B) 1.4422

(C) 1.7321

(D) 2.0801

(E) 5.1962

The correct answer is (E). The surface area of a sphere is proportional to the square of the radius $(A \propto r^2)$, so if the surface area increases by a factor of 3, the radius increases by a factor of $\sqrt{3}$. Since the volume is proportional to the cube of the radius $(V \propto r^3)$, when the radius increases by a factor of $\sqrt{3}$, the volume increases by a factor of $\sqrt{3}^3 = 5.1962$.

Practice Test 1

YOUR NAME (PRINT):

LAST   FIRST   MI

| Correct ● | Incorrect ⊘ ⊗ ⊘ ◑ ⊛ ○ ◎ ● | **Make sure you use a No. 2 pencil.** Each answer must be marked in the corresponding row on the answer sheet. Each bubble must be filled in completely and darkly within the lines. Extra marks on your answer sheet may be marked as incorrect answers and lower your score. |

○ Literature	○ Mathematics Level 1	○ German
○ Biology E	○ Mathematics Level 2	○ Italian
○ Biology M	○ U.S. History	○ Latin
○ Chemistry	○ World History	○ Modern Hebrew
○ Physics	○ French	○ Spanish

1 Ⓐ Ⓑ Ⓒ Ⓓ Ⓔ   21 Ⓐ Ⓑ Ⓒ Ⓓ Ⓔ   41 Ⓐ Ⓑ Ⓒ Ⓓ Ⓔ   61 Ⓐ Ⓑ Ⓒ Ⓓ Ⓔ   81 Ⓐ Ⓑ Ⓒ Ⓓ Ⓔ

2 Ⓐ Ⓑ Ⓒ Ⓓ Ⓔ   22 Ⓐ Ⓑ Ⓒ Ⓓ Ⓔ   42 Ⓐ Ⓑ Ⓒ Ⓓ Ⓔ   62 Ⓐ Ⓑ Ⓒ Ⓓ Ⓔ   82 Ⓐ Ⓑ Ⓒ Ⓓ Ⓔ

3 Ⓐ Ⓑ Ⓒ Ⓓ Ⓔ   23 Ⓐ Ⓑ Ⓒ Ⓓ Ⓔ   43 Ⓐ Ⓑ Ⓒ Ⓓ Ⓔ   63 Ⓐ Ⓑ Ⓒ Ⓓ Ⓔ   83 Ⓐ Ⓑ Ⓒ Ⓓ Ⓔ

4 Ⓐ Ⓑ Ⓒ Ⓓ Ⓔ   24 Ⓐ Ⓑ Ⓒ Ⓓ Ⓔ   44 Ⓐ Ⓑ Ⓒ Ⓓ Ⓔ   64 Ⓐ Ⓑ Ⓒ Ⓓ Ⓔ   84 Ⓐ Ⓑ Ⓒ Ⓓ Ⓔ

5 Ⓐ Ⓑ Ⓒ Ⓓ Ⓔ   25 Ⓐ Ⓑ Ⓒ Ⓓ Ⓔ   45 Ⓐ Ⓑ Ⓒ Ⓓ Ⓔ   65 Ⓐ Ⓑ Ⓒ Ⓓ Ⓔ   85 Ⓐ Ⓑ Ⓒ Ⓓ Ⓔ

6 Ⓐ Ⓑ Ⓒ Ⓓ Ⓔ   26 Ⓐ Ⓑ Ⓒ Ⓓ Ⓔ   46 Ⓐ Ⓑ Ⓒ Ⓓ Ⓔ   66 Ⓐ Ⓑ Ⓒ Ⓓ Ⓔ   86 Ⓐ Ⓑ Ⓒ Ⓓ Ⓔ

7 Ⓐ Ⓑ Ⓒ Ⓓ Ⓔ   27 Ⓐ Ⓑ Ⓒ Ⓓ Ⓔ   47 Ⓐ Ⓑ Ⓒ Ⓓ Ⓔ   67 Ⓐ Ⓑ Ⓒ Ⓓ Ⓔ   87 Ⓐ Ⓑ Ⓒ Ⓓ Ⓔ

8 Ⓐ Ⓑ Ⓒ Ⓓ Ⓔ   28 Ⓐ Ⓑ Ⓒ Ⓓ Ⓔ   48 Ⓐ Ⓑ Ⓒ Ⓓ Ⓔ   68 Ⓐ Ⓑ Ⓒ Ⓓ Ⓔ   88 Ⓐ Ⓑ Ⓒ Ⓓ Ⓔ

9 Ⓐ Ⓑ Ⓒ Ⓓ Ⓔ   29 Ⓐ Ⓑ Ⓒ Ⓓ Ⓔ   49 Ⓐ Ⓑ Ⓒ Ⓓ Ⓔ   69 Ⓐ Ⓑ Ⓒ Ⓓ Ⓔ   89 Ⓐ Ⓑ Ⓒ Ⓓ Ⓔ

10 Ⓐ Ⓑ Ⓒ Ⓓ Ⓔ   30 Ⓐ Ⓑ Ⓒ Ⓓ Ⓔ   50 Ⓐ Ⓑ Ⓒ Ⓓ Ⓔ   70 Ⓐ Ⓑ Ⓒ Ⓓ Ⓔ   90 Ⓐ Ⓑ Ⓒ Ⓓ Ⓔ

11 Ⓐ Ⓑ Ⓒ Ⓓ Ⓔ   31 Ⓐ Ⓑ Ⓒ Ⓓ Ⓔ   51 Ⓐ Ⓑ Ⓒ Ⓓ Ⓔ   71 Ⓐ Ⓑ Ⓒ Ⓓ Ⓔ   81 Ⓐ Ⓑ Ⓒ Ⓓ Ⓔ

12 Ⓐ Ⓑ Ⓒ Ⓓ Ⓔ   32 Ⓐ Ⓑ Ⓒ Ⓓ Ⓔ   52 Ⓐ Ⓑ Ⓒ Ⓓ Ⓔ   72 Ⓐ Ⓑ Ⓒ Ⓓ Ⓔ   92 Ⓐ Ⓑ Ⓒ Ⓓ Ⓔ

13 Ⓐ Ⓑ Ⓒ Ⓓ Ⓔ   33 Ⓐ Ⓑ Ⓒ Ⓓ Ⓔ   53 Ⓐ Ⓑ Ⓒ Ⓓ Ⓔ   73 Ⓐ Ⓑ Ⓒ Ⓓ Ⓔ   93 Ⓐ Ⓑ Ⓒ Ⓓ Ⓔ

14 Ⓐ Ⓑ Ⓒ Ⓓ Ⓔ   34 Ⓐ Ⓑ Ⓒ Ⓓ Ⓔ   54 Ⓐ Ⓑ Ⓒ Ⓓ Ⓔ   74 Ⓐ Ⓑ Ⓒ Ⓓ Ⓔ   94 Ⓐ Ⓑ Ⓒ Ⓓ Ⓔ

15 Ⓐ Ⓑ Ⓒ Ⓓ Ⓔ   35 Ⓐ Ⓑ Ⓒ Ⓓ Ⓔ   55 Ⓐ Ⓑ Ⓒ Ⓓ Ⓔ   75 Ⓐ Ⓑ Ⓒ Ⓓ Ⓔ   95 Ⓐ Ⓑ Ⓒ Ⓓ Ⓔ

16 Ⓐ Ⓑ Ⓒ Ⓓ Ⓔ   36 Ⓐ Ⓑ Ⓒ Ⓓ Ⓔ   56 Ⓐ Ⓑ Ⓒ Ⓓ Ⓔ   76 Ⓐ Ⓑ Ⓒ Ⓓ Ⓔ   96 Ⓐ Ⓑ Ⓒ Ⓓ Ⓔ

17 Ⓐ Ⓑ Ⓒ Ⓓ Ⓔ   37 Ⓐ Ⓑ Ⓒ Ⓓ Ⓔ   57 Ⓐ Ⓑ Ⓒ Ⓓ Ⓔ   77 Ⓐ Ⓑ Ⓒ Ⓓ Ⓔ   97 Ⓐ Ⓑ Ⓒ Ⓓ Ⓔ

18 Ⓐ Ⓑ Ⓒ Ⓓ Ⓔ   38 Ⓐ Ⓑ Ⓒ Ⓓ Ⓔ   58 Ⓐ Ⓑ Ⓒ Ⓓ Ⓔ   78 Ⓐ Ⓑ Ⓒ Ⓓ Ⓔ   98 Ⓐ Ⓑ Ⓒ Ⓓ Ⓔ

19 Ⓐ Ⓑ Ⓒ Ⓓ Ⓔ   39 Ⓐ Ⓑ Ⓒ Ⓓ Ⓔ   59 Ⓐ Ⓑ Ⓒ Ⓓ Ⓔ   79 Ⓐ Ⓑ Ⓒ Ⓓ Ⓔ   99 Ⓐ Ⓑ Ⓒ Ⓓ Ⓔ

20 Ⓐ Ⓑ Ⓒ Ⓓ Ⓔ   40 Ⓐ Ⓑ Ⓒ Ⓓ Ⓔ   60 Ⓐ Ⓑ Ⓒ Ⓓ Ⓔ   80 Ⓐ Ⓑ Ⓒ Ⓓ Ⓔ   100 Ⓐ Ⓑ Ⓒ Ⓓ Ⓔ

For automatic scoring and scaling, please visit **cloud.ivyglobal.com**.

SAT Math Level 2 Subject Test

Reference Materials

THE FORMULAS BELOW MAY BE USEFUL IN ANSWERING QUESTIONS ON THIS TEST.

$S = 4\pi r^2$ is the formula for the surface area of a sphere with a radius of r.

$V = \frac{1}{3}\pi r^2 h$ is the formula for the volume of a right circular cone with a radius of r and a height of h.

$V = \frac{4}{3}\pi r^3$ is the formula for the volume of a sphere with a radius of r.

$V = \frac{1}{3}Bh$ is the formula for the volume of a pyramid with a base area of B and a height of h.

When choosing an answer, find the CLOSEST answer possible. If the precise numerical value that you have found is not an answer choice, select the choice that is closest to your answer. Use the answer sheet and fill in the bubble corresponding to your choice.

Notes: (1) You ARE permitted the use of a graphing or scientific calculator, which you may use at your own discretion. You will also have to choose between degree or radian mode for some questions, so keep track of what mode your calculator is in.

(2) You may assume that figures are drawn as accurately as possible UNLESS it is explicitly stated that a figure is not drawn to scale. Furthermore, all figures are in a plane UNLESS it is stated otherwise.

(3) For any function f, unless otherwise specified, you may assume that a real number x is in the domain of f if and only if $f(x)$ is a real number. The range of f consists of all and only those real numbers of the form $f(x)$, where x is in the domain of f.

(4) Four formulas are provided in the box above for your reference.

GO ON TO THE NEXT PAGE

1. If the slope of the line containing the points (4, 5) and (a, 10) is 1, then $a =$

   (A)   8

   (B)   9

   (C)   10

   (D)   11

   (E)   12

2. The function $f(x) = \dfrac{7}{x(x+2)(x-5)(x-8)}$ has asymptotes at all of the following x-values EXCEPT

   (A) -2

   (B)   0

   (C)   5

   (D)   7

   (E)   8

3. If $3^y = 93.435$, then $y =$

   (A)   4.09

   (B)   4.13

   (C)   4.28

   (D)   4.54

   (E)   4.69

USE THIS SPACE FOR SCRATCH WORK.

GO ON TO THE NEXT PAGE

4. The mean weight of the 10 players on a professional hockey team is 190 pounds. When a new player is signed, the range of the players' weights increases to 100 pounds. Which of the following must be true?

    (A)   The new player weighs 190 pounds.

    (B)   The new player's weight did not change the mean.

    (C)   The new player weighs either the most or the least on the team.

    (D)   The new player weighs less than 190 pounds.

    (E)   The new player weighs more than 190 pounds.

5. If $\sin^2 \theta = 0.882$, then $\cos^2 \theta =$

    (A)   0.118

    (B)   0.441

    (C)   0.882

    (D)   1.065

    (E)   1.134

6. If $g(x) = 3x - 5$ and $g(a) = 2a$, then $a =$

    (A)   0

    (B)   1

    (C)   3

    (D)   5

    (E)   8

GO ON TO THE NEXT PAGE

USE THIS SPACE FOR SCRATCH WORK.

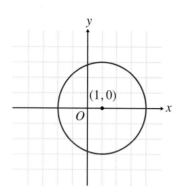

7. A circle with center (1,0) and radius 3 is shown above. Which of the following equations does NOT represent a line of symmetry of the circle?

(A) $x = 1$

(B) $y = 0$

(C) $y = x - 1$

(D) $y = -x + 1$

(E) $y = -x - 1$

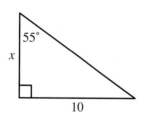

Note: Figure not drawn to scale.

8. In the triangle shown above, what is the value of x?

(A) $10 \sin 55°$

(B) $\dfrac{1}{10} \tan 55°$

(C) $10 \cot 55°$

(D) $\dfrac{1}{10} \csc 55°$

(E) $\dfrac{1}{10} \cot 55°$

GO ON TO THE NEXT PAGE

USE THIS SPACE FOR SCRATCH WORK.

9. Point A is located at $(10, 5)$ and point B is located at $(-3, -7)$. Which of the following is an equation of a line perpendicular to the line that passes through A and B ?

(A) $y = \frac{7}{2}x + 3$

(B) $y = -\frac{2}{7}x + 3$

(C) $y = \frac{12}{13}x + 3$

(D) $y = \frac{13}{12}x + 3$

(E) $y = -\frac{13}{12}x + 3$

10. $\frac{a}{b} + \frac{b}{a} =$

(A) 1

(B) 2

(C) $\frac{1}{ab}$

(D) $\frac{(a+b)^2}{ab}$

(E) $\frac{a^2 + b^2}{ab}$

GO ON TO THE NEXT PAGE

11. If $x+y=5$, $y+z=7$, and $x+z=-2$, then $x+y+z=$

   (A)   4

   (B)   5

   (C)   6

   (D)   7

   (E)   8

12. If $h(x) = x^n (x^2 - 4) + 21$, for which of the following values of n does h have at least one real root?

   (A)   0

   (B)   1

   (C)   2

   (D)   4

   (E)   There is no such value of n.

13. A salesman sells 15 cars for an average price of $32,500. If he wants to increase his average sale price to $40,000, for how much money must he sell his 16th and final car?

   (A) $36,250

   (B) $47,500

   (C) $72,500

   (D) $112,500

   (E) $152,500

GO ON TO THE NEXT PAGE

USE THIS SPACE FOR SCRATCH WORK.

14. If $a : b = -6za : yb$, then

(A) $|y| = |6a|$

(B) $|y| = |6z|$

(C) $y = -6$

(D) $y = -6za$

(E) $y = b$

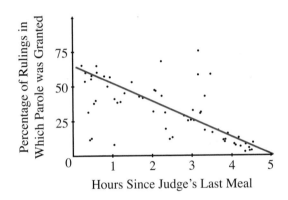

Hours Since Judge's Last Meal

15. The linear regression above shows the number of hours since a judge's last meal and the percentage of rulings in which that judge granted parole. Which of the following is a reasonable interpretation of these data?

(A)   When judges have not eaten a meal recently, they are more likely to grant parole.

(B)   When judges have not eaten a meal recently, they are less likely to grant parole.

(C)   When judges have eaten a meal recently, they are less likely to grant parole.

(D)   The amount of time since judges' last meals has no effect on their rulings.

(E)   The data have no outliers.

GO ON TO THE NEXT PAGE

USE THIS SPACE FOR SCRATCH WORK.

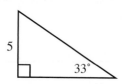

Note: Figure not drawn to scale.

16. A cord of lights is strung around a triangular garden with the dimensions shown above. What is the length of cord needed, to the nearest foot?

(A)   17

(B)   20

(C)   22

(D)   27

(E)   30

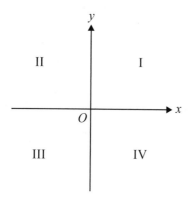

17. If a point (x, y) satisfies the inequalities $y < 2x - 4$ and $y \leq -x + 7$, then (x, y) could be in any quadrant EXCEPT

(A)   I

(B)   II

(C)   III

(D)   IV

(E)   The point (x, y) could be in any quadrant.

GO ON TO THE NEXT PAGE

USE THIS SPACE FOR SCRATCH WORK.

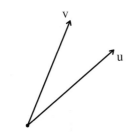

Note: Figure not drawn to scale.

18. If vector $\mathbf{u} = \langle 6,\ 5 \rangle$ and vector $\mathbf{v} = \langle 3, 7 \rangle$, then $2\mathbf{u} - \mathbf{v} =$

   (A) $\langle 0,\ 9 \rangle$

   (B) $\langle 3,\ -2 \rangle$

   (C) $\langle 9,\ 3 \rangle$

   (D) $\langle -3,\ 2 \rangle$

   (E) $\langle -9,\ 3 \rangle$

19. On which of the following intervals is the function
$f(x) = 2x^4 + 3x^3 - 9x^2 + x + 3$ increasing?

   (A) $0 < x < 1$

   (B) $-\dfrac{1}{2} < x < 0$

   (C) $-3 < x < -\dfrac{1}{2}$

   (D) $x < -3$

   (E)   None of the above

GO ON TO THE NEXT PAGE

USE THIS SPACE FOR SCRATCH WORK.

20. The intersection of a sphere with a plane could form which of the following?

I. A point
II. A parabola
III. A circle

(A) I only

(B) II only

(C) III only

(D) I and III only

(E) I, II, and III

$$\frac{1}{d_o}+\frac{1}{d_i}=\frac{1}{f}$$

21. The Thin Lens Equation is shown above, where d_o is the distance from the lens to the object, d_i is the distance from the lens to the image, and f is the focal length of the lens. Which of the following expressions is equivalent to f?

(A) $\frac{1}{d_o}+\frac{1}{d_i}$

(B) d_o+d_i

(C) $\frac{d_o+d_i}{d_o d_i}$

(D) $\frac{d_o d_i}{d_o+d_i}$

(E) $\frac{1}{d_o d_i}$

22. If $g(x)=7x^3+4x$, and $f(x)$ is the inverse of $g(x)$, then $f(-201)=$

(A) −4

(B) −3

(C) −2

(D) −1

(E) 4

GO ON TO THE NEXT PAGE

23. If $i^2 = -1$, and if $(2i+5)i^k = 5i-2$, then k could equal

(A) 4

(B) 5

(C) 6

(D) 7

(E) 8

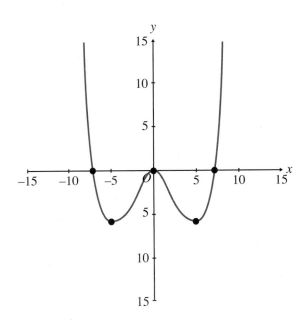

24. The function f, shown above, satisfies which of the following relationships for all real numbers x?

(A) $f(x) = f(-x)$

(B) $f(x) = -f(x)$

(C) $f(x) = -f(-x)$

(D) $f(x) = f(f(x))$

(E) None of the above

GO ON TO THE NEXT PAGE

USE THIS SPACE FOR SCRATCH WORK.

25. There is a 0.4 probability that Candidate A wins the election and a 0.6 probability that Candidate B wins the election. If Candidate A wins, there is a 0.3 probability that new parks will be built. If Candidate B wins, there is a 0.8 probability that new parks will be built. What is the probability that new parks will be built?

(A)   0.12

(B)   0.24

(C)   0.28

(D)   0.48

(E)   0.60

26. If $f(x) = 4^x - 5^x$ and $g(x) = 2^{2x} + 5^x$, then $(fg)(1) =$

(A)   −9

(B)   −7

(C)   0

(D)   9

(E)   41

27. A number's prime factors include n, $n + 3$, and $n + 11$, for some value of n. This number could be

(A)   42

(B)   110

(C)   130

(D)   429

(E)   3,330

GO ON TO THE NEXT PAGE

USE THIS SPACE FOR SCRATCH WORK.

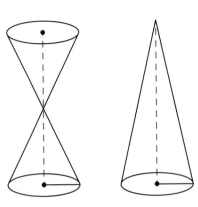

28. A cone and an hourglass, which is composed of two smaller, identical cones, have the same height and the same radius, as shown in the figure above. The hourglass's volume is what percentage of the cone's volume?

(A) 67%

(B) 75%

(C) 100%

(D) 125%

(E) 133%

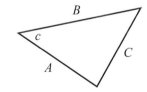

Note: Figure not drawn to scale.

29. If $A = 3$, $B = 4$, and $c = 45°$, what is the length of side C?

(A) 2.500

(B) 2.750

(C) 2.833

(D) 3.167

(E) 5.000

GO ON TO THE NEXT PAGE

USE THIS SPACE FOR SCRATCH WORK.

30. If $\sin^{-1}(\cos a) = -\dfrac{\pi}{6}$, which of the following is a possible value of a?

(A)　$-\dfrac{\pi}{3}$

(B)　$-\dfrac{1}{2}$

(C)　$\dfrac{\pi}{3}$

(D)　$\dfrac{4\pi}{3}$

(E)　$\dfrac{7\pi}{3}$

31. If $f(x)$ has three x-intercepts and $g(x)$ has four x-intercepts, what is the maximum number of x-intercepts that the function fg could have?

(A)　1

(B)　3

(C)　4

(D)　7

(E)　12

32. A function is defined recursively such that for any integer n, $f(n) = f(n-1) + 3$. If $f(0) = 2$, then $f(10) =$

(A)　5

(B)　12

(C)　13

(D)　29

(E)　32

GO ON TO THE NEXT PAGE

USE THIS SPACE FOR SCRATCH WORK.

33. Each person in a group of 7 people shakes hands with each other person, except for 2 pairs of people who have already met. How many handshakes take place?

(A)   19

(B)   26

(C)   34

(D)   358

(E)   2,520

34. Given $\log_4 m = 3$ and $\log_2 n = 5$, then the product of m and n is equal to

(A) 2^8

(B) 2^{11}

(C) 2^{15}

(D) 2^{22}

(E) 2^{30}

35. What is the period of the function $f(x) = 3\sin\left(2x + \frac{\pi}{2}\right) - 1$?

(A) 2π

(B) $\frac{3\pi}{2}$

(C) π

(D) $\frac{\pi}{2}$

(E) $\frac{\pi}{3}$

GO ON TO THE NEXT PAGE

36. If p and q are distinct prime numbers, how many positive factors does pq^2 have?

(A)   4

(B)   6

(C)   8

(D)   10

(E)   12

USE THIS SPACE FOR SCRATCH WORK.

Test Number	Attempt 1	Attempt 2
1	85	91
2	81	90
3	89	
4	88	97
5	92	

37. The chart above shows one student's test results in her physics class. Students in this class may retake any test one time, and the average of the two attempts is considered the final score on that test. If this student wants to retake Test 3 to get her total average test score to at least 90, what is the lowest she can score?

(A)   91

(B)   92

(C)   93

(D)   94

(E)   95

GO ON TO THE NEXT PAGE

USE THIS SPACE FOR SCRATCH WORK.

38. What is the domain of the function $f(x) = \dfrac{x-2}{\sqrt{2x-5}}$

   (A) $x > \dfrac{5}{2}$

   (B) $x \geq \dfrac{5}{2}$

   (C) $x > 2$

   (D) $x \geq 2$

   (E) $x \neq \dfrac{5}{2}$

39. If a line is represented by the parametric equations
   $x = 2t + 3$ and $y = 3t - 5$, what is the slope of the line?

   (A) $-\dfrac{19}{2}$

   (B) $-\dfrac{3}{2}$

   (C) $-\dfrac{2}{3}$

   (D) $\dfrac{2}{3}$

   (E) $\dfrac{3}{2}$

40. A cube has a volume of 343 m³. What is the maximum possible straight-line distance between two points that lie on its surface?

   (A)   7.2 m

   (B)   12.1 m

   (C)   21.3 m

   (D)   49.0 m

   (E)   147.2 m

GO ON TO THE NEXT PAGE

USE THIS SPACE FOR SCRATCH WORK.

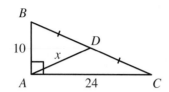

Note: Figure not drawn to scale.

41. In triangle *ABC* above, *AB* = 10, *AC* = 24, and *BD* = *CD*. What is the value of *x*?

(A)   7

(B)   10

(C)   12

(D)   13

(E)   26

42. Which of the following equations represents a conic section?

    I. $x^2 + y^2 = 1$

    II. $\dfrac{x^2}{a^2} + \dfrac{y^2}{b^2} = 1$

    III. $\dfrac{x^2}{a^2} - \dfrac{y^2}{b^2} = 1$

(A)   I only

(B)   II only

(C)   I and III

(D)   II and III

(E)   I, II, and III

43. Which of the following is true about the function $g(x) = \dfrac{1}{x^2} - \dfrac{1}{x}$?

    (A) $g(x)$ has two horizontal asymptotes.

    (B) $g(x)$ is symmetric about the y-axis.

    (C) $g(x)$ has a removable discontinuity at $x = 0$.

    (D) $g(x)$ is negative if and only if $x > 0$.

    (E) $g(x)$ is negative if and only if $x > 1$.

44. The point P has coordinates $(1, 3)$, and the point Q has coordinates $(3, 3)$. Both points are found on the perimeter of a square in the xy-plane. What is the minimum possible area of the square?

    (A)   1

    (B)   2

    (C)   4

    (D)   8

    (E)   9

45. Which of the following is equivalent to $\tan^2 x$?

    (A) $\csc^2 x - 1$

    (B) $\csc^2 x + 1$

    (C) $\sec^2 x - 1$

    (D) $\sec^2 x + 1$

    (E) $\csc^2 x + \sec^2 x$

GO ON TO THE NEXT PAGE

USE THIS SPACE FOR SCRATCH WORK.

$$f(x) = \begin{cases} 2x+1 \, , \, x < 0 \\ \sqrt{x} \quad , \, 0 \leq x < 9 \, ? \\ -x \quad \, , \, x \geq 9 \end{cases}$$

46. What is the maximum value of the function above?

    (A)   1

    (B)   2

    (C)   3

    (D)   9

    (E)   The function does not attain a maximum value.

x	$f(x)$
−7	2
−4	3
−1	−2
2	0.5
8	1

47. Five values of the function f are given in the table above. Given that the domain of f is $\{ x : x \in \mathbb{R}, x \neq 0, x \neq -2 \}$, which of the following can be inferred?

    (A)   The graph of f has at least 1 x-intercept.

    (B) f is increasing for $2 \leq x \leq 8$.

    (C)   the graph of f has at least two vertical asymoptotes.

    (D) f is continuous on the interval $2 < x < \infty$.

    (E)   The graph of f has no y-intercept.

USE THIS SPACE FOR SCRATCH WORK.

48. If $f(x) = -g(-x)$ for all real numbers x, what is the value of $g(f(4))$, given that $(-4, 7)$ is a point on the graph of g?

(A) $f(7)$

(B) $-f(7)$

(C) $f(-7)$

(D) $-f(-7)$

(E) $f(f(7))$

49. $\begin{bmatrix} 4 & 2 & 2 \end{bmatrix} \times \begin{bmatrix} 2 & 3 \\ 3 & 2 \\ 2 & 1 \end{bmatrix} =$

(A) $\begin{bmatrix} 18 & 18 \end{bmatrix}$

(B) $\begin{bmatrix} 20 & 10 \end{bmatrix}$

(C) $\begin{bmatrix} 8 & 12 \\ 6 & 4 \\ 4 & 2 \end{bmatrix}$

(D) $\begin{bmatrix} 20 \\ 10 \\ 6 \end{bmatrix}$

(E)   The product does not exist.

GO ON TO THE NEXT PAGE

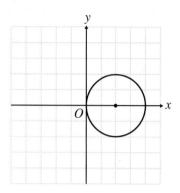

50. In polar coordinates, which of the following is an equation for the circle shown above?

(A) $r = 2$

(B) $r = 2 \cos \theta$

(C) $r = 2 \sin \theta$

(D) $r = 4 \cos \theta$

(E) $r = 4 \sin \theta$

STOP

**If you complete this test before the end of your allotted time,
you may check your work.**

Answers and Scoring

Scoring Your Test
Part 1

The easiest way to score your test is to use our Cloud scoring tool. The Cloud tool also provides more detailed results by showing you how you performed on specific kinds of questions. To score your test by hand, follow the directions below.

 For more detailed scoring results, please visit **cloud.ivyglobal.com.**

Answers

1. B	11. B	21. D	31. D	41. D
2. D	12. B	22. B	32. E	42. E
3. B	13. E	23. B	33. A	43. E
4. C	14. B	24. A	34. B	44. B
5. A	15. B	25. E	35. C	45. C
6. D	16. C	26. A	36. B	46. E
7. E	17. B	27. C	37. E	47. E
8. C	18. C	28. C	38. A	48. B
9. E	19. B	29. C	39. E	49. A
10. E	20. D	30. D	40. B	50. D

Raw Scores

To score your test, first use the answer key to mark each of your responses as correct or incorrect. Don't mark or count questions you left blank. Then, calculate your raw score for each section by subtracting one fourth the number of incorrect responses from the number of correct responses. Scores should be rounded to the nearest whole number, with .5 and above rounding up. Use the tables below to help you calculate your scores:

Scores	
Number Correct	_____ −
Number incorrect	_____ / 4 = _____
Raw Score	= _____
Scaled Score	_____

Scaled Scores

Once you have found your raw score for each test, convert it into an approximate scaled test score using the following chart. To find a scaled test score for each section, find the row in the Raw Score column which corresponds to your raw score for that section, then check the column for the section you are scoring in the same row. For example, if you had a raw score of 31, your scaled score would be 580. Keep in mind that these scaled scores are estimates only. Your actual SAT Subject Test in Mathematics Level 2 score will be scaled against the scores of all other students at your grade level taking the test on your test date.

			Scaled Score				
Raw Score	Scaled Score	Raw Score	Scaled Score	Raw Score	Scaled Score	Raw Score	Scaled Score
50	800	34	710	18	560	2	440
49	800	33	700	17	560	1	430
48	800	32	690	16	550	0	410
47	800	31	680	15	540	−1	390
46	800	30	670	14	530	−2	370
45	800	29	660	13	530	−3	360
44	800	28	650	12	520	−4	340
43	800	27	640	11	510	−5	340
42	790	26	630	10	500	−6	330
41	790	25	630	9	500	−7	320
40	780	24	620	8	490	−8	320
39	770	23	610	7	480	−9	320
38	750	22	600	6	480	−10	320
37	740	21	590	5	470	−11	310
36	730	20	580	4	460	−12	310
35	720	19	570	3	450		

Explanations
Part 2

1. The correct answer is (B). The slope of a line between two points is equal to the difference in y-values divided by the difference in x-values. In this case, the slope of the line is equal to $\frac{10-5}{a-4} = 1$. You can multiply both sides by $a - 4$ and solve for a to find that $a = 9$.

2. The correct answer is (D). To find the locations of the vertical asymptotes, set the denominator of this function equal to 0 and solve for x. The denominator is already factored, so you can see that it is equal to 0 when x is equal to 0, –2, 5, or 8. However, the denominator is not equal to 0 when $x = 7$, so there is no asymptote there.

3. The correct answer is (B). You can take the logarithm with base 3 of both sides to get $y = \log_3 93.435 = 4.13$. To evaluate this logarithm, it may be helpful to remember that $\log_3 93.435 = \frac{\log 93.435}{\log 3}$.

4. The correct answer is (C). If the range of the players' weights increases after a new player is added to the team, then the new player must weigh either the most or the least. The question does not give you any additional information about the new player's weight or the mean weight and whether it changed.

5. The correct answer is (A). Since $\sin^2 \theta + \cos^2 \theta = 1$, then $\cos^2 \theta = 1 - \sin^2 \theta = 1 - 0.882 = 0.118$, or (A).

6. The correct answer is (D). You know that $g(a) = 3a - 5$ for any value of a, so you can simply set $3a - 5 = 2a$ and solve to find $a = 5$.

7. The correct answer is (E). Any line that passes through the center of a circle is a line of symmetry of that circle. However, if a line does not pass through the center of the circle, it is not a line of symmetry. To solve this question, plug the center of the circle (1, 0) into each of the given equations to see which ones it satisfies. The point (1, 0) makes all of the given equations true except for (E), which results in –2 = 0.

8. The correct answer is (C). Since the cotangent of 55° is equal to the length of the adjacent side (x) divided by the length of the opposite side (10), you can rearrange for x to get $x = 10 \cot 55°$.

9. The correct answer is (E). Find the slope of the line that contains points A and B: $\frac{-7-5}{-3-10} = \frac{-12}{-13} = \frac{12}{13}$. The line perpendicular to this line has a slope that is the negative reciprocal of this slope: $-\frac{13}{12}$. The only answer option that has a slope of $-\frac{13}{12}$ is (E).

10. The correct answer is (E). To add fractions, you must first get them into a form with a common denominator. You can multiply the first fraction by $\frac{a}{a}$ and the second fraction by $\frac{b}{b}$ that they both have a denominator of ab. Finally, simply add the numerators: $\frac{a^2}{ab} + \frac{b^2}{ab} = \frac{a^2+b^2}{ab}$.

11. The correct answer is (B). Add the first three equations together to get $x + y + y + z + x + z = 5 + 7 - 2$, which simplifies to $2x + 2y + 2z = 10$. Dividing both sides by 2 gives you $x + y + z = 5$.

12. The correct answer is (B). If a polynomial function has an odd degree, it is guaranteed to have at least one real root. If $n = 1$ then the degree of the polynomial (after expanding) is 3, which is odd. However, if $n = 0, 2,$ or 4, then the degree of the polynomial will be even, so it is not guaranteed to have a real root. You can confirm that these options do not have any real roots by graphing them and noticing that the entire function lies above the x-axis in every case.

13. The correct answer is (E). The average of a set equals the sum of the numbers in the set divided by the number of elements in the set. The salesman has sold 15 cars for a sum of $32,500 \times 15 = 487,500$. He wants to sell 16 cars for an average of 40,000, which means a sum of $40,000 \times 16 = 640,000$. Therefore, the 16th and final car must be sold for $640,000 - 487,500 = 152,500$.

14. The correct answer is (B). Because a and b must be scaled by the same factor to remain in the same ratio with one another, $-6z = y$, so their absolute values are also equal: $\left|-6z\right| = \left|y\right|$.

15. The correct answer is (B). A linear regression analysis shows the correlation between two variables. This graph shows a negative correlation: as "Hours since judge's last meal" increases, the "Percentage of rulings in which parole was granted" decreases. Another way to phrase this is "When judges have not eaten a meal recently, they are less likely to grant parole."

16. The correct answer is (C). Since the sine of 33° is equal to the length of the opposite side divided by the length of the hypotenuse, $\sin 33° = \frac{5}{\text{hypotenuse}}$.

Solving this equation gives hypotenuse ≈ 9.18. Find the length of the remaining side in a similar way (using cosine or tangent) to get a length of 7.7. Add the three sides to find the perimeter: $9.18 + 7.7 + 5 = 21.9$, which is the length of cord needed.

17. The correct answer is (B). The easiest way to solve this question is to graph the two inequalities and look at their intersection. You can graph the line $y = 2x - 4$ and shade in the space below the line, and then graph the line $y = -x + 7$ and shade in the space below (and equal to) that line, as shown in the diagram below. As you can see, the region that lies below both lines (the darkest shaded region in the figure below) does not intersect quadrant II at all, so there is no point in that quadrant that satisfies both inequalities.

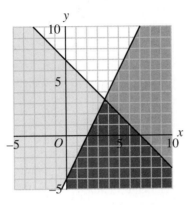

18. The correct answer is (C). First, to get $2u$, you can multiply $2 \times \langle 6, 5 \rangle = \langle 12, 10 \rangle$. Then, you can subtract $v : \langle 12, 10 \rangle - \langle 3, 7 \rangle = \langle (12 - 3), (10 - 7) \rangle = \langle 9, 3 \rangle$

19. The correct answer is (B). The easiest way to solve this problem is to simply graph the equation given. The graph is increasing (going up to the right) over the entire interval in (B), but not over any of the other listed intervals.

20. The correct answer is (D). If a plane is tangent to a sphere, a point is formed by their intersection. Any other intersection of a plane and a sphere will form a circle. If you thought that (II) was true, you may have been thinking of the intersection of a plane and a cone.

21. The correct answer is (D). Simplify the equation on the left side by adding the fractions. Multiply the first fraction by $\dfrac{d_i}{d_i}$ and the second fraction by $\dfrac{d_0}{d_0}$ so that they have a common denominator, and then add them to get $\dfrac{d_i + d_0}{d_i d_0}$. Since this expression is equal to $\dfrac{1}{f}$, you can take the reciprocal of both sides to get $f = \dfrac{d_i d_0}{d_i + d_0}$.

If you picked (B), you might have thought that the reciprocal of $\dfrac{1}{d_0} + \dfrac{1}{d_i}$ was $d_0 + d_i$. If you picked (A) or (C), you found an expression equivalent to $\dfrac{1}{f}$ instead of f.

22. The correct answer is (B). Because f is the inverse of g, you need to find a value of x such that $g(x) = -201$. To do this, simply set $g(x) = 7x^3 + 4x = -201$ and rearrange it to get $7x^3 + 4x + 201 = 0$.

You can use synthetic division or polynomial long division to factor this as $(x + 3)(7x^2 - 21x + 67) = 0$, meaning that $x = -3$ is the only solution, since the quadratic equation $7x^2 - 21x + 67 = 0$ has no real solutions. Alternatively, you could simply plug each answer option into your calculator to see which one satisfies $7x^3 + 4x = -201$.

23. The correct answer is (B). Remember that since $i^2 = -1$, you also know that $i^3 = i^2 i = -i$ and $i^4 = i^2 i^2 = 1$. The easiest way to solve this is to test each option. You know $i^6 = i^4 i^2 = -1$ and $i^4 = 1$, and multiplying $2i + 5$ by either of those will not result in $5i - 2$. Plugging in 5 will give you $(2i + 5)i^5 = 2i^6 + 5i^5 = -2 + 5i$, or $5i - 2$.

24. The correct answer is (A). The figure shows you that this function is symmetrical across the y-axis (or, in other words, it is "even"). This means that f takes on the same value at $-x$ that it does at x, for any real number x. Algebraically, you can write this as $f(x) = f(-x)$.

     (B) is incorrect; this is only true for the function $f(x) = 0$. (C) is incorrect; this is true for a function that has 180° rotational symmetry around the origin (an "odd" function). (D) is incorrect; this is true for functions such as constant functions and the function $f(x) = x$.

25. The correct answer is (E). To calculate the probability that new parks will be built, you must first calculate two conditional probabilities: the probability that new parks will be built given that Candidate A wins the election and the probability that new parks will be built given that Candidate B wins the election. The probability that Candidate A will win the election and then build parks is $0.4 \times 0.3 = 0.12$. The probability that Candidate B will win the election and then build parks is $0.6 \times 0.8 = 0.48$. In total, the probability that new parks will be built is $0.12 + 0.48 = 0.60$.

26. The correct answer is (A). Since $(fg)(1) = f(1) \times g(1)$, you can evaluate each function separately to get $f(1) = 4 - 5 = -1$ and $g(1) = 22 + 5 = 9$, so $f(1) \times g(1) = -1 \times 9 = -9$.

     If you got (D), you may have evaluated $f(1)$ as $5 - 4$ instead of $4 - 5$.

27. The correct answer is (C). Since n, $n + 3$ and $n + 11$ are all prime, you can test the first several prime numbers to determine that n must equal 2, so that $2 + 3 = 5$ and $2 + 11 = 13$. The resultant product must be at least $2 \times 5 \times 13 = 130$. (A) and (B) are less than this, while (D) and (E) do not have all three of 2, 5, and 13 as factors.

28. The correct answer is (C). If the bigger cone has radius r and height h then it has volume $\frac{1}{3}\pi r^2 h$. This also means that each of the smaller cones has radius r and height $\frac{h}{2}$, so combined they have volume $2\left(\frac{1}{3}\pi r^2 \frac{h}{2}\right) = \frac{1}{3}\pi r^2 h$. Since the two smaller cones have the same total volume as the larger cone, they are 100% of its volume.

29. The correct answer is (C). The law of cosines states that $C^2 = A^2 + B^2 - 2AB \cos c$. Therefore $C^2 = 9 + 16 - 2(12) \cos(45) = 25 - 24\left(\frac{1}{\sqrt{2}}\right) \approx 8.03$ so $C \approx 2.83$.

30. The correct answer is (D). First, solve for $\cos(a)$: $\cos(a) = \sin\left(-\frac{\pi}{6}\right) = -\frac{1}{2}$. You can plug each of the answer choices into your calculator to find which one has a cosine of $-\frac{1}{2}$ or you can use the complementary angles identity.

31. The correct answer is (D). If the function fg has an x-intercept at some point a, then $(fg)(a) = f(a) \times g(a) = 0$, meaning that either $f(a) = 0$ or $g(a) = 0$. This means that fg has x-intercepts exactly where either f or g has an x-intercept, which occurs at $3 + 4 = 7$ points, at most. The function fg could have fewer than 7 x-intercepts if some of the x-intercepts of f and g are the same.

32. The correct answer is (E). Based on the equation given, you know that the value of the function increases by 3 whenever n increases by 1. Since $f(0) = 2$, then $f(10)$ will be 30 more than that, or 32.

33. The correct answer is (A). If one person shakes hands with the other 6 people, there will be 6 handshakes total. Then, another person shakes hands with the 5 remaining people (not counting the first person, since that handshake has already happened), and so on. In total, there will be $6 + 5 + 4 + 3 + 2 + 1 = 21$ total handshakes if everyone shakes hands with everyone else. However, since two pairs have already met, there will be two fewer handshakes, meaning there will be $21 - 2 = 19$ in total.

34. The correct answer is (B). Rewrite the logarithmic expressions as $m = 4^3$ and $n = 2^5$, respectively. Then, $m \times n = (2^2)^3 \times 2^5 = 2^6 \times 2^5 = 2^{11}$.

    If you picked (A), you might have thought that $m = 2^3$.

35. The correct answer is (C). The period of a trigonometric function is equal to 2π divided by the constant in front of the x term, which in this case is 2. Therefore, this function has period $\frac{2\pi}{2} = \pi$.

    Alternatively, you could graph the function and measure the distance between two crests or two troughs of the wave.

36. The correct answer is (B). Every positive factor of a number must be made up of the prime factors of a number. The factors of pq^2 are $1, p, q, q^2, pq$, and pq^2, for a total of 6. You know that none of these six are equal because you are told that p and q are not equal (distinct).

37. The correct answer is (E). Calculate the final scores for Tests 1, 2, 4, and 5. The student will score 88 on Test 1 (88 is the average of her two scores on Test 1), 85.5 on Test 2, 92.5 on Test 4, and 92 on Test 5. To get an average score of 90 across all 5 tests, she must earn a total score of $5 \times 90 = 450$ on her 5 tests. So far, the total score of these four tests is $88 + 85.5 + 92.5 + 92 = 358$, so the student needs a score of $450 - 358 = 92$ to achieve this. To earn a 92 on Test 3, she must score at least a 95 on her second attempt, since the average of 89 and 95 is 92. Therefore, 95 is the correct answer.

38. The correct answer is (A). The domain of a function consists of all x-values that produce outputs. In this case, you know that the number inside the square root must be positive for the square root to make sense: $2x - 5 \geq 0$, so $x \geq \frac{5}{2}$. The number in the denominator cannot be 0, which you can write as $2x - 5 \neq 0$, or $x \neq \frac{5}{2}$. The numbers that satisfy both of these conditions are $x > \frac{5}{2}$.

If you picked (B), you may have only accounted for the square root. If you picked (E), you may have only accounted for the denominator not being equal to 0.

39. The correct answer is (E). Eliminate t and write the equation of the line in terms of x and y. The easiest way to do this is to write $y = 3t - 5 = \frac{3}{2}(2t + 3) - \frac{19}{2} = \frac{3}{2}x - \frac{19}{2}$, so the slope is $\frac{3}{2}$. You could also simply notice that for every unit increase in t, y increases by 3 and x increases by 2, meaning that the rise over the run is $\frac{3}{2}$.

If you picked (C), you confused x and y. If you picked (E), you found the y-intercept.

40. The correct answer is (B). First, find the side length of the cube by taking the cube root of the volume of the cube: $\sqrt[3]{343} = 7$. The maximum possible straight-line distance between two points on the cube's surface is the diagonal between the front bottom right vertex and the back top left vertex (or any vertices on opposite corners of the cube). To find this distance, you can use the formula for distance in three-dimensional space—simply square the distance you have to move in each dimension, add them, and take the square root: $d^2 = 7^2 + 7^2 + 7^2$, so $d = \sqrt{3 \times 7^2} \cong 12.12$

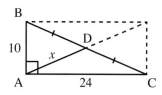

41. The correct answer is (D).) Use the Pythagorean Theorem to find that the length of the hypotenuse, BC, is equal to $\sqrt{10^2 + 24^2} = 26$. If you know that the length of a median from a right angle to the hypotenuse is always half the length of the hypotenuse, you know that x must equal 13. This is true because you can extend the triangle to form a rectangle, and you know that the two diagonals of a rectangle must bisect each other, so x must have the same length as BD and CD, as you can see in the figure above.

Otherwise, you can find the angles in the triangle as follows:

Since $BD = CD = 13$, because each is half the length of the hypotenuse, use the cosine law in the triangle ABD as follows:

$$(AD)^2 = (AB)^2 + (BD)^2 - 2(AB)(BD)\cos B$$
$$x^2 = 10^2 + 13^2 - 2(10)(13)\frac{10}{26}$$
$$x = \sqrt{169} = 13$$

42. The correct answer is (E). (I) is an equation of a circle because x and y are both squared and have the same coefficient. (II) is an equation of an ellipse because x and y are both squared and have positive coefficients that differ in magnitude. (III) is an equation of a hyperbola because x and y are both squared and one coefficient is positive and one is negative. Circles, ellipses, and hyperbolas are all conic sections.

43. The correct answer is (E). Check each of the answer choices and decide which one is true. You may find it helpful to graph the function. (A) is false because the function only has one horizontal asymptote, at $y = 0$. (B) is false because the function behaves differently for positive and negative values of x. (C) is false because $g(x)$ has an asymptote at $x = 0$, not a removable discontinuity. (D) is false because $g(x)$ is positive when $0 < x < 1$. (E) is true, which you can see by looking at the graph or by noticing that $\dfrac{1}{x} > \dfrac{1}{x^2}$ whenever $x > 1$.

44. The correct answer is (B). The minimum area of a square with two of its vertices at $(1, 3)$ and $(3, 3)$ is the area of the smallest square that has those two vertices, which means those vertices must be opposite corners of the square. Therefore, the diagonal of this square has length 2. To find the side length of the square, instead of using the Pythagorean theorem, you can use the diagonal as the hypotenuse of the 45-45-90 $\left(x - x - x\sqrt{2} \right)$ special triangle formed by two sides of the square and the diagonal. This shortcut gives you the length of the sides of the square, which is $\dfrac{2}{\sqrt{2}} = \sqrt{2}$. The area of this square is $\sqrt{2} \times \sqrt{2} = 2$.

(C) is the maximum area of a square with two of its vertices at $(1, 3)$ and $(3, 3)$, and you may have picked this answer because you assumed these points were on the same edge of the square, meaning its sides were 2 units long.

45. The correct answer is (C). You can start by writing $\tan^2 x$ as $\dfrac{\sin^2 x}{\cos^2 x}$. You can rewrite $\sin^2 x$ as $1 - \cos^2 x$ (because of

the

identity $\sin^2 x + \cos^2 x = 1$), to get $\dfrac{1 - \cos^2 x}{\cos^2 x} = \dfrac{1}{\cos^2 x} - \dfrac{\cos^2 x}{\cos^2 x} = \sec^2 x - 1$.

46. The correct answer is (E). First find the maximum value attained by the function on each of the three intervals that it is divided into. On the first interval, the function approaches the value 1 as x approaches 0, since $2(0) + 1 = 1$. On the second interval, the function is increasing, so it approaches its maximum value of 3 as x approaches 9. However, it never attains this maximum value, since $x = 9$ is included in the third of the three intervals, so $f(9) = -9$, not 3. On the third interval, the function begins at -9 and decreases, so it never hits any value larger than 3. Overall, the function attains values arbitrarily close to 3, but never hits it, meaning that it does not attain a maximum value.

If you picked (C), you might have thought that $x = 9$ was included in the second interval.

47. The correct answer is (E).Look at each of the answer choices in order and decide which one must be true. For the graph of f to have an x-intercept, there must be some value of x such that $f(x) = 0$. However, there is no x-value of 0 in the given table, so this does not need to be true. The table tells you nothing about the behaviour of the function between $x = 2$ and $x = 8$, so you cannot tell whether it is increasing on this interval, even though the value at $x = 8$ is higher than the value at $x = 2$. Option (C) may be tempting, because there are two x-values where the function is undefined, but these do not need to be asymptotes – they could be removable discontinuities, or "holes." The table tells you nothing about whether the function is continuous (or what it does at all) on the interval $2 < x < \infty$. However, you know that the function has no y-intercept because it is undefined at $x = 0$, so there is no way for it to cross the y-axis. Therefore, (E) is correct.

48. The correct answer is (B). Keeping in mind that $f(x) = -g(-x)$ and $g(-4)$, transform the expression $g(f(4))$ as follows: $g(f(4)) = g(-g(-4)) = -(-g(-7)) = -f(7)$.

49. The correct answer is (A). The first matrix has dimensions 1×3, and the second matrix has dimensions 3×2. The product matrix of two matrices of dimensions $a \times b$ and $b \times c$ will have dimensions $a \times c$, which in this case is 1×2. To find the value of the elements in the resultant matrix, multiply the elements of each row of the first matrix by the elements of each column of the second matrix, and sum the products together, as follows:

$$[4 \quad 2 \quad 2] \times \begin{bmatrix} 2 & 3 \\ 3 & 2 \\ 2 & 1 \end{bmatrix} =$$

$$[(4 \times 2) + (2 \times 3) + (2 \times 2) \quad (4 \times 3) + (2 \times 2) + (2 \times 1)]$$

$$= [18 \quad 18]$$

50. The correct answer is (D). In rectangular coordinates, the equation of a circle with radius 2 centered at (2, 0) is $(x - 2)^2 + y^2 = 4$. First, expand and simplify this equation:

$$(x - 2)^2 + y^2 = 4$$
$$x^2 - 4x + 4 + y^2 = 4$$
$$x^2 - 4x + y^2 = 0$$

Next, convert x and y to polar coordinates (r and θ) using the facts that $x^2 + y^2 = r^2$ and $x = r \cos \theta$. Rearrange the above equation to make it easier to use these facts:

$$(x^2 + y^2) - 4x = 0.$$
$$r^2 - 4r \cos \theta = 0$$

Finally, since all the answer choices are in the form $r =$, rearrange and simplify to solve for r:

$$r^2 = 4r \cos \theta$$
$$r = 4 \cos \theta$$

Practice Test 2

YOUR NAME (PRINT): _____

LAST   FIRST   MI

| Correct ● | Incorrect ⬤ ⊗ ⊘ ◕ ✪ ○ ◒ ◓ | **Make sure you use a No. 2 pencil.** Each answer must be marked in the corresponding row on the answer sheet. Each bubble must be filled in completely and darkly within the lines. Extra marks on your answer sheet may be marked as incorrect answers and lower your score. |

○ Literature	○ Mathematics Level 1	○ German
○ Biology E	○ Mathematics Level 2	○ Italian
○ Biology M	○ U.S. History	○ Latin
○ Chemistry	○ World History	○ Modern Hebrew
○ Physics	○ French	○ Spanish

1 Ⓐ Ⓑ Ⓒ Ⓓ Ⓔ   21 Ⓐ Ⓑ Ⓒ Ⓓ Ⓔ   41 Ⓐ Ⓑ Ⓒ Ⓓ Ⓔ   61 Ⓐ Ⓑ Ⓒ Ⓓ Ⓔ   81 Ⓐ Ⓑ Ⓒ Ⓓ Ⓔ

2 Ⓐ Ⓑ Ⓒ Ⓓ Ⓔ   22 Ⓐ Ⓑ Ⓒ Ⓓ Ⓔ   42 Ⓐ Ⓑ Ⓒ Ⓓ Ⓔ   62 Ⓐ Ⓑ Ⓒ Ⓓ Ⓔ   82 Ⓐ Ⓑ Ⓒ Ⓓ Ⓔ

3 Ⓐ Ⓑ Ⓒ Ⓓ Ⓔ   23 Ⓐ Ⓑ Ⓒ Ⓓ Ⓔ   43 Ⓐ Ⓑ Ⓒ Ⓓ Ⓔ   63 Ⓐ Ⓑ Ⓒ Ⓓ Ⓔ   83 Ⓐ Ⓑ Ⓒ Ⓓ Ⓔ

4 Ⓐ Ⓑ Ⓒ Ⓓ Ⓔ   24 Ⓐ Ⓑ Ⓒ Ⓓ Ⓔ   44 Ⓐ Ⓑ Ⓒ Ⓓ Ⓔ   64 Ⓐ Ⓑ Ⓒ Ⓓ Ⓔ   84 Ⓐ Ⓑ Ⓒ Ⓓ Ⓔ

5 Ⓐ Ⓑ Ⓒ Ⓓ Ⓔ   25 Ⓐ Ⓑ Ⓒ Ⓓ Ⓔ   45 Ⓐ Ⓑ Ⓒ Ⓓ Ⓔ   65 Ⓐ Ⓑ Ⓒ Ⓓ Ⓔ   85 Ⓐ Ⓑ Ⓒ Ⓓ Ⓔ

6 Ⓐ Ⓑ Ⓒ Ⓓ Ⓔ   26 Ⓐ Ⓑ Ⓒ Ⓓ Ⓔ   46 Ⓐ Ⓑ Ⓒ Ⓓ Ⓔ   66 Ⓐ Ⓑ Ⓒ Ⓓ Ⓔ   86 Ⓐ Ⓑ Ⓒ Ⓓ Ⓔ

7 Ⓐ Ⓑ Ⓒ Ⓓ Ⓔ   27 Ⓐ Ⓑ Ⓒ Ⓓ Ⓔ   47 Ⓐ Ⓑ Ⓒ Ⓓ Ⓔ   67 Ⓐ Ⓑ Ⓒ Ⓓ Ⓔ   87 Ⓐ Ⓑ Ⓒ Ⓓ Ⓔ

8 Ⓐ Ⓑ Ⓒ Ⓓ Ⓔ   28 Ⓐ Ⓑ Ⓒ Ⓓ Ⓔ   48 Ⓐ Ⓑ Ⓒ Ⓓ Ⓔ   68 Ⓐ Ⓑ Ⓒ Ⓓ Ⓔ   88 Ⓐ Ⓑ Ⓒ Ⓓ Ⓔ

9 Ⓐ Ⓑ Ⓒ Ⓓ Ⓔ   29 Ⓐ Ⓑ Ⓒ Ⓓ Ⓔ   49 Ⓐ Ⓑ Ⓒ Ⓓ Ⓔ   69 Ⓐ Ⓑ Ⓒ Ⓓ Ⓔ   89 Ⓐ Ⓑ Ⓒ Ⓓ Ⓔ

10 Ⓐ Ⓑ Ⓒ Ⓓ Ⓔ   30 Ⓐ Ⓑ Ⓒ Ⓓ Ⓔ   50 Ⓐ Ⓑ Ⓒ Ⓓ Ⓔ   70 Ⓐ Ⓑ Ⓒ Ⓓ Ⓔ   90 Ⓐ Ⓑ Ⓒ Ⓓ Ⓔ

11 Ⓐ Ⓑ Ⓒ Ⓓ Ⓔ   31 Ⓐ Ⓑ Ⓒ Ⓓ Ⓔ   51 Ⓐ Ⓑ Ⓒ Ⓓ Ⓔ   71 Ⓐ Ⓑ Ⓒ Ⓓ Ⓔ   81 Ⓐ Ⓑ Ⓒ Ⓓ Ⓔ

12 Ⓐ Ⓑ Ⓒ Ⓓ Ⓔ   32 Ⓐ Ⓑ Ⓒ Ⓓ Ⓔ   52 Ⓐ Ⓑ Ⓒ Ⓓ Ⓔ   72 Ⓐ Ⓑ Ⓒ Ⓓ Ⓔ   92 Ⓐ Ⓑ Ⓒ Ⓓ Ⓔ

13 Ⓐ Ⓑ Ⓒ Ⓓ Ⓔ   33 Ⓐ Ⓑ Ⓒ Ⓓ Ⓔ   53 Ⓐ Ⓑ Ⓒ Ⓓ Ⓔ   73 Ⓐ Ⓑ Ⓒ Ⓓ Ⓔ   93 Ⓐ Ⓑ Ⓒ Ⓓ Ⓔ

14 Ⓐ Ⓑ Ⓒ Ⓓ Ⓔ   34 Ⓐ Ⓑ Ⓒ Ⓓ Ⓔ   54 Ⓐ Ⓑ Ⓒ Ⓓ Ⓔ   74 Ⓐ Ⓑ Ⓒ Ⓓ Ⓔ   94 Ⓐ Ⓑ Ⓒ Ⓓ Ⓔ

15 Ⓐ Ⓑ Ⓒ Ⓓ Ⓔ   35 Ⓐ Ⓑ Ⓒ Ⓓ Ⓔ   55 Ⓐ Ⓑ Ⓒ Ⓓ Ⓔ   75 Ⓐ Ⓑ Ⓒ Ⓓ Ⓔ   95 Ⓐ Ⓑ Ⓒ Ⓓ Ⓔ

16 Ⓐ Ⓑ Ⓒ Ⓓ Ⓔ   36 Ⓐ Ⓑ Ⓒ Ⓓ Ⓔ   56 Ⓐ Ⓑ Ⓒ Ⓓ Ⓔ   76 Ⓐ Ⓑ Ⓒ Ⓓ Ⓔ   96 Ⓐ Ⓑ Ⓒ Ⓓ Ⓔ

17 Ⓐ Ⓑ Ⓒ Ⓓ Ⓔ   37 Ⓐ Ⓑ Ⓒ Ⓓ Ⓔ   57 Ⓐ Ⓑ Ⓒ Ⓓ Ⓔ   77 Ⓐ Ⓑ Ⓒ Ⓓ Ⓔ   97 Ⓐ Ⓑ Ⓒ Ⓓ Ⓔ

18 Ⓐ Ⓑ Ⓒ Ⓓ Ⓔ   38 Ⓐ Ⓑ Ⓒ Ⓓ Ⓔ   58 Ⓐ Ⓑ Ⓒ Ⓓ Ⓔ   78 Ⓐ Ⓑ Ⓒ Ⓓ Ⓔ   98 Ⓐ Ⓑ Ⓒ Ⓓ Ⓔ

19 Ⓐ Ⓑ Ⓒ Ⓓ Ⓔ   39 Ⓐ Ⓑ Ⓒ Ⓓ Ⓔ   59 Ⓐ Ⓑ Ⓒ Ⓓ Ⓔ   79 Ⓐ Ⓑ Ⓒ Ⓓ Ⓔ   99 Ⓐ Ⓑ Ⓒ Ⓓ Ⓔ

20 Ⓐ Ⓑ Ⓒ Ⓓ Ⓔ   40 Ⓐ Ⓑ Ⓒ Ⓓ Ⓔ   60 Ⓐ Ⓑ Ⓒ Ⓓ Ⓔ   80 Ⓐ Ⓑ Ⓒ Ⓓ Ⓔ   100 Ⓐ Ⓑ Ⓒ Ⓓ Ⓔ

For automatic scoring and scaling, please visit **cloud.ivyglobal.com**.

SAT Math Level 2 Subject Test

Reference Materials

THE FORMULAS BELOW MAY BE USEFUL IN ANSWERING QUESTIONS ON THIS TEST.

$S = 4\pi r^2$ is the formula for the surface area of a sphere with a radius of r.

$V = \frac{1}{3}\pi r^2 h$ is the formula for the volume of a right circular cone with a radius of r and a height of h.

$V = \frac{4}{3}\pi r^3$ is the formula for the volume of a sphere with a radius of r.

$V = \frac{1}{3}Bh$ is the formula for the volume of a pyramid with a base area of B and a height of h.

When choosing an answer, find the CLOSEST answer possible. If the precise numerical value that you have found is not an answer choice, select the choice that is closest to your answer. Use the answer sheet and fill in the bubble corresponding to your choice.

Notes: (1) You ARE permitted the use of a graphing or scientific calculator, which you may use at your own discretion. You will also have to choose between degree or radian mode for some questions, so keep track of what mode your calculator is in.

(2) You may assume that figures are drawn as accurately as possible UNLESS it is explicitly stated that a figure is not drawn to scale. Furthermore, all figures are in a plane UNLESS it is stated otherwise.

(3) For any function f, unless otherwise specified, you may assume that a real number x is in the domain of f if and only if $f(x)$ is a real number. The range of f consists of all and only those real numbers of the form $f(x)$, where x is in the domain of f.

(4) Four formulas are provided in the box above for your reference.

GO ON TO THE NEXT PAGE

1. If $4y - 3 = \dfrac{12}{k}(y - 1) + 1$ for all y, then $k =$

   (A) 1

   (B) 2

   (C) 3

   (D) 4

   (E) 6

2. What is the slope of the line that passes through the points $(5, -3)$ and $(-4, 2)$?

   (A) -0.56

   (B) -0.44

   (C) -0.11

   (D) 0.11

   (E) 0.56

Mean	Median	Mode
76%	75%	72%

3. The mean, median, and mode of the scores on a science test are shown in the table above. If a student takes the test at a later date and receives a score of 82%, which of the measures of center could change?

   I. Mean
   II. Median
   III. Mode

   (A) I only

   (B) II only

   (C) III only

   (D) I and II only

   (E) I, II, and III

GO ON TO THE NEXT PAGE

USE THIS SPACE FOR SCRATCH WORK.

4. A coupon gives half off the price of a movie ticket. The coupon also charges a $3 service charge on the discounted price. If the original price of the ticket is $8, what will the total cost be if the coupon is used?

(A) $1
(B) $4
(C) $7
(D) $13
(E) $19

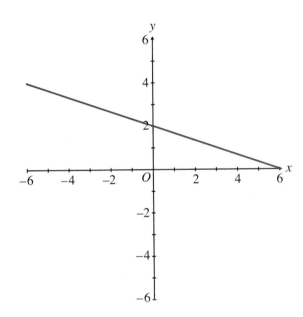

5. What is the slope of a line perpendicular to the line shown above?

(A) $-\dfrac{1}{3}$
(B) $\dfrac{1}{3}$
(C) -3
(D) 3
(E) 9

GO ON TO THE NEXT PAGE

USE THIS SPACE FOR SCRATCH WORK.

6. What is a possible value of x if $\sqrt{x^2 - 60^2} = 11$?

    (A)   59
    (B)   61
    (C)   71
    (D)   3,611
    (E)   3,721

7. A cake requires 2 eggs for every $1\frac{1}{2}$ cups of flour, and $\frac{1}{2}$ a cup of butter for every egg. If a baker uses 9 cups of flour, how many cups of butter does she use?

    (A)   1
    (B)   3
    (C)   6
    (D)   12
    (E)   24

8. If a line with a slope of 2 is reflected across the x-axis and then reflected across the y-axis, its slope becomes

    (A)   2
    (B) -2
    (C) $\frac{1}{2}$
    (D) $-\frac{1}{2}$
    (E)   Cannot be determined from the given information.

GO ON TO THE NEXT PAGE

$$2, -6, 18, \ldots$$

9.   What is the common ratio of the geometric series above?

(A)   −8

(B)   −3

(C)   2

(D)   3

(E)   24

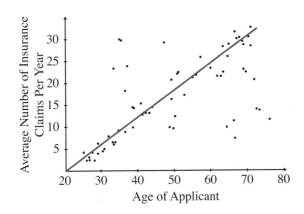

10.   The scatterplot above shows a linear regression analysis conducted by a health insurance company. Based on these data, which of the following can the company reasonably conclude?

(A)   As applicants age, the number of claims they make decreases.

(B)   As applicants age, the number of claims they make becomes less varied.

(C)   Any given applicant will age approximately 10 years for every claim they make.

(D)   A 40-year-old will make approximately twice as many claims as a 30-year-old.

(E)   A 40-year-old will make approximately one-third as many claims as a 60-year-old.

GO ON TO THE NEXT PAGE

Note: Figure not drawn to scale.

11. A wheelchair ramp, shown in the diagram above, has angle $a = 11°$. If the ramp is 10 feet long, how high off the ground is the top of the ramp?

(A)   0.19 feet

(B)   0.52 feet

(C)   0.98 feet

(D)   1.91 feet

(E)   9.82 feet

12. $\dfrac{\sqrt{16x}}{\sqrt{4x}} =$

(A)   2

(B)   4

(C) $2x$

(D) $4x$

(E) $2\sqrt{x}$

13. Which of the following systems of equations has $(2, 3)$ as a solution for (x, y)?

(A) $\begin{aligned} y &= -x - 1 \\ y &= 2x - 7 \end{aligned}$

(B) $\begin{aligned} y &= -x + 1 \\ y &= 2x - 7 \end{aligned}$

(C) $\begin{aligned} y &= x + 1 \\ y &= 2x + 7 \end{aligned}$

(D) $\begin{aligned} y &= -x + 1 \\ y &= -2x + 7 \end{aligned}$

(E) $\begin{aligned} y &= x + 1 \\ y &= -2x + 7 \end{aligned}$

GO ON TO THE NEXT PAGE

USE THIS SPACE FOR SCRATCH WORK.

$$y = \frac{x^2 + 2x + 1}{x^2 - 1}$$

14. In the function above, which of the following occurs at $x = -1$?

(A)   A vertical asymptote

(B)   A horizontal asymptote

(C)   A removable discontinuity at which the function is undefined

(D)   A removable discontinuity at which the function is defined

(E)   No discontinuity

15. If $(5.23)^a = 10$, what is the value of a ?

(A)   0.36

(B)   0.72

(C)   1.39

(D)   1.91

(E)   2.82

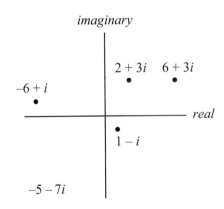

16. The magnitude $|a + bi|$ of a complex number $a + bi$ is equal to $\sqrt{a^2 + b^2}$. Which of the complex numbers, shown on the complex plane above, has the largest magnitude?

(A) $2 + 3i$

(B) $6 + 3i$

(C) $1 - i$

(D) $-5 - 7i$

(E) $-6 + i$

GO ON TO THE NEXT PAGE

USE THIS SPACE FOR SCRATCH WORK.

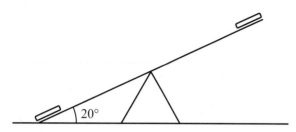

Note: Figure not drawn to scale.

17. A 12-foot long see-saw balanced on its midpoint at rest position makes an angle of 20° with the ground, as shown above. How high off the ground is the midpoint of the see-saw?

(A)   2.05 feet

(B)   3.00 feet

(C)   5.20 feet

(D)   5.64 feet

(E)   6.00 feet

18. Which of the following statements is NOT true about the graph of $y = \log_2 x$?

(A)   It has a vertical asymptote.

(B)   Its domain is all real numbers.

(C)   Its range is all real numbers.

(D)   Its x-intercept is $x = 1$.

(E)   It has no y-intercept.

GO ON TO THE NEXT PAGE

USE THIS SPACE FOR SCRATCH WORK.

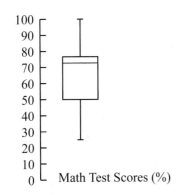

19. Which of the following must be true about students' scores on a recent math test, as shown the boxplot above?

(A) The mean test score is 72%.

(B) The range of test scores is 28%.

(C) Three-quarters of all students scored between 26% and 72%.

(D) Half of all students scored between 50% and 78%.

(E) One-quarter of all students scored between 72% and 100%.

20. If $f(x) = ax^b$, and $f(c) = d$, then $f(2c) =$

(A) $2d$

(B) $2ad$

(C) $2^b d$

(D) $2^b ad$

(E) $(2d)^b$

21. Which of the following does NOT uniquely determine a plane?

(A) Two non-collinear points

(B) A line and a point not on the line

(C) Three non-collinear points

(D) Two parallel lines

(E) Two perpendicular lines

GO ON TO THE NEXT PAGE

USE THIS SPACE FOR SCRATCH WORK.

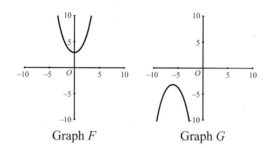

Graph F Graph G

22. Graph F shows a portion of the graph of $f(x) = x^2 + 3$. Graph G shows a portion of the graph of the function $g(x)$, which was created by transforming $f(x)$ in which of the following ways?

(A) Horizontal shift 6 to the left, reflection across the y-axis

(B) Horizontal shift 6 to the left, reflection across the x-axis

(C) Horizontal shift 6 to the right, reflection across the y-axis

(D) Horizontal shift 6 to the right, reflection across the x-axis

(E) Horizontal shift 6 to the right, vertical shift 6 down

23. If a cylinder and a sphere have the same volume and the same radius, what is the cylinder's height, h, in terms of its radius, r?

(A) $h = \dfrac{4}{3}r$

(B) $h = \dfrac{3}{4}r$

(C) $h = \dfrac{4}{3r}$

(D) $h = \dfrac{3}{4r}$

(E) $h = \dfrac{3}{4}r^2$

GO ON TO THE NEXT PAGE

USE THIS SPACE FOR SCRATCH WORK.

24. If $a + 2b < a - 2b$, which of the following must be true?

 I. a is positive
 II. b is positive
 III. b is negative

(A) I only

(B) II only

(C) III only

(D) I and II only

(E) I and III only

25. A lattice point is a point (x, y) such that both x and y are integers. How many lattice points does the line $y = \frac{3}{2}x + 2$ pass through for $-50 < x < 50$?

(A) 33

(B) 34

(C) 48

(D) 49

(E) 50

26. If $f(x) = \frac{2x + 6}{3x - 4}$ and $g(x) = \frac{1}{2x}$, then $g(f(x)) =$

(A) $\dfrac{3x - 4}{4x + 12}$

(B) $\dfrac{3x - 4}{x + 3}$

(C) $\dfrac{-12x^2 - 2x}{8x^2 - 3x}$

(D) $\dfrac{-8x^2 + 3x}{12x^2 + 2x}$

(E) $\dfrac{4x + 12}{3x - 4}$

GO ON TO THE NEXT PAGE

27. Five sprinters on a high school track team are deciding which four of them will form the 4×100 meter relay team. If the fastest sprinter must be on the team, how many different teams of 4 are possible?

(A)   4

(B)   5

(C)   10

(D)   24

(E)   120

USE THIS SPACE FOR SCRATCH WORK.

28. If $2 \cos x = \sin 2x$, then x could equal

(A)   0

(B) $\dfrac{\pi}{2}$

(C) π

(D) $\dfrac{2\pi}{3}$

(E) 2π

29. If $f(x) = \log_5 x^2$ for $x > 0$, what is the value of $f^{-1}(3)$?

(A) $\sqrt{3}$

(B) $3\sqrt{3}$

(C) $5\sqrt{3}$

(D) $3\sqrt{5}$

(E) $5\sqrt{5}$

GO ON TO THE NEXT PAGE

USE THIS SPACE FOR SCRATCH WORK.

30. If the hypotenuse of a right triangle inscribed in a circle is equal to the diameter of the circle, then the triangle's two remaining sides

    I. must be equal in length
    II. must form a rectangle if mirrored across the hypotenuse
    III. must have a combined length greater than the diameter of the circle

(A)   II only

(B)   III only

(C)   I and III only

(D)   II and III only

(E)   I, II, and III

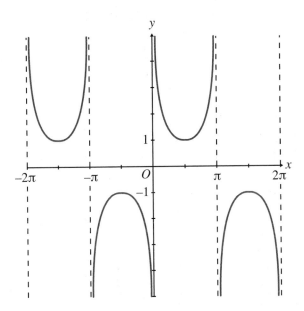

31. What trigonometric function is represented by the graph above?

(A) $y = \sin x$

(B) $y = \cos x$

(C) $y = \sec x$

(D) $y = \csc x$

(E) $y = \cot x$

GO ON TO THE NEXT PAGE

32. Four of the vertices of a cube are located at $(1, 3, 4)$, $(4, 3, 4)$, $(1, 0, 1)$, and $(4, 0, 1)$. All of the following must be vertices of the cube EXCEPT

    (A) $(1, 3, 1)$

    (B) $(4, 0, 4)$

    (C) $(1, 0, 4)$

    (D) $(1, 4, 3)$

    (E) $(4, 3, 1)$

USE THIS SPACE FOR SCRATCH WORK.

33. A function g is idempotent if $g(x) = g(g(x))$ for all real numbers x. Which of the following functions is idempotent?

    I. $f(x) = 3$
    II. $f(x) = x$
    III. $f(x) = 3x$

    (A) I only

    (B) II only

    (C) I and II only

    (D) II and III only

    (E) I, II, and III

        If x is divisible by 4, then x^2 is also divisible by 4.

34. Which of the following can be inferred from the statement above?

    (A) If x is not divisible by 4, then x^2 is divisible by 4.

    (B) If x is not divisible by 4, then x^2 is not divisible by 4.

    (C) If x^2 is divisible by 4, then x is divisible by 4.

    (D) If x^2 is not divisible by 4, then x is divisible by 4.

    (E) If x^2 is not divisible by 4, then x is not divisible by 4.

GO ON TO THE NEXT PAGE

35. What is the maximum number of identical spheres that can be positioned so that every sphere touches every other sphere?

(A)   3

(B)   4

(C)   5

(D)   6

(E)   8

36. Line L passes through the points (a, b) and $(2a, 2b)$, and line M passes through the points (b, a) and $(2b, 2a)$. If a and b are both nonzero, then lines L and M *must* be

(A)   parallel

(B)   perpendicular

(C)   the same line

(D)   inverse functions

(E)   none of the above

37. Which of the following trigonometric functions has the longest period?

(A) $y = 3 \sin (2x)$

(B) $y = 2 \sin (x + \pi)$

(C) $y = \cos (3x)$

(D) $y = \cos \left(\frac{x}{2}\right)$

(E) $y = 4 + \cos x$

38. If p is an integer larger than 1, which of the following must be an even integer?

(A) $2p + 1$

(B) $3p + 1$

(C) p^2

(D) $p^2 + p$

(E) $p^3 + p^2 + p$

GO ON TO THE NEXT PAGE

39. A bacterial colony doubles in mass every half hour. If the colony initially weighs 2 grams, after how much time will it weigh 40 grams?

    (A) 2h 9m 39s

    (B) 2h 20m 0s

    (C) 4h 18m 12s

    (D) 4h 19m 18s

    (E) 5h 0m 0s

40. In a group of 20 people, 85% are right-handed. Three people are selected at random from the group. What is the probability that all three people selected are right-handed?

    (A) 61.4%

    (B) 59.6%

    (C) 38.6%

    (D) 6.3%

    (E) 0.7%

GO ON TO THE NEXT PAGE

USE THIS SPACE FOR SCRATCH WORK.

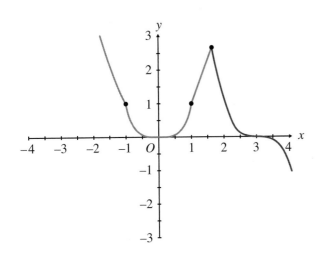

41. What piecewise function is represented by the spline shown above?

(A) $y = \begin{cases} x^2, & x \le -1 \text{ or } 1 \le x \le 1.62 \\ x^4, & -1 < x < 1 \\ -x^3 + 3, & x > 1.62 \end{cases}$

(B) $y = \begin{cases} x^2, & x \le -1 \text{ or } 1 \le x \le 1.62 \\ x^4, & -1 < x < 1 \\ -x^3, & x > 1.62 \end{cases}$

(C) $y = \begin{cases} x^2, & x \le -1 \text{ or } 1 \le x \le 1.62 \\ x^4, & -1 < x < 1 \\ -(x-3)^3, & x > 1.62 \end{cases}$

(D) $y = \begin{cases} x^2, & x \le -1 \text{ or } 1 \le x \le 1.62 \\ x^4, & x > 1.62 \\ -x^3, & -1 < x < 1 \end{cases}$

(E) $y = \begin{cases} x^2, & x \le 1.62 \\ -(x-3)^3, & x > 1.62 \end{cases}$

USE THIS SPACE FOR SCRATCH WORK.

42. If $\cos \alpha = 1 - 2 \sin^2 18°$, what is a possible value for α?

    (A)   9°

    (B)   18°

    (C)   36°

    (D)   72°

    (E)   108°

43. If the circles given by $(x - 2)^2 + (y - 4)^2 = 25$ and $(x - 10)^2 + (y - 4)^2 = k$ are tangent to each other, then $k =$

    (A)   1

    (B)   3

    (C)   4

    (D)   6

    (E)   9

USE THIS SPACE FOR SCRATCH WORK.

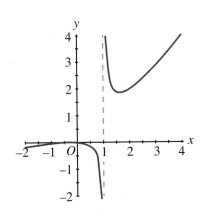

44. A portion of the graph $\dfrac{f}{g}$ is shown above. Which of the following could be portions of the graphs of f and g?

(A)

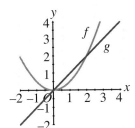

(C)

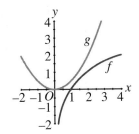

(B)

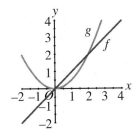

(D)

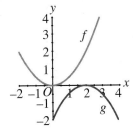

(E)

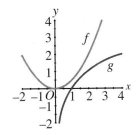

GO ON TO THE NEXT PAGE

45. The points in the rectangular coordinate plane are transformed in such a way that each point $P(x, y)$ is moved to the point $P'\left(\frac{x}{2}, 2y\right)$. What condition describes ALL points $P(x, y)$ such that P and P' are the same distance from the origin?

(A) $x = 2y$

(B) $x = \pm 2y$

(C) $2x = y$

(D) $2x = \pm y$

(E) $x = y = 0$

USE THIS SPACE FOR SCRATCH WORK.

46. If $f(x) = x^2 + bx + c$ for all real numbers x, and if $f(-1) = 2$ and $f(1) = 4$, what is the y-intercept of f?

(A) -1

(B) 0

(C) 1

(D) 2

(E) 3

$$A = \begin{bmatrix} 2 & 3 \end{bmatrix} \quad B = \begin{bmatrix} -1 & 0 \\ 4 & 1 \\ 2 & 2 \end{bmatrix} \quad C = \begin{bmatrix} 7 \\ 4 \\ 1 \end{bmatrix} \quad D = \begin{bmatrix} 5 & 1 & -1 \\ -2 & -4 & 0 \end{bmatrix}$$

47. Given the four matrices above, which of the following matrix products is undefined?

(A) AD

(B) CA

(C) BD

(D) DB

(E) CB

GO ON TO THE NEXT PAGE

USE THIS SPACE FOR SCRATCH WORK.

48. If f is a rational function with a single vertical asymptote at $x = a$, and g is a rational function with a single vertical asymptote at $x = b$, where $a \neq b$, then the function fg must have

 (A) vertical asymptotes at $x = a$ and $x = b$ only

 (B) vertical asymptotes at $x = a$ and $x = b$, and possibly others

 (C) a vertical asymptote at either $x = a$ or $x = b$

 (D) no vertical asymptotes

 (E) Cannot be determined from the given information.

49. The sum of two real numbers is equal to their product. How many pairs of real numbers satisfy this relationship?

 (A) 0

 (B) 1

 (C) 2

 (D) 4

 (E) Infinitely many

50. If the ellipse $\dfrac{x^2}{4} + \dfrac{y^2}{6} = 1$ is stretched horizontally by a factor of 2, its new equation is

 (A) $x^2 + \dfrac{y^2}{6} = 1$

 (B) $\dfrac{x^2}{2} + \dfrac{y^2}{6} = 1$

 (C) $\dfrac{x^2}{8} + \dfrac{y^2}{6} = 1$

 (D) $\dfrac{x^2}{16} + \dfrac{y^2}{6} = 1$

 (E) $\dfrac{x^2}{4} + \dfrac{y^2}{3} = 1$

STOP

If you complete this test before the end of your allotted time, you may check your work.

Answers and Scoring

Scoring Your Test
Part 1

The easiest way to score your test is to use our Cloud scoring tool. The Cloud tool also provides more detailed results by showing you how you performed on specific kinds of questions. To score your test by hand, follow the directions below.

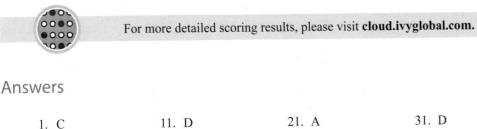

For more detailed scoring results, please visit **cloud.ivyglobal.com.**

Answers

1. C	11. D	21. A	31. D	41. C
2. A	12. A	22. B	32. D	42. C
3. E	13. E	23. A	33. C	43. E
4. C	14. C	24. C	34. E	44. E
5. D	15. C	25. D	35. B	45. B
6. B	16. D	26. A	36. D	46. D
7. C	17. A	27. A	37. D	47. E
8. A	18. B	28. B	38. D	48. E
9. B	19. D	29. E	39. A	49. E
10. D	20. C	30. B	40. B	50. D

Raw Scores

To score your test, first use the answer key to mark each of your responses as correct or incorrect. Don't mark or count questions you left blank. Then, calculate your raw score for each section by subtracting one fourth the number of incorrect responses from the number of correct responses. Scores should be rounded to the nearest whole number, with .5 and above rounding up. Use the tables below to help you calculate your scores:

Scores	
Number Correct	_____ −
Number incorrect	_____ / 4 = _____
Raw Score	= _____
Scaled Score	_____

Scaled Scores

Once you have found your raw score for each test, convert it into an approximate scaled test score using the following chart. To find a scaled test score for each section, find the row in the Raw Score column which corresponds to your raw score for that section, then check the column for the section you are scoring in the same row. For example, if you had a raw score of 31, your scaled score would be 580. Keep in mind that these scaled scores are estimates only. Your actual SAT Subject Test in Mathematics Level 2 score will be scaled against the scores of all other students at your grade level taking the test on your test date.

			Scaled Score				
Raw Score	Scaled Score	Raw Score	Scaled Score	Raw Score	Scaled Score	Raw Score	Scaled Score
50	800	34	710	18	560	2	440
49	800	33	700	17	560	1	430
48	800	32	690	16	550	0	410
47	800	31	680	15	540	−1	390
46	800	30	670	14	530	−2	370
45	800	29	660	13	530	−3	360
44	800	28	650	12	520	−4	340
43	800	27	640	11	510	−5	340
42	790	26	630	10	500	−6	330
41	790	25	630	9	500	−7	320
40	780	24	620	8	490	−8	320
39	770	23	610	7	480	−9	320
38	750	22	600	6	480	−10	320
37	740	21	590	5	470	−11	310
36	730	20	580	4	460	−12	310
35	720	19	570	3	450		

Explanations

Part 2

1. The correct answer is (C). Expand the brackets on the right side by distributing $\frac{12}{k}$ and rearranging the order of terms to get $\frac{12}{k}y + \left(1 - \frac{12}{k}\right)$. Since this is equal to $4y - 3$ for all values of y, you know the coefficient of y must be the same on both sides, so $4 = \frac{12}{k}$, meaning $k = 3$. Instead, you could have rearranged the equation to isolate for $\frac{12}{k}$ and then solved for k.

2. The correct answer is (A). To find the slope of this line, take the difference in the y-values and divide it by the difference in the x-values: $\frac{2-(-3)}{-4-5} = -\frac{5}{9} = -0.56$.

   If you picked (E), you missed the minus sign.

3. The correct answer is (E). Because the actual scores are not given, it is impossible to be certain that any of the measures will not change. Because 82% is higher than the mean, the mean will increase. If, for example, the previous scores are 74%, 75%, and 79%, then the median will change from 75% to 77%. If, for example, the previous scores are 72%, 72%, and 82%, then the mode is 72%, but after the second 82% grade is entered, the mode becomes 72% and 82%. Therefore, any of the three measures of center could change.

4. The correct answer is (C). Since the original ticket price is $8, and the coupon gives the user half off the price, the ticket will cost $4. However, because of the $3 service charge to use the coupon, the total cost will be $4 + $3 = $7.

5. The correct answer is (D). First find the slope of the line in the diagram: $\frac{2-0}{0-6} = -\frac{1}{3}$. The slope of a perpendicular line is the negative reciprocal of this, which is 3.

   If you picked (A), you found the slope of the line in the diagram or a line parallel to it.

6. The correct answer is (B). Square both sides of the equation to get $x^2 - 60^2 = 121$, or $x^2 = 3,721$. Take the square root of both sides to get $x = \pm 61$. However, -61 is not an answer choice, so you know $x = 61$.

   If you picked (E), you solved for x^2 instead of x.

7. The correct answer is (C). First, convert the question into ratios: eggs to flour is 2 : 1.5, and eggs to butter is 1 : 0.5. Multiply the second ratio by 2 to set the eggs part of each ratio equal to one another. Eliminate the eggs to get a flour to butter ratio of 1.5 : 1. The baker uses 9 cups of flour, which requires $\frac{9}{1.5} = 6$ cups of butter.

8. The correct answer is (A). The easiest way to solve this question is to draw a picture. If you draw any line with a slope of 2 and reflect it across the x-axis, its slope will become -2. If you then reflect this line across the y-axis, its slope goes back to 2. In general, reflecting a line across either axis will make the slope the negative of what it was before.

9. The correct answer is (A). To find the common ratio of a geometric series, simply divide the second term by the first. In this question, that gives you -3. To confirm that this is the correct ratio, you can divide the third term by the second, which will also give you -3.

10. The correct answer is (D). You can see that the line of best fit passes through (approximately) the points (30, 5) and (40, 10), meaning that a 40-year-old will make approximately twice as many claims as a 30-year-old.

    (A) is incorrect, because the number of claims increases as applicants age, which you can tell since the line of best fit has a positive slope. (B) is incorrect because the line of best fit does not tell you anything about the variance of the number of claims, and the data points seem to vary more after about age 35, not less. (C) is incorrect because making claims does not cause applicants to age. (E) is incorrect because a 40-year-old will make approximately 10 claims while a 60-year-old will make approximately 20 claims, which is half as many, not one-third.

11. The correct answer is (D). You know that the sine of angle a is equal to the length of the opposite side divided by the length of the hypotenuse. If you let x represent the height that the top of the ramp is off the ground, you can write $\sin(11°) = \frac{x}{10}$. Since $\sin(11°) = 0.191$, you know that $x = 1.91$, so the top of the ramp is 1.91 feet off the ground.

12. The correct answer is (A). Taking the square root of the numerator and denominator of a fraction is the same as taking the square root of the entire fraction, so this is equal to $\sqrt{\frac{16x}{4x}} = \sqrt{\frac{16}{4}} = \sqrt{4} = 2$.

13. The correct answer is (E). The easiest way to solve this question is to plug $x = 2$ and $y = 3$ into the five systems of equations and find the system for which these values satisfy both equations. The equations in (E) become $3 = 2 + 1$ and $3 = -2(2) + 7$, both of which are true, so (E) is the correct answer. The other answer choices all have at least one equation that is not satisfied by $x = 2$ and $y = 3$.

14. The correct answer is (C). Plug $x = -1$ into the given equation to determine what occurs at that point. Both the numerator and denominator are 0, meaning the function is undefined. This allows you to eliminate (D) and (E). Also, it does not make sense for a horizontal asymptote to occur at a certain x-value—horizontal asymptotes occur at certain y-values, along horizontal lines—which allows you to eliminate (B). Finally, you know that the discontinuity at this point is a removable one (or a "hole") and not an asymptote because the numerator of the rational function is also equal to 0. Asymptotes only occur when the numerator is nonzero while the denominator is zero. Alternatively, you could graph the function and look closely at $x = -1$.

15. The correct answer is (C). Take the log (base 10) of both sides of this equation, to get $\log_{10} 5.23^a = 1$. Using log laws, you can rewrite this equation as $a \log_{10} 5.23 = 1$, and then divide both sides by $\log_{10} 5.23$ to get $a = \dfrac{1}{\log_{10} 5.23} = 1.39$. If you picked (B), you found $\dfrac{1}{a}$.

16. The correct answer is (D). Since the magnitude of a complex number is equal to its distance from the origin–the given formula is the distance formula—it's easy to look at the picture and realize that $-5 - 7i$ is the farthest from the origin, and therefore has the greatest magnitude. Alternatively, calculate the magnitude of each of the answer options using the formula provided. The magnitude of $2 + 3i$ is $\sqrt{2^2 + 3^2} = \sqrt{13} = 3.61$. Similarly, the magnitudes of the other answer options are, in order, 6.71, 1.41, 7.75, and 6.08, so $-5 - 7i$ has the greatest magnitude.

17. The correct answer is (A). Since you know the see-saw is 12 feet long, you know that the distance from the left end of the see-saw to its midpoint is 6 feet. You can draw a right-angled triangle using the left half of the see-saw, the ground, and a vertical line from the ground to the midpoint of the see-saw. Since you know that sine of an angle is equal to the length of the opposite side divided by the length of the hypotenuse, you can write $\sin 20° = \dfrac{x}{6}$, where x is the height of the midpoint of the see-saw off the ground. Solving for x gives you $x = 6 \sin 20° = 2.05$ feet.

If you picked (D), you found the horizontal distance between the end of the see-saw and the point on the ground below the midpoint of the see-saw.

18. The correct answer is (B). Evaluate each of these answers one by one. It may be helpful to graph the function $y = \log_2 x$ on your graphing calculator first. (B) is false because logarithms are not defined at 0 or at negative numbers, so the domain does not include all real numbers.

If you picked (D), you may have forgotten to plug in $y = 0$ to find that $x = 1$. If you picked (E), you missed that the function has an asymptote along the y-axis.

19. The correct answer is (D). The bottom of the box on the boxplot represents the 25th percentile of test scores, and the top of the box represents the 75th percentile, which means that exactly half of the class scored between these two scores, 50% and 78%.

(A) is incorrect because the middle line of a boxplot represents the median, not the mean. (B) is incorrect because the highest test score is 100% and the lowest is 26%, so the range is 74%. (C) is incorrect because 26% is the minimum score and 72% is the median score, so exactly half the class scored within this range. (E) is incorrect because 72% is the median score and 100% is the maximum score, so exactly half the class scored within this range.

20. The correct answer is (C). You know that $f(c) = ac^b = d$. Now, you can evaluate $f(2c) = a(2c)^b = a(2^b)(c^b) = ac^b \times 2^b = d \times 2^b$, which is option (C).

21. The correct answer is (A). Any two points determine a line between them, but there are infinitely many different planes that pass through that line, so two points do not uniquely determine a plane. For each other answer choice, there is only one plane that passes through the given objects, so each one uniquely determines a plane.

22. The correct answer is (B). The easiest way to solve this question is to imagine starting at $f(x)$ and to think about what steps you would need to take to transform it into $g(x)$. You would need to start by moving it to the left by 6 units, since the vertex of $f(x)$ is at $x = 0$ and the vertex of $g(x)$ is at $x = -6$. Next, you would have to reflect it across the x-axis so that it opens downward instead of upward. Since the y-coordinate of the vertex of $f(x)$ was $y = 3$, and the y-coordinate of the vertex of $g(x)$ is $y = -3$, you don't need to shift it vertically at all, so this set of transformations is your final answer—a shift by 6 units to the left, and then a reflection across the x-axis, or (B).

23. The correct answer is (A). The formula for the volume of a cylinder is $\pi r^2 h$ and the formula for the volume of a sphere is $\frac{4}{3}\pi r^3$. You can set these equal and rearrange for h in terms of r:

$$\pi r^2 h = \frac{4}{3}\pi r^3$$
$$h = \frac{4}{3}r$$

24. The correct answer is (C). Rearrange the inequality by subtracting a and adding $2b$ to both sides to get $4b < 0$. This means that b must be negative. However, this gives you no information about a, so a can be anything. Therefore, the correct answer is (III) only.

25. The correct answer is (D). By looking at the given equation, you can figure out that a point on the graph will be a lattice point when x is even (since then y will be an integer), but not when x is odd. Now, you can simply count the even numbers between −50 and 50—there are 24 negative ones, 24 positive ones, and 0, for a total of 49. Therefore, the given line passes through 49 lattice points in this range.

If you picked (A) or (B), you may have thought x needed to be divisible by 3. If you picked (C) or (E), you may have miscounted the even numbers.

26. The correct answer is (A). Plug the expression for $f(x)$ into the place of x in the expression for $g(x)$ and simplify:

$$g(f(x)) = g\left(\frac{2x+6}{3x-4}\right) = \frac{1}{2\left(\frac{2x+6}{3x-4}\right)} = \frac{3x-4}{4x+12}$$

27. The correct answer is (A). Since you know that the fastest sprinter must be on every team, there are three spots remaining that need to be filled by the four remaining sprinters. There are four ways to do this, since you could either leave out the first sprinter, the second sprinter, the third sprinter, or the fourth sprinter. Therefore, there are four ways to make this team.

If you picked (B), you may have forgotten that the fastest sprinter must be on every team. If you picked (D), you may have thought the order of the remaining three sprinters mattered. If you picked (E), you may have thought that all five sprinters were on the team and that the order mattered.

28. The correct answer is (B). Using the double angle formula, you know that $\sin 2x = 2 \sin x \cos x$, which means you can rewrite the given expression as $2 \cos x = 2 \sin x \cos x$. Cancelling out $2 \cos x$ on both sides gives you $\sin x = 1$, which means that $x = \dfrac{\pi}{2}$.

29. The correct answer is (E). Rewrite the function, using log laws, as $f(x) = 2 \log_5 x$. Now, you are trying to find what x is if $f(x) = 3$, since this is the definition of the inverse function. You can plug in $f(x) = 3$ and simplify to get $3 = 2 \log_5 x$, divide both sides by 2 to get $\dfrac{3}{2} = \log_5 x$, and then put 5 to the power of each side to get $5^{\frac{3}{2}} = 5^{\log_5 x}$. Since $5^{\log_5 x} = x$, you know that $x = 5^{\frac{3}{2}} = 5\sqrt{5}$.

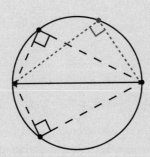

30. The correct answer is (B). Use the diagram above to help you visualize a few examples of the given situation. No matter where the third vertex of the triangle is, it will have a 90° angle. This means that the point where the two legs meet along the circumference of the circle is variable, so the two sides do not need to be equal in length, eliminating option I. As you can see, reflecting a triangle across the hypotenuse of the circle does not necessarily result in a rectangle, but may result in a kite shape. This eliminates option II. However, in any triangle, the sum of the length of any two sides must be greater than the length of the third. Since the diameter of the circle is one side of the triangle, the sum of the other two sides must be greater than it. This means that the answer is (B), III only.

31. The correct answer is (D). You know right away that this is not sine or cosine, since the graphs of those functions look like waves. This lets you eliminate (A) and (B). Also, the graph of cot x looks like a mirrored version of tan x, which does not look like this, so you can eliminate (E) as well. Now, you have to decide whether this is $\csc x = \dfrac{1}{\sin x}$ or $\sec x = \dfrac{1}{\cos x}$. You can see that the given function has an asymptote at $x = 0$, which means that the denominator must evaluate to 0 at $x = 0$. This is true of sin x but not cos x, meaning that the answer must be csc x.

32. The correct answer is (D). Based on the four coordinates given, you know the side length of this cube must be 3, since that is the distance between $(1, 3, 4)$ and $(4, 3, 4)$ and also between $(1, 0, 1)$ and $(4, 0, 1)$. This means that the edges of the cube must be parallel with the x, y, and z axes. There are two options for the x-coordinate (1 or 4), two options for the y-coordinate (0 or 3), and two options for the z-coordinate (1 or 4). This tells you that the other four vertices are all the possible combinations of these that aren't already listed: $(1, 3, 1)$, $(1, 0, 4)$, $(4, 3, 1)$, and $(4, 0, 4)$. The remaining answer choice is $(1, 4, 3)$, which is not a vertex.

33. The correct answer is (C). Evaluate the three options one by one to determine which are correct by checking whether they satisfy $f(x) = f(f(x))$. If $f(x) = 3$ for all real numbers x, then $f(f(x)) = f(3) = 3 = f(x)$, so the function in (I) is idempotent. If $f(x) = x$, then $f(f(x)) = f(x)$, so this function is also idempotent. If $f(x) = 3x$, then $f(f(x)) = f(3x) = 3(3x) = 9x \neq f(x)$, so this function is not idempotent. This means that only the functions in (I) and (II) are idempotent.

34. The correct answer is (E). The easiest way to solve this question, and logic questions like it, is not to try to work through each answer choice to see whether it is true or false. This will take too much time and effort. Instead, memorize the four basic logical if-then statements. If a statement "if P then Q" is true, then its contrapositive "if not Q, then not P" is also true. Its converse "if Q then P" is not necessarily true, and neither is its inverse "if not P, then not Q."

In this question, $P = $ "x is divisible by 4" and $Q = $ "x^2 is divisible by 4." Therefore, (B) is the inverse and (C) is the converse of the given statement, so neither one can be concluded from the original statement. (A) and (D) also do not obey this inference rule, so they are also not necessarily true.

35. The correct answer is (B). You can arrange three spheres at the vertices of an equilateral triangle so that each one touches the other two. You can then put a fourth sphere on top of those three, so that their centers are at the vertices of a tetrahedron. There is no way to extend this to have five identical spheres that are all adjacent, so 4 is the maximum possible number of spheres.

36. The correct answer is (D). You know the slope of line L is $\frac{2b-b}{2a-a} = \frac{b}{a}$ and the slope of line M, similarly, is $\frac{a}{b}$. Also, you can find the y-intercept, c, of each line with the equation $b = \left(\frac{b}{a}\right)a + c$ for L and $a = \left(\frac{a}{b}\right)b + c$ for M. Solving both of these tells you that both lines have a y-intercept of 0, so they pass through the origin. This means that L has the equation $y = \frac{b}{a}x$ and M has the equation $y = \frac{a}{b}x$, so L and M are inverse functions. Geometrically, this means the lines are reflections of each other across the line $y = x$.

(A) is incorrect because the lines only have the same slope if $a = b$. (B) is incorrect because the lines only have slopes that are negative reciprocals of each other if $a = -b$. (C) is incorrect because the lines have different slopes.

37. The correct answer is (D). In a trigonometric function of the form $f(x) = a\sin(kx - p) + q$ (or cosine instead of sine), the period is equal to $\frac{2\pi}{k}$, and the other numbers do not affect it. The period of the function in (A) is $\frac{2\pi}{2} = \pi$. The period of the function in (B) is $\frac{2\pi}{1} = 2\pi$. In (C), it is $\frac{2\pi}{3}$. In (D), it is $\frac{2\pi}{\frac{1}{2}} = 4\pi$. In (E), it is $\frac{2\pi}{1} = 2\pi$. Out of all of these, (D) has the longest period.

38. The correct answer is (D). To solve this question, you can look at each option individually, knowing that every integer larger than 1 is either odd or even. In answer choice (D), you know that if p is odd then p^2 is also odd, so $p^2 + p$ is even. If p is even, p^2 is also even, so in either case, $p^2 + p$ must be even. Therefore, (D) is correct.

(A) is incorrect because you know that any number multiplied by 2 will be even, and adding 1 to that number will make it odd. (B) is incorrect because if p is even then $3p + 1$ will be odd. (C) is incorrect because if p is odd, then p^2 is also odd. (E) is incorrect because if p is odd then p^3 and p^2 are also odd, and adding three odd numbers together will produce an odd number.

39. The correct answer is (A). Since you know that the initial quantity is 2, the growth factor is 2, and the mass doubles twice per hour, you can set up an equation to model the growth of the bacteria: $y = 2 \times 2^{2t}$, where t is the number of hours that have passed and y is the mass of the colony. You want to find t when $y = 40$. Plugging this in and simplifying, you get $40 = 2 \times 2^{2t}$, or $20 = 2^{2t}$. Take the log base 2 of both sides, and then divide both sides by 2, to get $t = \frac{\log_2 20}{2} = 2.161$ hours. Now, you just have to convert this into minutes and seconds. You know that 0.161 hours $= 0.161 \times 60$ minutes $= 9.66$ minutes, which is roughly 9 minutes and 39 seconds. In total, the mass of the colony will take around 2 hours, 9 minutes, and 39 seconds to reach 40 grams.

40. The correct answer is (B). If 85% of the 20 people are right-handed, this means 17 of them are right-handed. The probability that the first person you select is right-handed is $\frac{17}{20}$. After choosing this person, the probability that the next person you select is right-handed will be $\frac{16}{19}$. The probability that the third person will be right-handed is $\frac{15}{18}$. Multiplying all these numbers together (since you need to pick a right-handed person in all 3 instances) gives you $\frac{17 \times 16 \times 15}{20 \times 19 \times 18} = 59.6\%$.

If you picked (A), you may have thought there was an 85% chance of choosing a right-handed person in all three trials.

41. The correct answer is (C). You should notice from the picture that the function looks like x^2 or x^4 between -1 and 1. This allows you to eliminate (D). Also, the curve clearly changes (there is a sharp corner) at $x = -1$ and $x = 1$, so you can eliminate (E) since this is saying that it is the same polynomial everywhere to the left of $x = 1.62$. Next, you can look at the polynomial on the right side (to the right of $x = 1.62$). It goes down, flattens out, and then goes down more. You should recognize this as a cubic polynomial with a negative coefficient on the x^3 term (since it goes downwards instead of upwards). Also, its x-intercept is $x = 3$, meaning that you can eliminate (A) and (B) since these both have different x-intercepts (the x-intercept of the cubic function in (A) is $\sqrt[3]{3}$, and the x-intercept of the cubic function in (B) is 0). Therefore, (C) is correct.

42. The correct answer is (C). The fastest way to solve this problem is to notice that the given equation looks like the double angle formula: $\cos a = 1 - \sin^2 \frac{a}{2}$. In this case, since $\frac{a}{2} = 18°$, you know that $a = 36°$. If you didn't notice this, you could just plug the right-hand side into your calculator and then take the inverse cosine of both sides.

43. The correct answer is (E). In general, the circle $(x - h)^2 + (y - k)^2 = r^2$ has its center at (h, k), so you know that these circles are centered at $(2, 4)$ and $(10, 4)$, meaning they are 8 units apart. Since the circles are tangent to each other, the sum of their radii must be 8 (since the distance between their centers is the radius of the first one plus the radius of the second one). The first circle has a radius of $\sqrt{25} = 5$, so the radius of the second circle must be 3. However, since k is the square of the radius, $k = 3^2 = 9$.

If you got (B), you may have thought k was the radius.

44. The correct answer is (E). Examine characteristics of the given graph to determine information about f and g. The given graph has an asymptote at $x = 1$, meaning that $g(1)$ must be equal to 0 (since g is in the denominator of $\frac{f}{g}$). The only graph that has $g(1) = 0$ is (E). (Note that in (C), the labels are switched so that $f(1) = 0$ but $g(1) = \frac{1}{2}$).

45. The correct answer is (B). To solve this question, write a formula for the distance of (x, y) to the origin, write a different formula for the distance of $\left(\frac{x}{2}, y\right)$ to the origin, and set them equal. The distance from (x, y) to the origin is $\sqrt{x^2 + y^2}$, and the distance from $\left(\frac{x}{2}, 2y\right)$ to the origin is $\sqrt{\left(\frac{x}{2}\right)^2 + (2y)^2} = \sqrt{\frac{x^2}{4} + 4y^2}$. Setting these equal to each other and squaring both sides gives you $x^2 + y^2 = \frac{x^2}{4} + 4y^2$. Combine like terms to get $\frac{3}{4}x^2 = 3y^2$, or $y^2 - \frac{1}{4}x^2 = 0$. Factor this as a difference of squares to get $\left(y - \frac{1}{2}x\right)\left(y + \frac{1}{2}x\right) = 0$, so either $x = 2y$ or $x = -2y$. Combining these solutions gives you $x = \pm 2y$.

If you got (A), you may have tried to take the square root of both sides of $y^2 = \frac{1}{4}x^2$ without considering the possibility of negative values of x or y.

46. The correct answer is (D). Finding the y-intercept of a parabola means finding the value of the equation when $x = 0$, which in this case is equal to c. You can plug in the given values and simplify:

$f(-1) = 2 = (-1)^2 + b(-1) + c = 1 - b + c$, so $c - b = 1$. Also, $f(1) = 4 = 1^2 + b(1) + c = 1 + b + c$, so $c + b = 3$.

Adding the equations $c - b = 1$ and $c + b = 3$ together, you can see that $2c = 4$, so $c = 2$, which is the y-intercept.

47. The correct answer is (E). For the product of two matrices to be defined, the number of columns of the first matrix must equal the number of rows of the second. You can avoid doing any calculations for this question by identifying the dimensions of each matrix and determining whether the number of columns of the first matrix equals or does not equal the number of rows of the second. Matrix A is a 1×2 matrix, B is 3×2, C is 3×1, and D is 2×3. Therefore, (A) is defined, because a multiplication of matrices A and D with dimensions $(1 \times 2) \times (2 \times 3)$ results in matrix AD with dimensions 1×3. (B), (C), and (D) are also all defined. (E) is undefined because matrix C has 1 column and matrix B has 3 rows, and $1 \neq 3$.

48. The correct answer is (E). When you are trying to evaluate whether a certain claim must be true, you should try to find situations in which it is not true—if you can find any, then you know the statement doesn't always have to be true. For this question, you should go through the answer options and try to find a counterexample to each one. If

$f(x) = \dfrac{1}{x - a}$ and $g(x) = \dfrac{1}{x - b}$, they both have the required asymptotes. The function $(fg)(x) = \dfrac{1}{(x - a)(x - b)}$

has asymptotes at both $x = a$ and $x = b$. This allows you to eliminate (C) and (D). However, if $f(x) = \dfrac{x - b}{x - a}$ and

$g(x) = \dfrac{x - a}{x - b}$, then $(fg)(x) = \dfrac{(x - a)(x - b)}{(x - a)(x - b)}$, which has no asymptotes, only removable discontinuities (or "holes")

at $x = a$ and $x = b$. This allows you to eliminate (A) and (B). Since none of these answers must be true, the correct answer is (E).

49. The correct answer is (E). Write out this relationship algebraically. Call the two numbers a and b, so that $ab = a + b$. The easiest way to see that this has infinitely many solutions (a, b) is to rearrange it as $ab - a = b$, or, by factoring the left side, $a(b - 1) = b$. You can divide both sides by $b - 1$ to get $a = \dfrac{b}{b - 1}$. You have now written a as a function of b, so any value that you plug in for b (other than $b = 1$) will give you an a-value that satisfies the original equation, meaning that there are infinitely many pairs that satisfy it.

50. The correct answer is (D). The general equation of an ellipse is $\dfrac{x^2}{a^2} + \dfrac{y^2}{b^2} = 1$, where a is half the length of the horizontal axis and b is half the length of the vertical axis. In the original equation, the length of the horizontal axis of the ellipse is $2a = 2 \times \sqrt{4} = 4$. Since the ellipse is stretched horizontally by a factor of 2, the new length of its horizontal axis should be $2 \times 4 = 8$, meaning that $2a = 8$ and so $a = 4$ and $a^2 = 16$. The vertical axis is unaffected, so b does not change.

Practice Test 3

YOUR NAME (PRINT): _____

LAST   FIRST   MI

Correct ●	Incorrect ◐ ⊗ ⊘ ◓ ✪ ○ ◒ ◍	**Make sure you use a No. 2 pencil.** Each answer must be marked in the corresponding row on the answer sheet. Each bubble must be filled in completely and darkly within the lines. Extra marks on your answer sheet may be marked as incorrect answers and lower your score.

○ Literature
○ Biology E
○ Biology M
○ Chemistry
○ Physics

○ Mathematics Level 1
○ Mathematics Level 2
○ U.S. History
○ World History
○ French

○ German
○ Italian
○ Latin
○ Modern Hebrew
○ Spanish

---

1 Ⓐ Ⓑ Ⓒ Ⓓ Ⓔ   21 Ⓐ Ⓑ Ⓒ Ⓓ Ⓔ   41 Ⓐ Ⓑ Ⓒ Ⓓ Ⓔ   61 Ⓐ Ⓑ Ⓒ Ⓓ Ⓔ   81 Ⓐ Ⓑ Ⓒ Ⓓ Ⓔ

2 Ⓐ Ⓑ Ⓒ Ⓓ Ⓔ   22 Ⓐ Ⓑ Ⓒ Ⓓ Ⓔ   42 Ⓐ Ⓑ Ⓒ Ⓓ Ⓔ   62 Ⓐ Ⓑ Ⓒ Ⓓ Ⓔ   82 Ⓐ Ⓑ Ⓒ Ⓓ Ⓔ

3 Ⓐ Ⓑ Ⓒ Ⓓ Ⓔ   23 Ⓐ Ⓑ Ⓒ Ⓓ Ⓔ   43 Ⓐ Ⓑ Ⓒ Ⓓ Ⓔ   63 Ⓐ Ⓑ Ⓒ Ⓓ Ⓔ   83 Ⓐ Ⓑ Ⓒ Ⓓ Ⓔ

4 Ⓐ Ⓑ Ⓒ Ⓓ Ⓔ   24 Ⓐ Ⓑ Ⓒ Ⓓ Ⓔ   44 Ⓐ Ⓑ Ⓒ Ⓓ Ⓔ   64 Ⓐ Ⓑ Ⓒ Ⓓ Ⓔ   84 Ⓐ Ⓑ Ⓒ Ⓓ Ⓔ

5 Ⓐ Ⓑ Ⓒ Ⓓ Ⓔ   25 Ⓐ Ⓑ Ⓒ Ⓓ Ⓔ   45 Ⓐ Ⓑ Ⓒ Ⓓ Ⓔ   65 Ⓐ Ⓑ Ⓒ Ⓓ Ⓔ   85 Ⓐ Ⓑ Ⓒ Ⓓ Ⓔ

6 Ⓐ Ⓑ Ⓒ Ⓓ Ⓔ   26 Ⓐ Ⓑ Ⓒ Ⓓ Ⓔ   46 Ⓐ Ⓑ Ⓒ Ⓓ Ⓔ   66 Ⓐ Ⓑ Ⓒ Ⓓ Ⓔ   86 Ⓐ Ⓑ Ⓒ Ⓓ Ⓔ

7 Ⓐ Ⓑ Ⓒ Ⓓ Ⓔ   27 Ⓐ Ⓑ Ⓒ Ⓓ Ⓔ   47 Ⓐ Ⓑ Ⓒ Ⓓ Ⓔ   67 Ⓐ Ⓑ Ⓒ Ⓓ Ⓔ   87 Ⓐ Ⓑ Ⓒ Ⓓ Ⓔ

8 Ⓐ Ⓑ Ⓒ Ⓓ Ⓔ   28 Ⓐ Ⓑ Ⓒ Ⓓ Ⓔ   48 Ⓐ Ⓑ Ⓒ Ⓓ Ⓔ   68 Ⓐ Ⓑ Ⓒ Ⓓ Ⓔ   88 Ⓐ Ⓑ Ⓒ Ⓓ Ⓔ

9 Ⓐ Ⓑ Ⓒ Ⓓ Ⓔ   29 Ⓐ Ⓑ Ⓒ Ⓓ Ⓔ   49 Ⓐ Ⓑ Ⓒ Ⓓ Ⓔ   69 Ⓐ Ⓑ Ⓒ Ⓓ Ⓔ   89 Ⓐ Ⓑ Ⓒ Ⓓ Ⓔ

10 Ⓐ Ⓑ Ⓒ Ⓓ Ⓔ   30 Ⓐ Ⓑ Ⓒ Ⓓ Ⓔ   50 Ⓐ Ⓑ Ⓒ Ⓓ Ⓔ   70 Ⓐ Ⓑ Ⓒ Ⓓ Ⓔ   90 Ⓐ Ⓑ Ⓒ Ⓓ Ⓔ

11 Ⓐ Ⓑ Ⓒ Ⓓ Ⓔ   31 Ⓐ Ⓑ Ⓒ Ⓓ Ⓔ   51 Ⓐ Ⓑ Ⓒ Ⓓ Ⓔ   71 Ⓐ Ⓑ Ⓒ Ⓓ Ⓔ   81 Ⓐ Ⓑ Ⓒ Ⓓ Ⓔ

12 Ⓐ Ⓑ Ⓒ Ⓓ Ⓔ   32 Ⓐ Ⓑ Ⓒ Ⓓ Ⓔ   52 Ⓐ Ⓑ Ⓒ Ⓓ Ⓔ   72 Ⓐ Ⓑ Ⓒ Ⓓ Ⓔ   92 Ⓐ Ⓑ Ⓒ Ⓓ Ⓔ

13 Ⓐ Ⓑ Ⓒ Ⓓ Ⓔ   33 Ⓐ Ⓑ Ⓒ Ⓓ Ⓔ   53 Ⓐ Ⓑ Ⓒ Ⓓ Ⓔ   73 Ⓐ Ⓑ Ⓒ Ⓓ Ⓔ   93 Ⓐ Ⓑ Ⓒ Ⓓ Ⓔ

14 Ⓐ Ⓑ Ⓒ Ⓓ Ⓔ   34 Ⓐ Ⓑ Ⓒ Ⓓ Ⓔ   54 Ⓐ Ⓑ Ⓒ Ⓓ Ⓔ   74 Ⓐ Ⓑ Ⓒ Ⓓ Ⓔ   94 Ⓐ Ⓑ Ⓒ Ⓓ Ⓔ

15 Ⓐ Ⓑ Ⓒ Ⓓ Ⓔ   35 Ⓐ Ⓑ Ⓒ Ⓓ Ⓔ   55 Ⓐ Ⓑ Ⓒ Ⓓ Ⓔ   75 Ⓐ Ⓑ Ⓒ Ⓓ Ⓔ   95 Ⓐ Ⓑ Ⓒ Ⓓ Ⓔ

16 Ⓐ Ⓑ Ⓒ Ⓓ Ⓔ   36 Ⓐ Ⓑ Ⓒ Ⓓ Ⓔ   56 Ⓐ Ⓑ Ⓒ Ⓓ Ⓔ   76 Ⓐ Ⓑ Ⓒ Ⓓ Ⓔ   96 Ⓐ Ⓑ Ⓒ Ⓓ Ⓔ

17 Ⓐ Ⓑ Ⓒ Ⓓ Ⓔ   37 Ⓐ Ⓑ Ⓒ Ⓓ Ⓔ   57 Ⓐ Ⓑ Ⓒ Ⓓ Ⓔ   77 Ⓐ Ⓑ Ⓒ Ⓓ Ⓔ   97 Ⓐ Ⓑ Ⓒ Ⓓ Ⓔ

18 Ⓐ Ⓑ Ⓒ Ⓓ Ⓔ   38 Ⓐ Ⓑ Ⓒ Ⓓ Ⓔ   58 Ⓐ Ⓑ Ⓒ Ⓓ Ⓔ   78 Ⓐ Ⓑ Ⓒ Ⓓ Ⓔ   98 Ⓐ Ⓑ Ⓒ Ⓓ Ⓔ

19 Ⓐ Ⓑ Ⓒ Ⓓ Ⓔ   39 Ⓐ Ⓑ Ⓒ Ⓓ Ⓔ   59 Ⓐ Ⓑ Ⓒ Ⓓ Ⓔ   79 Ⓐ Ⓑ Ⓒ Ⓓ Ⓔ   99 Ⓐ Ⓑ Ⓒ Ⓓ Ⓔ

20 Ⓐ Ⓑ Ⓒ Ⓓ Ⓔ   40 Ⓐ Ⓑ Ⓒ Ⓓ Ⓔ   60 Ⓐ Ⓑ Ⓒ Ⓓ Ⓔ   80 Ⓐ Ⓑ Ⓒ Ⓓ Ⓔ   100 Ⓐ Ⓑ Ⓒ Ⓓ Ⓔ

For automatic scoring and scaling, please visit **cloud.ivyglobal.com**.

SAT Math Level 2 Subject Test

Reference Materials

THE FORMULAS BELOW MAY BE USEFUL IN ANSWERING QUESTIONS ON THIS TEST.

$S = 4\pi r^2$ is the formula for the surface area of a sphere with a radius of r.

$V = \frac{1}{3}\pi r^2 h$ is the formula for the volume of a right circular cone with a radius of r and a height of h.

$V = \frac{4}{3}\pi r^3$ is the formula for the volume of a sphere with a radius of r.

$V = \frac{1}{3}Bh$ is the formula for the volume of a pyramid with a base area of B and a height of h.

When choosing an answer, find the CLOSEST answer possible. If the precise numerical value that you have found is not an answer choice, select the choice that is closest to your answer. Use the answer sheet and fill in the bubble corresponding to your choice.

Notes: (1) You ARE permitted the use of a graphing or scientific calculator, which you may use at your own discretion. You will also have to choose between degree or radian mode for some questions, so keep track of what mode your calculator is in.

(2) You may assume that figures are drawn as accurately as possible UNLESS it is explicitly stated that a figure is not drawn to scale. Furthermore, all figures are in a plane UNLESS it is stated otherwise.

(3) For any function f, unless otherwise specified, you may assume that a real number x is in the domain of f if and only if $f(x)$ is a real number. The range of f consists of all and only those real numbers of the form $f(x)$, where x is in the domain of f.

(4) Four formulas are provided in the box above for your reference.

GO ON TO THE NEXT PAGE

1.   What is the range of possible values of x if $10x - 3 < 17$?

(A) $x < 1.4$

(B) $x > 1.4$

(C) $x < 2$

(D) $x > 2$

(E) $x < -2$

USE THIS SPACE FOR SCRATCH WORK.

2.   If one student can type 80 words per minute and another student can type 60 words per minute, how many total words can both students type in an hour?

(A) 14,000

(B)   8,400

(C)   4,800

(D)   4,200

(E)   140

3.   If the y-intercept of a line is $(0, a)$ and its x-intercept is $(a, 0)$, where $a > 0$, then the slope of the line is

(A) −2

(B) −1

(C)   0

(D)   1

(E)   2

GO ON TO THE NEXT PAGE

USE THIS SPACE FOR SCRATCH WORK.

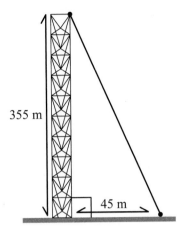

Note: Figure not drawn to scale.

4. A radio tower is 355 meters tall and is stabilized by a guy-wire
    stretched from the top of the tower to the level ground 45 meters away
    from its base. What is the length of the wire, to the nearest meter?

    (A) 352
    (B) 353
    (C) 357
    (D) 358
    (E) 359

5. The mean age of 10 members of a club is 29.5. When 5 new
    members join the club, the mean age of the club becomes 24.4.
    What is the mean age of the 5 new members?

    (A) 13.8
    (B) 14.0
    (C) 14.2
    (D) 15.0
    (E) 15.2

GO ON TO THE NEXT PAGE

USE THIS SPACE FOR SCRATCH WORK.

6. $(4t - 1)\left(\dfrac{4t + 1}{2}\right) =$

   (A) $8t^2 - \dfrac{1}{2}$

   (B) $16t^2 - 1$

   (C) $8t^2 - 4t - \dfrac{1}{2}$

   (D) $16t^2 + 8t - 1$

   (E) $32t^2 - 2$

7. If $\sin^2 \theta = 0.433$, $\cos^2 \theta =$

   (A) 0.187
   (B) 0.217
   (C) 0.433
   (D) 0.567
   (E) 1.875

8. If line L is perpendicular to both line M and line N, and all three lines are in the same plane, which of the following statements must be true?

   (A) Lines M and N are parallel.
   (B) Lines M and N are perpendicular.
   (C) Lines M and N are the same line.
   (D) The slope of line M is the negative of the slope of line N.
   (E) None of the above.

9. If $f(x) = 2x - 3$ and $f(g(3)) = 5$, then $g(x)$ could equal

   (A) $2x - 2$
   (B) $2x - 3$
   (C) $3x - 3$
   (D) $3x - 4$
   (E) $5x - 1$

GO ON TO THE NEXT PAGE

USE THIS SPACE FOR SCRATCH WORK.

10. Which of the following expressions is equivalent to $\sec x$?

(A) $\dfrac{\tan x}{\sin x}$

(B) $\dfrac{\sin x}{\tan x}$

(C) $\dfrac{\cot x}{\sin x}$

(D) $\dfrac{\cot x}{\cos x}$

(E) $\dfrac{\cos x}{\cot x}$

11. If $\dfrac{1}{x} + \dfrac{2}{y} = \dfrac{4}{z}$, then, the value of x in terms of y and z is equal to

(A) $\dfrac{yz}{2(2y - z)}$

(B) $\dfrac{2(2y - z)}{yz}$

(C) $\dfrac{yz}{2(2y + z)}$

(D) $\dfrac{2(2y + z)}{yz}$

(E) $\dfrac{z - 2y}{4}$

GO ON TO THE NEXT PAGE

USE THIS SPACE FOR SCRATCH WORK.

Circumference = 28.5"   Circumference = 9.25"

Note: Figures not drawn to scale.

12. A baseball has a circumference of 9.25 inches, and a basketball has a circumference of 28.5 inches. The surface area of the basketball is how many times as large as the surface area of the baseball.

    (A)   3.1
    (B)   9.5
    (C)   9.6
    (D)   29.2
    (E)   90.1

13. If $f(x) = \dfrac{3}{x-1}$, then $f\left(\dfrac{1}{x}\right) =$

    (A) $\dfrac{3}{1-x}$

    (B) $\dfrac{3x}{x-1}$

    (C) $\dfrac{3x}{1-x}$

    (D) $\dfrac{1}{3x}$

    (E) $\dfrac{1-x}{3x}$

GO ON TO THE NEXT PAGE

USE THIS SPACE FOR SCRATCH WORK.

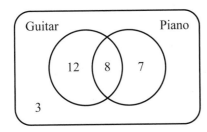

14. The Venn diagram above shows the number of students in a 30-student class who play guitar and piano. What is the probability that a student chosen at random from the class does NOT play both guitar and piano?

(A) 0.10
(B) 0.27
(C) 0.50
(D) 0.67
(E) 0.73

15. The Twin Sisters are two adjacent mountains. The first peak has an altitude of 1,650 meters, and the second peak has an altitude of 1,600 meters. If the first peak is 400 meters west and 200 meters north of the second peak, what is the distance, to the nearest meter, from the first peak to the second?

(A) 59 m
(B) 416 m
(C) 444 m
(D) 447 m
(E) 450 m

GO ON TO THE NEXT PAGE

USE THIS SPACE FOR SCRATCH WORK.

```
1 | 7 9
2 | 2 5 5 9
3 | 0 1 4 4 6 7 7 8
4 | 0 0 1 2 4 7
5 | 2
```

Note: 1 | 7 represents 17.

16. The stem-and-leaf plot above shows the heights of 21 daffodil plants in a garden, in centimeters. What is the median height?

(A) 4 cm

(B) 30 cm

(C) 34 cm

(D) 36 cm

(E) 37 cm

**US FEDERAL
REVENUES ($3.3 trillion)**

■ Payroll Taxes

■ Corporate Income Taxes

■ Individual Income Taxes

■ Other

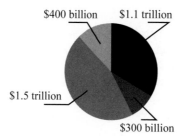

$400 billion $1.1 trillion

$1.5 trillion

$300 billion

17. The pie chart above shows US federal revenues. What is the difference between the central angle of the section that represents Individual Taxes and the central angle of the section that represents Corporate Taxes?

(A) 32.73°

(B) 43.64°

(C) 44.24°

(D) 119.40°

(E) 130.91°

GO ON TO THE NEXT PAGE

18. If d is the greatest common factor of m and n, where all three are positive integers, what is the least common multiple of m and n?

(A) mnd

(B) mn

(C) $\dfrac{mn}{d}$

(D) d

(E) Cannot be determined from the given information.

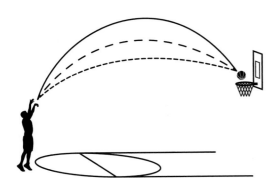

19. A basketball player shoots a basketball in a parabola from a height of 2.5 m and with an initial velocity of 10 m/s. The height of the basketball can be modelled by the equation $h = -5t^2 + 10t + 2.5$, where t is the time of the basketball's flight in seconds. How many seconds does it take for the basketball to enter the net, at a height of 3.05 m?

(A) 0.057 s
(B) 0.225 s
(C) 1.000 s
(D) 1.943 s
(E) 2.225 s

20. If the distance between boat A and boat B is 50 meters, and boat B is 50 meters away from the dock, then the distance between boat A and the dock could be any of the following EXCEPT

(A)　　0 meters
(B)　　10 meters
(C)　　50 meters
(D)　　80 meters
(E)　120 meters

GO ON TO THE NEXT PAGE

21. If $f(x)$ is a linear function and $g(x)$ is a quadratic function, then which of the following could represent $(f + g)(x)$?

USE THIS SPACE FOR SCRATCH WORK.

(A)
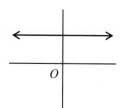

(B)
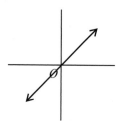

(C)
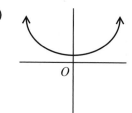

(D)

(E)
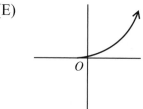

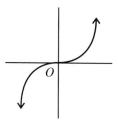

Note: figure not drawn to scale.

22. In the triangle shown above, $c =$

(A) 1.54

(B) 2.73

(C) 3.00

(D) 3.27

(E) 4.78

GO ON TO THE NEXT PAGE

USE THIS SPACE FOR SCRATCH WORK.

23. $\dfrac{\left(x^2 + x^{\frac{1}{2}}\right)^3}{x^2} =$

    (A) $x^2 + x^{\frac{1}{2}}$

    (B) $x^3 + x^{\frac{3}{2}}$

    (C) $x^3 + 3x^{\frac{9}{4}} + 3x^{\frac{3}{2}} + x^{\frac{3}{4}}$

    (D) $x^4 + 3x^{\frac{5}{2}} + 3x + x^{-\frac{1}{2}}$

    (E) $x^6 + 3x^{\frac{9}{2}} + 3x^3 + x^{\frac{3}{2}}$

24. A factory produces square tiles with a diagonal of 12 cm. Tiles with diagonals 14 cm and longer or 10 cm and shorter are discarded. Which of the following inequalities models the range of side lengths s, in cm, of tiles that can be produced without being discarded?

    (A) $|s - 12| < 2$

    (B) $|s - 2| < 12$

    (C) $|s - 6\sqrt{2}| > \sqrt{2}$

    (D) $|s - 6\sqrt{2}| < \sqrt{2}$

    (E) $|s - 6\sqrt{2}| \leq \sqrt{2}$

25. If $-\dfrac{\pi}{2} < \theta < 0$, which of the following inequalities is true?

    (A) $\sin\theta < \cos\theta < \tan\theta$

    (B) $\cos\theta < \sin\theta < \tan\theta$

    (C) $\sin\theta < \tan\theta < \cos\theta$

    (D) $\tan\theta < \cos\theta < \sin\theta$

    (E) $\tan\theta < \sin\theta < \cos\theta$

GO ON TO THE NEXT PAGE

USE THIS SPACE FOR SCRATCH WORK.

26. What value does $\dfrac{2x-100}{3x+10}$ approach as x approaches infinity?

   (A)　−10

   (B)　$\dfrac{2}{3}$

   (C)　2

   (D)　3

   (E)　It does not approach a unique value.

27. For which of the following values of x is $\dfrac{\sin 2x}{\csc 2x}$ negative?

   (A)　0.7854
   (B)　1.5708
   (C)　3.7783
   (D)　4.2046
   (E)　None of the above

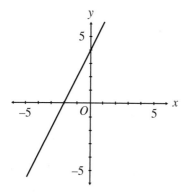

28. If the line above intersects a circle at exactly one point, then the center of the circle could be any of the following EXCEPT

   (A)　$(1, 6)$
   (B)　$(3, 5)$
   (C)　$(5, 3)$
   (D)　$(2, 1)$
   (E)　$(0, 0)$

GO ON TO THE NEXT PAGE

29. If $f(2 - 3x) = 3x + 2$ for all real numbers x, then $f(x) =$

(A) $x + 4$

(B) $-x + 4$

(C) $-9x - 12$

(D) $\frac{3}{2}x - 2$

(E) $6x + 7$

30. What is the sum of the infinite geometric series
$\frac{1}{3} + \frac{1}{6} + \frac{1}{12} + \frac{1}{24} + \ldots$?

(A) $\frac{1}{2}$

(B) $\frac{2}{3}$

(C) 1

(D) $\frac{4}{3}$

(E) 2

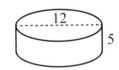

Note: Figure not drawn to scale.

31. What is the greatest linear distance between two points on the surface of the cylinder above?

(A) 11

(B) 12

(C) 13

(D) 15

(E) 17

GO ON TO THE NEXT PAGE

USE THIS SPACE FOR SCRATCH WORK.

32. If $f(x)$ is defined for all real numbers x, and $xf(x)$ has two x-intercepts, how many x-intercepts does $x^6 f(x)$ have?

(A) 0
(B) 2
(C) 5
(D) 6
(E) 7

$$f(x) = \frac{1}{2}x^2 + x - 2$$

33. What is the difference between the maximum and minimum values of the function f, shown above, where $-6 \leq x \leq 2$?

(A)   2.5
(B)   8
(C)   12.5
(D)   18
(E)   32

34. If $x_0 = 0$ and $x_{n+1} = (x_n - 1)^2$, then $x_4 =$

(A) -676
(B)   0
(C)   1
(D)   4
(E)   676

35. If the parabola represented by $y = -(x - 2)^2 + 5$ is translated 3 units to the left and then reflected across the x-axis, what is its new equation?

(A) $y = -(x + 1)^2 - 5$
(B) $y = (x - 1)^2 + 5$
(C) $y = (x - 5)^2 - 5$
(D) $y = -(x + 2) + 2$
(E) $y = (x + 1)^2 - 5$

GO ON TO THE NEXT PAGE

USE THIS SPACE FOR SCRATCH WORK.

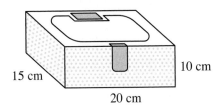

15 cm   20 cm   10 cm

Note: Figure not drawn to scale.

36. A company wants to reduce the volume of its box of cookies from 3000 cm³ to 1536 cm³ by reducing each dimension by a certain identical percentage. What is the percentage by which each dimension must be reduced?

(A) 10%
(B) 20%
(C) 48%
(D) 51%
(E) 80%

37. If $f(x) = 8 \cdot 2^x$ and $g(x) = a \cdot 2^x$, what is the value of a if $g(x + 2) = f(x)$ for all real numbers x?

(A) −2
(B) $\frac{1}{2}$
(C) 1
(D) 2
(E) 8

38. After a conference, 15% of attendees were sent survey A and 15% of attendees were sent survey B. No attendee received both surveys. Of the recipients of survey A, 80% responded. Of the recipients of survey B, 40% responded. If 2,106 attendees in total responded to the two surveys, how many attendees were at the conference?

(A) 380
(B) 5,265
(C) 11,700
(D) 29,250
(E) 37,908

USE THIS SPACE FOR SCRATCH WORK.

39. Which of the following equations represents a sphere?

(A) $x^2 + y^2 = 1$
(B) $x + y + z = 1$
(C) $x^2 + y^2 + z^2 = 1$
(D) $x^3 + y^3 + z^3 = 1$
(E) $x^4 + y^4 + z^4 = 1$

40. If n is an odd integer, then whenever n^2 is divided by 8, the remainder must always be

(A) 1
(B) 5
(C) 1 or 5
(D) 3 or 7
(E) 1, 3, 5, or 7

41. For which of the following functions is $f(x^2) = f(x)^2$ for all real numbers x ?

     I. $f(x) = x$
     II. $f(x) = 5x$
     III. $f(x) = x^2$

(A) I only
(B) II only
(C) III only
(D) I and III only
(E) I, II, and III

42. A line segment starts at the origin and extends for 13 units at an angle of 112.62° (measured counterclockwise from the positive x-axis). What are the (x, y) coordinates of the endpoint of the line segment?

(A) (5, 12)
(B) (12, 5)
(C) (−5, 12)
(D) (−12, 5)
(E) (−5, −12)

GO ON TO THE NEXT PAGE

USE THIS SPACE FOR SCRATCH WORK.

43. How many points of intersection occur between $f(x) = \frac{1}{4}\tan x$ and $g(x) = 4\sin 2x$ for $0 \leq x \leq 2\pi$?

   (A) 3
   (B) 5
   (C) 7
   (D) 9
   (E) 10

44. If $f(x) = \log_7(ax+5)$ and $f(4) = 2$, then $a =$

   (A) -4
   (B)   0
   (C)   4
   (D)   7
   (E) 11

45. How many ways can 8 people be divided into two groups of 4?

   (A)   24
   (B)   32
   (C)   70
   (D)   120
   (E) 1,680

46. If the point $(-3, 4)$ is reflected across the line $y = 2x$, what are its new coordinates?

   (A) $(5, 0)$
   (B) $(3, 1)$
   (C) $(3, -4)$
   (D) $(2, -6)$
   (E) $(6, 2)$

GO ON TO THE NEXT PAGE

$$9y + 6 = 2x - 30$$
$$y = ax^2 - b$$

USE THIS SPACE FOR SCRATCH WORK.

47. For which of the following values of a and b do the above equations have two points of intersection?

    (A) $a = -2, b = 5$
    (B) $a = -4, b = 3$
    (C) $a = 2, b = -5$
    (D) $a = 2, b = -3$
    (E) $a = 4, b = 3$

48. Let $f(x) = xe^{x-k}$. If $f(4) = 29.556$, what is the approximate value of k?

    (A) 7
    (B) 4
    (C) 3
    (D) 2
    (E) 1

49. A curve in the xy-plane is defined by the parametric equations $x = t^2 - 4$ and $y = t + 2$, for all real values of t. Which of the following equations describes this curve?

    (A) $x = \sqrt{y+4}$
    (B) $x = y - 2$
    (C) $x = y^2$
    (D) $x = y^2 - 4y$
    (E) $x = y^2 - 4y + 4$

GO ON TO THE NEXT PAGE

50. The area of an ellipse is given by the formula $A = \pi ab$, where a and b are the lengths of the semimajor and semiminor axes of the ellipse. What is the area of the ellipse represented by the equation $\frac{x^2}{25} + \frac{y^2}{49} = 1$ in the xy-plane?

(A) 2π

(B) 5π

(C) 7π

(D) 24π

(E) 35π

STOP

If you complete this test before the end of your allotted time, you may check your work.

Answers and Scoring

Scoring Your Test
Part 1

The easiest way to score your test is to use our Cloud scoring tool. The Cloud tool also provides more detailed results by showing you how you performed on specific kinds of questions. To score your test by hand, follow the directions below.

 For more detailed scoring results, please visit **cloud.ivyglobal.com.**

Answers

1. C	11. A	21. C	31. C	41. D
2. B	12. B	22. B	32. B	42. C
3. B	13. C	23. D	33. C	43. C
4. D	14. E	24. D	34. B	44. E
5. C	15. E	25. E	35. E	45. C
6. A	16. D	26. B	36. B	46. A
7. D	17. E	27. E	37. D	47. B
8. A	18. C	28. A	38. C	48. D
9. A	19. D	29. B	39. C	49. D
10. A	20. E	30. B	40. A	50. E

Raw Scores

To score your test, first use the answer key to mark each of your responses as correct or incorrect. Don't mark or count questions you left blank. Then, calculate your raw score for each section by subtracting one fourth the number of incorrect responses from the number of correct responses. Scores should be rounded to the nearest whole number, with .5 and above rounding up. Use the tables below to help you calculate your scores:

Scores	
Number Correct	_____ −
Number incorrect	_____ / 4 = _____
Raw Score	= _____
Scaled Score	_____

Scaled Scores

Once you have found your raw score for each test, convert it into an approximate scaled test score using the following chart. To find a scaled test score for each section, find the row in the Raw Score column which corresponds to your raw score for that section, then check the column for the section you are scoring in the same row. For example, if you had a raw score of 31, your scaled score would be 580. Keep in mind that these scaled scores are estimates only. Your actual SAT Subject Test in Mathematics Level 2 score will be scaled against the scores of all other students at your grade level taking the test on your test date.

Scaled Score							
Raw Score	Scaled Score	Raw Score	Scaled Score	Raw Score	Scaled Score	Raw Score	Scaled Score
50	800	34	710	18	560	2	440
49	800	33	700	17	560	1	430
48	800	32	690	16	550	0	410
47	800	31	680	15	540	−1	390
46	800	30	670	14	530	−2	370
45	800	29	660	13	530	−3	360
44	800	28	650	12	520	−4	340
43	800	27	640	11	510	−5	340
42	790	26	630	10	500	−6	330
41	790	25	630	9	500	−7	320
40	780	24	620	8	490	−8	320
39	770	23	610	7	480	−9	320
38	750	22	600	6	480	−10	320
37	740	21	590	5	470	−11	310
36	730	20	580	4	460	−12	310
35	720	19	570	3	450		

Explanations
Part 2

1. The correct answer is (C). Add 3 to both sides to get $10x < 20$, then divide by 10 to get $x < 2$.

   If you chose (A), you might have subtracted 3 from the right side instead of adding 3.

2. The correct answer is (B). Each minute, one student types 80 words and the other student types 60 words, which means that together they type 140 words each minute. In an hour, they will be able to type 140 words × 60 minutes = 8,400 words.

3. The correct answer is (B). Use the two given points to find the slope of the line: $\frac{y_2 - y_1}{x_2 - x_1} = \frac{a - 0}{0 - a} = \frac{a}{-a} = -1$.

4. The correct answer is (D). The radio tower and the ground form two legs of a right triangle. The guy-wire forms the hypotenuse, which you can call c. Use the Pythagorean theorem to find that $c = \sqrt{355^2 + 45^2} = 358$.

   If you chose (A), you may have thought the tower formed the hypotenuse of the triangle. If you chose (C), you may have rounded incorrectly.

5. The correct answer is (C). If the mean age of 10 members is 29.5, the sum of all the ages must be $29.5 \times 10 = 295$. When 5 new members join, bringing the mean age to 24.4, the sum of all 15 members' ages must be $15 \times 24.4 = 366$. Subtract the original sum from 366 to find the total age of the 5 new members: $366 - 295 = 71$. Take the average: $\frac{71}{5} = 14.2$.

6. The correct answer is (A). Rewrite $(4t - 1)$ as $\frac{(4t - 1)}{1}$ and multiply to get $\frac{(4t - 1)(4t + 1)}{2}$. Then expand the expression in the numerator: $(4t - 1)(4t + 1) = 16t^2 + 4t - 4t - 1 = 16t^2 - 1$. Dividing by the 2 in the denominator gives you $8t^2 - \frac{1}{2}$.

   If you picked (B), you might have forgotten to divide by 2. If you picked (C), you might have forgotten that the $-4t$ and the $4t$ cancelled out.

7. The correct answer is (D). The easiest way to solve this question is to remember the identity $\sin^2 \theta + \cos^2 \theta = 1$. Since $\sin^2 \theta = 0.433$, you know that $\cos^2 \theta = 1 - 0.433 = 0.567$.

   Alternately, you can use your calculator to find $\sin^{-1} \sqrt{0.433}$ and then plug that into $\cos^2 \theta$.

8. The correct answer is (A). The only way that one line can intersect two other lines at $90°$, all in the same plane, is if the two other lines are parallel to each other. This is because if line L has a slope of m, then lines M and N must both have a slope of $\frac{-1}{m}$, and having the same slope means they are parallel to each other.

   (B) is false because if lines M and N are perpendicular, one of them must be parallel to line L, which means that line L cannot be perpendicular to both of them. (C) is not necessarily true, because though identical lines must also be parallel, there are non-identical parallel lines that also satisfy the situation given in the question, which means that (C) does not need to be true.

9. The correct answer is (A). First, find the value of $g(3)$. Let $k = g(3)$. Then you know that $f(k) = 2k - 3 = 5$, which you can rearrange to get $k = 4$, so $g(3) = 4$. Now, you just need to pick the answer option that evaluates to 4 when $x = 3$. Since $2(3) - 2 = 4$, you know that (A) is correct.

10. The correct answer is (A). First, you know that $\sec x = \frac{1}{\cos x}$. Solve this question by rewriting each answer in terms of $\sin x$ and $\cos x$. Since you know that $\tan x = \frac{\sin x}{\cos x}$, you can rewrite the expression in (A), $\frac{\tan x}{\sin x}$, as $\frac{\left(\frac{\sin x}{\cos x} \right)}{\sin x} = \frac{1}{\cos x}$, which is the answer. The expression in (B) is equal to $\cos x$, the expression in (C) is equal to $\frac{\cos x}{\sin^2 x}$, the expression in (D) is equal to $\frac{1}{\sin x}$, and the expression in (E) is equal to $\sin x$.

11. The correct answer is (A). First, isolate $\frac{1}{x}$ by subtracting $\frac{2}{y}$ from both sides to get $\frac{1}{x} = \frac{4}{z} - \frac{2}{y}$. Next, add the two fractions on the right by finding a common denominator:

$$\frac{1}{x} = \frac{4y}{yz} - \frac{2z}{yz} = \frac{4y - 2z}{yz} = \frac{2(2y - z)}{yz}.$$

Finally, take the reciprocal of both sides of the equation to get $x = \frac{yz}{2(2y - z)}$.

12. The correct answer is (B). The circumference of a sphere is proportional to its radius, but the surface area of a sphere is proportional to its radius squared. This means that the ratio of the circumferences of two spheres is equal to the ratio of their radii, and the ratio of their surface areas is equal to the square of the ratio of their radii. In this case, the ratio of the balls' circumferences is $\frac{28.5}{9.25} = 3.08$. This means that the ratio of the surface area of the balls is equal to $3.08^2 = 9.5$, so the basketball has a surface area approximately 9.5 times as large as the surface area of the baseball.

You could also work backwards to find the radius of each ball, then the surface area of each ball, and then find the ratio between them, but this is more time-consuming.

If you picked (A), you may have thought that the surface area of a sphere was proportional to its radius. If you picked (C), you may have rounded 3.081 to 3.1 before squaring it.

13. The correct answer is (C). To find an expression for $\frac{1}{x}$, plug $\frac{1}{x}$ in place of x in the expression for the original function. Therefore, $f\left(\frac{1}{x}\right) = \frac{3}{\left(\frac{1}{x} - 1\right)}$. You can then simplify this by multiplying the numerator and denominator by x, to get $\frac{3x}{1-x}$.

If you chose (A), you may have forgotten to multiply the numerator by x.

14. The correct answer is (E). To find the probability that a randomly chosen student does not play both instruments, find the number of students who do not play both instruments and divide it by the total number of students in the class, which is 30, as shown in the question. The 8 in the middle of the two circles represents the number of students who play both instruments, so the number of students who do NOT play both instruments is $30 - 8 = 22$. Therefore, the probability that a randomly selected student will not play both instruments is $\frac{22}{30} = 0.73$.

If you picked (A), you found the probability that a randomly selected student plays neither instrument. If you picked (B), you found the probability that a randomly selected student plays both instruments. If you picked (C), you found the probability that a randomly selected student plays piano. If you picked (D), you found the probability that a randomly selected student plays guitar.

15. The correct answer is (E). To find the distance between these two peaks, you should use the formula for distance in three dimensions. You know that the first peak is 400 meters west, 200 meters north, and 50 meters higher than the second peak, then the distance between them is $\sqrt{400^2 + 200^2 + 50^2} = 450$ meters.

16. The correct answer is (D). If there are 21 daffodils in the garden, then the 11th daffodil, in order of height, is the median: 36 cm.

17. The correct answer is (E). Find the central angle of each section by finding out what fraction of this total the section represents. For example, Corporate Income Taxes represents $\frac{0.3}{3.3} = 0.091$ of the circle. In degrees, this is approximately $0.091 \times 360° = 32.73°$. Individual Income Taxes represents $\frac{1.5}{3.3} = 0.455$ of the circle, which is $0.455 \times 360° = 163.64°$. Therefore, the magnitude of the difference of these angle measurements is $163.64° - 32.73° = 130.91°$.

18. The correct answer is (C). The least common multiple of two numbers is always equal to the product of the two numbers divided by their greatest common factor. Therefore, in this case, the least common multiple of m and n is equal to $\frac{mn}{d}$.

19. The correct answer is (D). To solve this question, set the ball's height equal to 3.05 and solve for t. This gives you $3.05 = -5t^2 + 10t + 2.5$, which you can rearrange to get $5t^2 - 10t + 0.55 = 0$. Using the quadratic formula, this gives you the solutions $t = \frac{10 \pm \sqrt{(-10)^2 - 4(5)(0.55)}}{10}$, so either $t = 0.057$ or $t = 1.943$. To decide between these two answers, you should remember that the ball will have a height of 3.05 meters twice—once on the way up, and once on the way down. Since you know it goes in the net on the way down, the answer will be the greater of the two numbers, which is 1.943.

If you picked (A), you found the first time the ball was 3.05 meters off the ground, when it was on the way up. If you picked (C), you found the time when the ball was at its maximum height. If you picked (E), you found the time when the ball hits the ground after going in the net.

20. The correct answer is (E). It is not possible for boat A to be 120 meters from the dock. If you were at boat A and wanted to get to the dock, you could travel 50 meters to boat B, and then another 50 meters to the dock, for a total of 100 meters, meaning that boat A could not be any more than 100 meters away from the dock. However, boat A could be less than 100 meters away from the dock—one way to think about this is to use the fact that the two boats and the dock could form an isosceles triangle, where two of the side lengths are 50 meters, but the third side length could have any measurement between 0 and 100 meters. Boat A could also be 0 meters from the dock, if it were at the dock.

21. The correct answer is (C). The sum of a quadratic polynomial with a linear polynomial is a quadratic polynomial, since the highest power of x will still be x^2. The only answer that represents a quadratic polynomial (a parabola) is option (C).

22. The correct answer is (B). Since you know two sides and the angle between them, you can use the law of cosines to find the length of the opposite side.

$$c^2 = a^2 + b^2 - 2ab \cos C$$
$$c = \sqrt{4^2 + 5^2 - 2(4)(5) \cos 33°}$$
$$c = 2.73$$

23. The correct answer is (D). This question requires you to use various exponent rules to simplify the given expression. Start by expanding the numerator. Remember to add the exponents when expressions with the same base are multiplied, and subtract exponents when expressions with the same base are divided. You should also remember that, when expanding a binomial to the power of 3, $(a + b)^3 = a^3 + 3a^2 b + 3ab^2 + b^3$:

$$\frac{\left(x^2 + x^{\frac{1}{2}}\right)^3}{x^2} = \frac{x^6 + 3x^4 x^{\frac{1}{2}} + 3x^2 x + x^{\frac{3}{2}}}{x^2}$$

$$= \frac{x^6 + 3x^{\frac{9}{2}} + 3x^3 + x^{\frac{3}{2}}}{x^2}$$

$$= x^4 + 3x^{\frac{5}{2}} + 3x + x^{-\frac{1}{2}}$$

24. The correct answer is (D). First, write the length of the diagonal in terms of the side length, s. Since the tiles are squares, the diagonal of a tile will have length $s\sqrt{2}$, which you can find using the Pythagorean Theorem or the 45-45-90 special triangle. The question tells you that for a tile not to be discarded, the length of the diagonal must be between 10 and 14 cm, but not equal to either of those values. You can write this as $10 < s\sqrt{2} < 14$, or $\left|s\sqrt{2} - 12\right| < 2$. This absolute value inequality says that the length of the diagonal must be less than 2 cm away from 12 cm; that is, between 10 and 14 cm. Finally, you can divide the entire inequality by $\sqrt{2}$ to get $\left|s - 6\sqrt{2}\right| < \sqrt{2}$.

If you picked (E), you may have thought that tiles with diagonals of exactly 10 or 14 cm would be kept.

25. The correct answer is (E). If $-\frac{\pi}{2} < \theta < 0$, then θ is in the fourth quadrant. In this range, $\sin\theta$ is negative and $\cos\theta$ is positive, so $\sin\theta < \cos\theta$. Additionally, you know that the tangent will always be negative because $\frac{\sin\theta}{\cos\theta}$ will always be negative. Since $\cos\theta < 1$ always, you know that dividing $\sin\theta$ by $\cos\theta$ will make it smaller (more negative), so $\tan\theta < \sin\theta$. Put these two inequalities together to get $\tan\theta < \sin\theta < \cos\theta$.

26. The correct answer is (B). As x approaches infinity, the linear terms in the numerator and denominator (the ones that contain an "x") also approach infinity, and the constant terms appear tiny in comparison. Because the constant terms are so small that they do not affect the value of this limit, the rational function approaches a value determined by the ratio of the linear terms. Since the linear term in the numerator has a coefficient of 2 and the linear term in the denominator has a coefficient of 3, the function approaches the value $\frac{2}{3}$.

27. The correct answer is (E). Since $\csc 2x = \frac{1}{\sin 2x}$, $\sin x$ and $\csc x$ will always have the same sign—if one is positive then the other is too, and if one is negative then the other is too. Therefore, the expression $\frac{\sin 2x}{\csc 2x}$ will always be a positive number divided by a positive number, or a negative number divided by a negative number. In either case, it will be positive.

28. The correct answer is (A). If the center of a circle is not on the line, then it is possible for the circle to only intersect the line once: when the line is tangent to the circle. So, to solve this question, you should find which of the answer options lies on the given line, since only circles centered on the line cannot be tangent to it. Plug the answers into the equation. (A) satisfies the equation of the line, plug the values into the equation. (A) satisfies the equation $y = 2x + 4$, because $6 = 2(1) + 4$. Therefore, the circle with the center $(1, 6)$ lies on the line, so the line intersects the circle twice.

29. The correct answer is (B). Because you are only given the rule for f when the input is in the form $2 - 3x$, you must write x in a form that looks like this to find what $f(x)$ is. Let $x = 2 - 3a$. Therefore, $f(x) = f(2 - 3a) = 3a + 2$. Now you can solve your original let-statement for a: $x = 2 - 3a$, so $x - 2 = -3a$, or $a = \frac{x-2}{-3}$. Next, substitute the resulting value of a into the first equation you found: $f(x) = 3a + 2 = 3(\frac{x-2}{-3}) + 2 = -x + 2 + 2 = -x + 4$.

30. The correct answer is (B). This series is convergent because its common ratio is $\frac{\frac{1}{6}}{\frac{1}{3}} = \frac{1}{2}$. The formula for the sum of a convergent series is $S = \frac{a}{1-r}$, where S is the sum, a is the first term in the series, and r is the common ratio. In this series, the first term is $\frac{1}{3}$ and the common ratio is $\frac{1}{2}$. Therefore, the sum of the series is $\frac{\frac{1}{3}}{1-\frac{1}{2}} = \frac{\frac{1}{3}}{\frac{1}{2}} = \frac{2}{3}$.

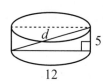

31. The correct answer is (C). The diagram above shows the greatest distance d between any two points on the surface of a cylinder. These two points are on opposite sides of the two bases. The distance d is the length of the diagonal line through the solid, which acts as the hypotenuse of a triangle, for which the two legs are the diameter of the base and the height of the cylinder. Using the Pythagorean theorem, $d = \sqrt{12^2 + 5^2} = 13$.

32. The correct answer is (B). A function has an x-intercept at any x-value where it evaluates to 0. The function $xf(x)$ evaluates to 0 at $x = 0$, and at any other values of x such that $f(x) = 0$. Because you are told that $xf(x)$ has two x-intercepts, you know that there is exactly one other value of x, call it a, such that $f(a) = 0$. The function $x^6 f(x)$ will also evaluate to 0 at $x = 0$ and $x = a$ (whatever a is), but not at any other values of x, since $x = a$ (and possibly $x = 0$) is the only zero (or x-intercept) of the function $f(x)$. Therefore, $x^6 f(x)$ must also have exactly two x-intercepts. In general, since $x = 0$ is already an x-intercept of the function $xf(x)$, multiplying this function by x will not add any more x-intercepts, since the function will still evaluate to 0 at the same x-values.

33. The correct answer is (C). A good first step to answering this question is to graph the given function. Since you have to find the maximum and minimum values of the function, it will help you to see which values of x you need to check. You will be able to see from the graph that the maximum value of the function occurs when $x = -6$ and the minimum value occurs when $x = -1$. Since $f(-6) = 10$ and $f(-1) = -2.5$, the difference between these values is 12.5.

If you didn't graph the function, you could have noticed that the function is a parabola that opens upward, meaning its minimum is its vertex. Then you could have found the x-coordinate of its vertex by using the formula $-\frac{b}{2a}$, and tested that point as well as the endpoints of the interval $-6 \leq x \leq 2$.

34. The correct answer is (B). Evaluate the terms of this sequence one by one, as follows. Start by finding that

$$x_1 = (x_0 - 1)^2 = (0 - 1)^2 = 1.$$

Now, you can use this to find that

$$x_2 = (x_1 - 1)^2 = (1 - 1)^2 = 0.$$

If you continue this pattern, you'll notice that $x_k = 0$ if k is even, and $x_k = 1$ if k is odd. Therefore, you know that $x_4 = 0$.

If you got (A), you may have thought that $(-1)^2 = -1$. If you got (C), you may have started with $x_1 = 0$ instead of $x_0 = 0$. If you got (E), you may have thought that the rule had a plus sign in it instead of a minus sign.

35. The correct answer is (E). Break this transformation into two steps. First, to translate the equation $y = -(x - 2)^2 + 5$ by 3 units to the left, add 3 to the constant in the parentheses with the x-variable to get $y = -(x + 1)^2 + 5$. Next, to reflect the equation across the x-axis, make the y-variable negative and keep the x-variable the same to get $-y = -(x + 1)^2 + 5$, then multiply both sides by -1 to get $y = (x + 1)^2 - 5$.

If you got (A), you may have forgotten to multiply the $(x + 1)^2$ term by -1. If you got (B), you may have forgotten to multiply the 5 by -1. If you got (C), you may have subtracted 3 from -2 instead of adding it.

36. The correct answer is (B). You know from the figure that the current dimensions of the box are 20, 15, and 10 cm. Since each dimension will get scaled by the same percentage, let r be the factor by which each dimension gets scaled. The new volume of the box will be $1536 = (20r)(15r)(10r) = 3000r^3$. Divide both sides by 3000 to get $r^3 = 0.512$, and so $r = 0.8$. This means that each dimension is 80% of its original length, so each dimension has been reduced by 20%.

If you picked (C), you might have only multiplied one of the dimensions by r. If you picked (E), you might have thought that r was the amount by which each dimension was reduced..

37. The correct answer is (D). The fact that $g(x + 2) = f(x)$ for all real numbers x tells you that $8 \times 2^x = a \times 2^{x+2}$. Simplifying the right side will give you $a \times 4 \times 2^x$, and dividing both sides of this equation by 2^x tells you that $8 = 4a$, so $a = 2$.

38. The correct answer is (C). If 15% of attendees received survey A and 80% of those responded, then $0.15 \times 0.8 = 0.12$ or 12% of attendees responded to survey A. Similarly, if 15% of attendees received survey B and 40% of those responded, $0.15 \times 0.4 = 0.06$ or 6% of attendees responded to survey B. A total of $12\% + 6\% = 18\%$ of attendees responded to surveys. If that percentage represents 2,106 attendees, then $\frac{2,106}{0.18} = 11,700$ attendees were at the conference.

39. The correct answer is (C). The equation of a sphere is $x^2 + y^2 + z^2 = r^2$, where r is the radius, which means (C) is the correct answer. If the equation of a sphere is not familiar to you, you can reason through the answer choices as follows. Choice (A) cannot be correct, as a sphere is three-dimensional and therefore requires three variables; choice (A) is in fact the equation for a circle. Choice (B) has three variables, but they are not of the correct degree; this equation produces a plane. The degrees of the variables in choice (D) are too great; this equation produces an unenclosed region. Similarly, the variables in choice (E) are of even higher degree. This equation produces an enclosed but non-spherical shape.

40. The correct answer is (A). The first few odd square numbers are 1, 9, 25, 49, and 81, all of which have a remainder of 1 when they are divided by 8. You can continue to test numbers until you are confident enough in your answer. To prove that this must always be true, recall that you can write any odd number in the form $2k + 1$, where k is an integer. When you square that, you get $(2k + 1)^2 = 4k^2 + 4k + 1 = 4(k^2 + k) + 1$. Since $k^2 + k$ must always be even (since k and k^2 are always either both even or both odd), you know that $4(k^2 + k)$ is 4 times an even number, which means it is divisible by 8. This tells you that the remainder of $4(k^2 + k) + 1$ must always be 1 when it is divided by 8.

41. The correct answer is (D). Test the given condition on each of these functions individually. If $f(x) = x$, then $f(x)^2 = (x)^2 = x^2$, and $f(x^2) = x^2$ also, so the condition is true for (I). If $f(x) = 5x$ then $f(x)^2 = (5x)^2 = 25x^2$, but $f(x^2) = 5x^2$, so the condition is not true for (II). If $f(x) = x^2$, then $f(x)^2 = (x^2)^2 = x^4$, and $f(x^2) = (x^2)^2 = x^4$, so the condition is true for (III) as well.

42. The correct answer is (C). Drawing a diagram of this situation might help. The line segment at an angle of 112.62° (counterclockwise from the positive x-axis) forms the hypotenuse of a triangle, in the second quadrant, whose legs are the x-axis and the perpendicular line from the x-axis to the point at the end of the 13-unit line segment. The angle between the hypotenuse and the x-axis is $180° - 112.62° = 67.38°$. The x-coordinate of the endpoint is equal to $13 \cos 67.38°$, which is approximately 5, but from your drawing you know the x-coordinate is negative, so this must be −5. The y-coordinate is equal to $13 \sin 67.38°$, which is approximately 12. Therefore, the endpoint is at (−5, 12).

43. The correct answer is (C). The easiest way to solve this question is to graph the two functions and count the points of intersection. The functions intersect at 0, 2π, and five other points in between, for a total of seven.

If you picked (B), you may not have counted the intersections at 0 and 2π. If you picked (A), you may have only counted the intersections where both functions intersect the x-axis (at 0, π, and 2π).

44. The correct answer is (E). Plug in the values $x = 4$ and $f(x) = 2$ to get $2 = \log_7(4a + 5)$ and then put 7 to the power of each side to get $7^2 = 4a + 5$, which you can solve to get $a = 11$.

45. The correct answer is (C). To count the number of ways that an unordered group of 4 people can be selected from a group of 8 people, use the combinations function, $\binom{8}{4} = \frac{8!}{4!(8-4)!} = \frac{8!}{4!4!} = 70$. Once you have selected one group of 4, you have already split the 8 people into 2 groups of 4 (since the other group is the remaining 4 people that you didn't pick), so the total number of ways is 70.

If you picked (E), you may have thought that the order in which the people were selected mattered, and used the formula for permutations rather than combinations.

46. The correct answer is (A). It may help to draw a diagram to solve this question. Call the given point P, the reflected point P', and the line of reflection line L. P and P' must be equidistant from L along a line, call it line R, that is perpendicular to L and is bisected by L at point I. In order to find the coordinates of P', you must first find the equation of R, then point I, and then the horizontal and vertical distances from P to I. These are the same distances from I to P', so they will allow you to find P'.

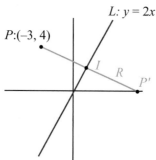

First, since line R is perpendicular to line L, its slope is the negative reciprocal of the slope of L. This means the slope of R is $-\frac{1}{2}$. Next, you know that point P lies on R, so you can plug P into the equation for R to find the y-intercept of R:

$$y = -\frac{1}{2}x + b$$

$$4 = -\frac{1}{2}(-3) + b$$

$$4 = \frac{3}{2} + b$$

$$b = 4 - \frac{3}{2} = \frac{5}{2}$$

Therefore, the equation of R is $y = -\frac{1}{2}x + \frac{5}{2}$. Next, you know that point I is the point of intersection of lines L and R, so you can solve L and R as a system of equations:

$$-\frac{1}{2}x + \frac{5}{2} = 2x$$

$$\frac{5}{2} = 2x + \frac{1}{2}x$$

$$\frac{5}{2} = \frac{5}{2}x$$

$$x = 1$$

Plug $x = 1$ into line L ($y = 2x$) to get $y = 2$. Therefore, point I is $(1, 2)$. The horizontal distance from P to I is $|x_P - x_I| = |-3 - 1| = 4$ units to the right. The vertical distance from P to I is $|y_P - y_I| = |4 - 2| = 2$ units down. Therefore, to find P', you can go 4 units to the right and 2 units down from I (since I is the midpoint of P and P'). This gives you the point $(1 + 4, 2 - 2) = (5, 0)$.

If you chose (C), you may have reflected P across the line $y = x$. If you chose (D) or (E), you may have thought the slope of line R was -2.

47. The correct answer is (B). The fastest way to solve this question is to start by rearranging the equation of the line into the form $y = \frac{2}{9}x - 4$, so you know that the y-intercept is –4. Also, since the quadratic equation has no linear term, you know that the parabola it represents is symmetric across the y-axis. Therefore, for the parabola and the line to have two points of intersection, either the vertex of the parabola must be above –4 and the parabola must open downward, or the vertex must be below –4 and the parabola must open upward. Because the given equation of the parabola is $y = ax^2 - b$, you know that the sign of a tells you whether the parabola opens upward or downward, and the y-coordinate of the vertex of the parabola is $-b$. This means that a pair of values for a and b will mean there are two points of intersection if a is negative and $b < 4$, or if a is positive and $b > 4$. Of the answer choices, (B) is the only option that satisfies either of these conditions.

You could also have substituted each value and then solved the resulting system of equations, but this would be very time-consuming.

48. The correct answer is (D). The easiest way to solve this question is to plug the values of x and $f(x)$ into the equation. This gives you $29.556 = 4e^{(4-k)}$. You can divide both sides of this equation by 4 to get $7.389 = e^{(4-k)}$. Next, take the natural log of both sides to get $2 = 4 - k$, and so $k = 2$.

49. The correct answer is (D). To eliminate the parameter, isolate t in the equation for y and then substitute the resultant expression into the equation for x: $y = t + 2$, so $t = y - 2$. Therefore,

$x = t^2 - 4$
$x = (y - 2)^2 - 4$
$x = (y^2 - 4y + 4) - 4$
$x = y^2 - 4y$.

50. The correct answer is (E). The general formula of an ellipse is $\dfrac{(x-h)^2}{a^2} + \dfrac{(y-k)^2}{b^2} = 1$, where $2a$ and $2b$ are the lengths of the major and minor axes. The semimajor and semiminor axes are half the length of the major and minor axes, so they have lengths a and b. In this case, $a^2 = 25$ and $b^2 = 49$, so $a = 5$ and $b = 7$. Therefore, the area of this ellipse is $\pi ab = 35\pi$.

Practice Test 4

YOUR NAME (PRINT):

LAST   FIRST   MI

| Correct ●   Incorrect ⊘ ⊗ ⊘ ◓ ✪ ◉ ⊜ ⊛ | **Make sure you use a No. 2 pencil.** Each answer must be marked in the corresponding row on the answer sheet. Each bubble must be filled in completely and darkly within the lines. Extra marks on your answer sheet may be marked as incorrect answers and lower your score. |

○ Literature	○ Mathematics Level 1	○ German
○ Biology E	○ Mathematics Level 2	○ Italian
○ Biology M	○ U.S. History	○ Latin
○ Chemistry	○ World History	○ Modern Hebrew
○ Physics	○ French	○ Spanish

1 Ⓐ Ⓑ Ⓒ Ⓓ Ⓔ   21 Ⓐ Ⓑ Ⓒ Ⓓ Ⓔ   41 Ⓐ Ⓑ Ⓒ Ⓓ Ⓔ   61 Ⓐ Ⓑ Ⓒ Ⓓ Ⓔ   81 Ⓐ Ⓑ Ⓒ Ⓓ Ⓔ

2 Ⓐ Ⓑ Ⓒ Ⓓ Ⓔ   22 Ⓐ Ⓑ Ⓒ Ⓓ Ⓔ   42 Ⓐ Ⓑ Ⓒ Ⓓ Ⓔ   62 Ⓐ Ⓑ Ⓒ Ⓓ Ⓔ   82 Ⓐ Ⓑ Ⓒ Ⓓ Ⓔ

3 Ⓐ Ⓑ Ⓒ Ⓓ Ⓔ   23 Ⓐ Ⓑ Ⓒ Ⓓ Ⓔ   43 Ⓐ Ⓑ Ⓒ Ⓓ Ⓔ   63 Ⓐ Ⓑ Ⓒ Ⓓ Ⓔ   83 Ⓐ Ⓑ Ⓒ Ⓓ Ⓔ

4 Ⓐ Ⓑ Ⓒ Ⓓ Ⓔ   24 Ⓐ Ⓑ Ⓒ Ⓓ Ⓔ   44 Ⓐ Ⓑ Ⓒ Ⓓ Ⓔ   64 Ⓐ Ⓑ Ⓒ Ⓓ Ⓔ   84 Ⓐ Ⓑ Ⓒ Ⓓ Ⓔ

5 Ⓐ Ⓑ Ⓒ Ⓓ Ⓔ   25 Ⓐ Ⓑ Ⓒ Ⓓ Ⓔ   45 Ⓐ Ⓑ Ⓒ Ⓓ Ⓔ   65 Ⓐ Ⓑ Ⓒ Ⓓ Ⓔ   85 Ⓐ Ⓑ Ⓒ Ⓓ Ⓔ

6 Ⓐ Ⓑ Ⓒ Ⓓ Ⓔ   26 Ⓐ Ⓑ Ⓒ Ⓓ Ⓔ   46 Ⓐ Ⓑ Ⓒ Ⓓ Ⓔ   66 Ⓐ Ⓑ Ⓒ Ⓓ Ⓔ   86 Ⓐ Ⓑ Ⓒ Ⓓ Ⓔ

7 Ⓐ Ⓑ Ⓒ Ⓓ Ⓔ   27 Ⓐ Ⓑ Ⓒ Ⓓ Ⓔ   47 Ⓐ Ⓑ Ⓒ Ⓓ Ⓔ   67 Ⓐ Ⓑ Ⓒ Ⓓ Ⓔ   87 Ⓐ Ⓑ Ⓒ Ⓓ Ⓔ

8 Ⓐ Ⓑ Ⓒ Ⓓ Ⓔ   28 Ⓐ Ⓑ Ⓒ Ⓓ Ⓔ   48 Ⓐ Ⓑ Ⓒ Ⓓ Ⓔ   68 Ⓐ Ⓑ Ⓒ Ⓓ Ⓔ   88 Ⓐ Ⓑ Ⓒ Ⓓ Ⓔ

9 Ⓐ Ⓑ Ⓒ Ⓓ Ⓔ   29 Ⓐ Ⓑ Ⓒ Ⓓ Ⓔ   49 Ⓐ Ⓑ Ⓒ Ⓓ Ⓔ   69 Ⓐ Ⓑ Ⓒ Ⓓ Ⓔ   89 Ⓐ Ⓑ Ⓒ Ⓓ Ⓔ

10 Ⓐ Ⓑ Ⓒ Ⓓ Ⓔ   30 Ⓐ Ⓑ Ⓒ Ⓓ Ⓔ   50 Ⓐ Ⓑ Ⓒ Ⓓ Ⓔ   70 Ⓐ Ⓑ Ⓒ Ⓓ Ⓔ   90 Ⓐ Ⓑ Ⓒ Ⓓ Ⓔ

11 Ⓐ Ⓑ Ⓒ Ⓓ Ⓔ   31 Ⓐ Ⓑ Ⓒ Ⓓ Ⓔ   51 Ⓐ Ⓑ Ⓒ Ⓓ Ⓔ   71 Ⓐ Ⓑ Ⓒ Ⓓ Ⓔ   81 Ⓐ Ⓑ Ⓒ Ⓓ Ⓔ

12 Ⓐ Ⓑ Ⓒ Ⓓ Ⓔ   32 Ⓐ Ⓑ Ⓒ Ⓓ Ⓔ   52 Ⓐ Ⓑ Ⓒ Ⓓ Ⓔ   72 Ⓐ Ⓑ Ⓒ Ⓓ Ⓔ   92 Ⓐ Ⓑ Ⓒ Ⓓ Ⓔ

13 Ⓐ Ⓑ Ⓒ Ⓓ Ⓔ   33 Ⓐ Ⓑ Ⓒ Ⓓ Ⓔ   53 Ⓐ Ⓑ Ⓒ Ⓓ Ⓔ   73 Ⓐ Ⓑ Ⓒ Ⓓ Ⓔ   93 Ⓐ Ⓑ Ⓒ Ⓓ Ⓔ

14 Ⓐ Ⓑ Ⓒ Ⓓ Ⓔ   34 Ⓐ Ⓑ Ⓒ Ⓓ Ⓔ   54 Ⓐ Ⓑ Ⓒ Ⓓ Ⓔ   74 Ⓐ Ⓑ Ⓒ Ⓓ Ⓔ   94 Ⓐ Ⓑ Ⓒ Ⓓ Ⓔ

15 Ⓐ Ⓑ Ⓒ Ⓓ Ⓔ   35 Ⓐ Ⓑ Ⓒ Ⓓ Ⓔ   55 Ⓐ Ⓑ Ⓒ Ⓓ Ⓔ   75 Ⓐ Ⓑ Ⓒ Ⓓ Ⓔ   95 Ⓐ Ⓑ Ⓒ Ⓓ Ⓔ

16 Ⓐ Ⓑ Ⓒ Ⓓ Ⓔ   36 Ⓐ Ⓑ Ⓒ Ⓓ Ⓔ   56 Ⓐ Ⓑ Ⓒ Ⓓ Ⓔ   76 Ⓐ Ⓑ Ⓒ Ⓓ Ⓔ   96 Ⓐ Ⓑ Ⓒ Ⓓ Ⓔ

17 Ⓐ Ⓑ Ⓒ Ⓓ Ⓔ   37 Ⓐ Ⓑ Ⓒ Ⓓ Ⓔ   57 Ⓐ Ⓑ Ⓒ Ⓓ Ⓔ   77 Ⓐ Ⓑ Ⓒ Ⓓ Ⓔ   97 Ⓐ Ⓑ Ⓒ Ⓓ Ⓔ

18 Ⓐ Ⓑ Ⓒ Ⓓ Ⓔ   38 Ⓐ Ⓑ Ⓒ Ⓓ Ⓔ   58 Ⓐ Ⓑ Ⓒ Ⓓ Ⓔ   78 Ⓐ Ⓑ Ⓒ Ⓓ Ⓔ   98 Ⓐ Ⓑ Ⓒ Ⓓ Ⓔ

19 Ⓐ Ⓑ Ⓒ Ⓓ Ⓔ   39 Ⓐ Ⓑ Ⓒ Ⓓ Ⓔ   59 Ⓐ Ⓑ Ⓒ Ⓓ Ⓔ   79 Ⓐ Ⓑ Ⓒ Ⓓ Ⓔ   99 Ⓐ Ⓑ Ⓒ Ⓓ Ⓔ

20 Ⓐ Ⓑ Ⓒ Ⓓ Ⓔ   40 Ⓐ Ⓑ Ⓒ Ⓓ Ⓔ   60 Ⓐ Ⓑ Ⓒ Ⓓ Ⓔ   80 Ⓐ Ⓑ Ⓒ Ⓓ Ⓔ   100 Ⓐ Ⓑ Ⓒ Ⓓ Ⓔ

For automatic scoring and scaling, please visit **cloud.ivyglobal.com**.

SAT Math Level 2 Subject Test

Reference Materials

THE FORMULAS BELOW MAY BE USEFUL IN ANSWERING QUESTIONS ON THIS TEST.

$S = 4\pi r^2$ is the formula for the surface area of a sphere with a radius of r.

$V = \frac{1}{3}\pi r^2 h$ is the formula for the volume of a right circular cone with a radius of r and a height of h.

$V = \frac{4}{3}\pi r^3$ is the formula for the volume of a sphere with a radius of r.

$V = \frac{1}{3}Bh$ is the formula for the volume of a pyramid with a base area of B and a height of h.

When choosing an answer, find the CLOSEST answer possible. If the precise numerical value that you have found is not an answer choice, select the choice that is closest to your answer. Use the answer sheet and fill in the bubble corresponding to your choice.

Notes: (1) You ARE permitted the use of a graphing or scientific calculator, which you may use at your own discretion. You will also have to choose between degree or radian mode for some questions, so keep track of what mode your calculator is in.

(2) You may assume that figures are drawn as accurately as possible UNLESS it is explicitly stated that a figure is not drawn to scale. Furthermore, all figures are in a plane UNLESS it is stated otherwise.

(3) For any function f, unless otherwise specified, you may assume that a real number x is in the domain of f if and only if $f(x)$ is a real number. The range of f consists of all and only those real numbers of the form $f(x)$, where x is in the domain of f.

(4) Four formulas are provided in the box above for your reference.

1. Which of the following linear functions does NOT have an *x*-intercept?

    (A) $y = x$
    (B) $y = 2x$
    (C) $y = -2x - 2$
    (D) $y = 2$
    (E) $x = 2$

USE THIS SPACE FOR SCRATCH WORK.

2. What is the range of possible values of *x* if $5x + 8 < 16$?

    (A) $x < \frac{8}{5}$
    (B) $x < \frac{5}{8}$
    (C) $x > \frac{5}{8}$
    (D) $x > \frac{8}{5}$
    (E) $x > \frac{16}{5}$

3. If $9y = y^{\frac{3}{2}}$, and $y \neq 0$, then $y =$

    (A)   3
    (B)   9
    (C)   27
    (D)   81
    (E)   243

$$14.3, -10.01, 7.007, -4.9049,\ldots$$

4. What is the common ratio of the geometric sequence above?

    (A) -1.43
    (B) -0.7
    (C)   0.7
    (D)   1.43
    (E)   4.29

GO ON TO THE NEXT PAGE

USE THIS SPACE FOR SCRATCH WORK.

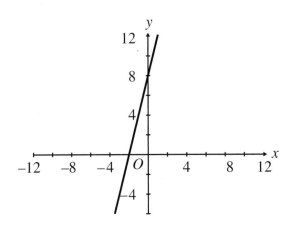

5. What is the slope of any line parallel to the line shown above?

    (A) −4
    (B) $-\frac{1}{4}$
    (C) $\frac{1}{4}$
    (D) 1
    (E) 4

6. A transport truck's cab weighs 25,000 pounds, its trailer weighs 10,000 pounds, and its driver weighs 200 pounds. In Presidio County, the total weight of a transport truck, including cargo, must not exceed 80,000 pounds. What is the maximum number of 20-pound garbage bags that the transport truck can carry without exceeding the total weight limit?

    (A) 2,238
    (B) 2,239
    (C) 2,240
    (D) 2,241
    (E) 2,250

GO ON TO THE NEXT PAGE

USE THIS SPACE FOR SCRATCH WORK.

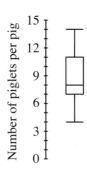

7. A pig farmer collects data on the number of piglets per mother pig. These data are summarized in the box plot above. What is the range of these data?

    (A) 4
    (B) 7
    (C) 8
    (D) 10
    (E) 14

8. If $f(x) = 3^{x-3} + 10x$, what is $f(0.5)$?

    (A) 0.06
    (B) 1.55
    (C) 5.06
    (D) 10.06
    (E) 20.59

9. $\dfrac{\sin 100°}{\sin 50° \cos 50°} =$

    (A) $\dfrac{1}{4}$

    (B) $\dfrac{1}{2}$

    (C) 1

    (D) 2

    (E) 4

GO ON TO THE NEXT PAGE

USE THIS SPACE FOR SCRATCH WORK.

10. Trail mix is made from nuts and raisins. Nuts cost $1.25 per ounce and raisins cost $1.50 per ounce. If a bag of trail mix weighs 1 pound and costs $22.50, how many ounces of nuts are in the trail mix? (16 ounces = 1 pound)

(A)   5
(B)   6
(C)   8
(D)   10
(E)   11

11. Which of the following pairs of integers does NOT share a prime factor?

(A)   126 and 124
(B)   140 and 49
(C)   216 and 147
(D)   255 and 182
(E)   264 and 231

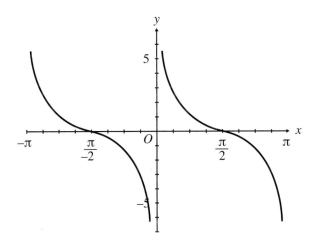

12. Which of the following trigonometric functions is graphed above?

(A) $\sin x$
(B) $\cos x$
(C) $\cot x$
(D) $\sec x$
(E) $\csc x$

GO ON TO THE NEXT PAGE

13. Ten people are leaving a party one by one. In how many different orders can they leave?

(A)   1
(B)   10
(C)   100
(D)   25,200
(E)   3,628,800

USE THIS SPACE FOR SCRATCH WORK.

14. Point P has coordinates $(3, 5, 5)$ and point Q has coordinates $(1, 2, -2)$. What is the distance between P and Q?

(A)   5.0
(B)   7.9
(C)   8.6
(D)   13.0
(E)   17.0

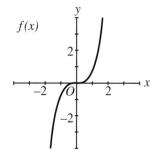
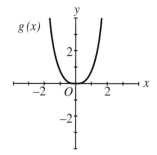

15. Which of the following is true about the functions f and g, shown above, for all values of x?

(A) $g(x) = f(|x|)$
(B) $g(x) > f(x)$
(C) $g(x) < f(x)$
(D) $g(x) = -f(x)$
(E) $g(x) = f(-x)$

GO ON TO THE NEXT PAGE

USE THIS SPACE FOR SCRATCH WORK.

16. If $\sin\theta = -\cos\theta$, then $\tan\theta =$

(A) -1

(B) 0

(C) $\frac{1}{2}$

(D) 1

(E) $-\frac{1}{2}$

17. If $x \neq 0$, which of the following is equivalent to $\dfrac{(x^3 + x^3)^{\frac{1}{3}}}{x^3}$?

(A) $\dfrac{\sqrt[3]{2}}{x^2}$

(B) $\dfrac{\sqrt[3]{2}}{x^{\frac{2}{3}}}$

(C) $\dfrac{\sqrt[3]{2}}{x^3}$

(D) $8x^6$

(E) $6x^8$

18. Which of the following points could be the intersection of the lines $\dfrac{y-3}{a} = x$ and $y = -\dfrac{1}{a}x + 3$ when graphed on the xy-plane?

(A) $(a, 0)$

(B) (a, a)

(C) $(a, -a)$

(D) $(0, 3)$

(E) $(3, 0)$

19. If $15 = 153^z$, what is the value of z?

(A) 0.40

(B) 0.54

(C) 0.68

(D) 0.81

(E) 0.86

GO ON TO THE NEXT PAGE

USE THIS SPACE FOR SCRATCH WORK.

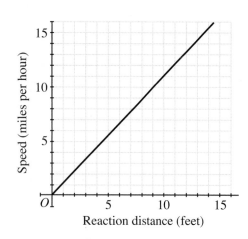

20. Reaction distance in feet, d_r, is modeled by the linear function shown in the graph above. Braking distance in feet, d_b, is modeled by the formula $d_b = 0.05r^2$, where r is the speed in miles per hour. What is the total stopping distance, $d_t = d_r + d_b$, required for a car travelling 20 miles per hour?

(A) 20 feet

(B) 22 feet

(C) 40 feet

(D) 42 feet

(E) 44 feet

21. If $p < q$, and p, q, and $p + q$ are all prime numbers, what is the value of p?

(A) 1

(B) 2

(C) 3

(D) 5

(E) 11

GO ON TO THE NEXT PAGE

USE THIS SPACE FOR SCRATCH WORK.

22. Which of the following is the root of the equation
$y = 12x^3 - 6x^2 + 3$?

(A) -3

(B) $-\dfrac{1}{2}$

(C) $\dfrac{1}{2}$

(D) 3

(E) 4

23. If $f(x) = 2g(x) + 3$ for every real number x, and if $g(0) = -2$, what is the value of $f(0)$?

(A) -1

(B) 0

(C) 1

(D) 3

(E) 7

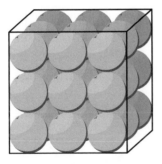

Note: Figure not drawn to scale.

24. A company packs oranges, which are spherical and have a diameter of 4 inches, in cubic boxes, as shown above. If the boxes have a volume of 8 ft³, how many oranges can be packed into one box? (12 inches = 1 foot)

(A) 27

(B) 64

(C) 144

(D) 216

(E) 512

GO ON TO THE NEXT PAGE

USE THIS SPACE FOR SCRATCH WORK.

25. A right triangle is inscribed in a circle. If the lengths of its two shortest sides are 6 and 7, what is the radius of the circle?

    (A) 1.80
    (B) 3.61
    (C) 4.61
    (D) 6.50
    (E) 9.22

26. If $k = \dfrac{a^b - b^a}{a - b}$, and $a = 3$ and $b = 5$, what is the value of k?

    (A) −118
    (B) −59
    (C) 0
    (D) 59
    (E) 118

GO ON TO THE NEXT PAGE

Population of Cities in Lane County in 2010	
Coburg	1,035
Cottage Grove	9,686
Creswell	5,031
Dunes City	1,303
Eugene	156,185
Florence	8,466
Junction City	5,392
Lowell	1,045
Oakridge	3,205
Springfield	59,403
Veneta	4,561
Westfir	253

Population of Cities in Multnomah County in 2010	
Fairview	8,920
Gresham	105,594
Lake Oswego	36,619
Maywood Park	752
Milwaukie	20,291
Portland	639,863
Troutdale	15,962
Wood Village	3,878

27. The charts above show the populations of all the cities in Lane County and Multnomah County, according to the 2010 census. Which of the following is true based on the data given?

   I. Multnomah County has a greater total city population than Lane County.
   II. Multnomah County has a greater average population per city than Lane County.
   III. Multnomah County has a greater range of city populations than Lane County.

   (A) I only
   (B) I and II only
   (C) I and III only
   (D) II and III only
   (E) I, II, and III

GO ON TO THE NEXT PAGE

USE THIS SPACE FOR SCRATCH WORK.

x	$f(x)$
-2	0
-1	5
0	-5
1	0
2	8

28. The table above shows five values for the polynomial function f. Which of the following conclusions can be inferred from the table?

    (A) f has a maximum of 8.
    (B) f has at least three roots.
    (C) f has an inverse function.
    (D) The degree of f is greater than 7.
    (E) The range of f is $y \in \mathbb{R}$.

29. If a fair coin is tossed three times, what is the probability that exactly two of the tosses will result in heads?

    (A) $\frac{1}{8}$
    (B) $\frac{1}{4}$
    (C) $\frac{3}{8}$
    (D) $\frac{1}{2}$
    (E) $\frac{2}{3}$

30. If the graph of $f(x) = x^2$ is shifted two units to the left and four units up to produce the graph of $g(x)$, then $g(x) =$

    (A) $f(x + 2) + 4$
    (B) $f(x - 2) + 4$
    (C) $f(x + 4) + 4$
    (D) $f(x - 4) + 4$
    (E) $f(x) + 2$

GO ON TO THE NEXT PAGE

USE THIS SPACE FOR SCRATCH WORK.

31. The vertices of an equilateral triangle in the xy-plane are at the points $(a, 0)$, $(-a, 0)$, and $(0, 3)$. If $a > 0$, what is the value of a?

(A) 3

(B) $\sqrt{3}$

(C) $\dfrac{\sqrt{3}}{2}$

(D) $\dfrac{1}{2}$

(E) $\dfrac{1}{3}$

32. A strawberry farm charges an admission price of $1.00 and charges $2.25 for each quart (or part thereof) of strawberries a customer picks. The farm also offers a discount of $0.15 for each container a customer returns. Which of the following represents the price, in dollars, of x quarts of strawberries and r containers returned? (Let $\lceil x \rceil$ represent the least integer that is greater than or equal to x.)

(A) $3.25 \lceil x \rceil - 0.15r$

(B) $2.25 \lceil x \rceil - 0.15r + 1.00$

(C) $2.25 \lceil x \rceil + 0.15r - 1.00$

(D) $0.15 \lceil x \rceil + 2.25r + 1.00$

(E) $1.00 \lceil x - 0.15r \rceil + 2.25$

GO ON TO THE NEXT PAGE

USE THIS SPACE FOR SCRATCH WORK.

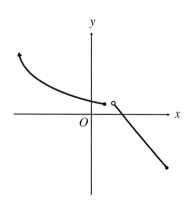

33. If the graph above shows the function $f(x)$, which of the following graphs shows the function $f^{-1}(x)$?

(A)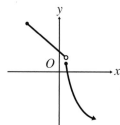

(B)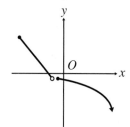

(C)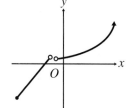

(D)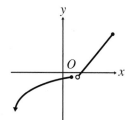

(E)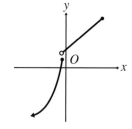

GO ON TO THE NEXT PAGE

USE THIS SPACE FOR SCRATCH WORK.

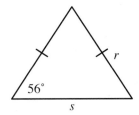

34. What is the value of $\frac{r}{s}$ in the triangle above?

    (A) 0.824
    (B) 0.894
    (C) 0.927
    (D) 1.118
    (E) 1.214

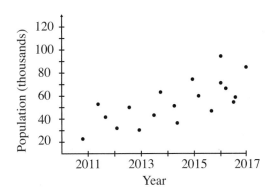

35. The scatterplot above shows the population of Northern red-legged
    frogs in a section of the Tsanchiifin wetlands over a period of 8 years.
    If the population of frogs can be approximated by the equation
    $y = mx + b$, where y is the population of frogs, in thousands, and x is
    the number of years since 2010, which of the following could be the
    values of m and b?

    (A) $m = 6, b = 30$
    (B) $m = 5, b = 28{,}000$
    (C) $m = 0.5, b = 28$
    (D) $m = 5{,}500, b = 28$
    (E) $m = 5{,}500, b = 30{,}000$

GO ON TO THE NEXT PAGE

USE THIS SPACE FOR SCRATCH WORK.

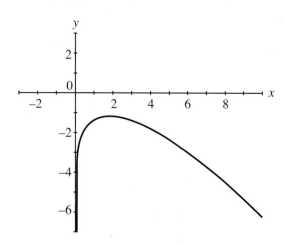

36. Which of the following logarithmic functions is represented by the graph shown above?

(A) $f(x) = \log_2 x$

(B) $f(x) = 2 - \log_2 x$

(C) $f(x) = x - \log_2 x$

(D) $f(x) = \log_2 x + x$

(E) $f(x) = \log_2 x - x$

37. A student has r red pens, b blue pens, and k black pens. The student has 13 pens in total, and at least one of each color. If $\frac{r}{b} > \frac{r}{k}$, which of the following must be true?

(A) The student has 11 red pens.

(B) The student has a total of at least 3 black and blue pens.

(C) The student has a total of at most 11 black and blue pens.

(D) The student has more blue pens than black pens.

(E) The student has an equal number of blue and black pens.

38. Which of the following lines is an asymptote of $f(x) = \frac{5x^2 + 2}{x - 1}$?

(A) $y = 1$

(B) $y = 5$

(C) $y = 5x + 5$

(D) $y = 5x + 2$

(E) This function has no asymptotes.

GO ON TO THE NEXT PAGE

USE THIS SPACE FOR SCRATCH WORK.

39. The volume of a cube is tripled. If the length of each side was originally a, what is the length of each new side?

(A) $a\sqrt[3]{3}$

(B) $a\sqrt[3]{3^2}$

(C) $2a\sqrt[3]{3}$

(D) $27a$

(E) $243a^3$

40. Which of the following is equivalent to $\sin^2 x \cos x - \cos x$?

(A) $-\cos^3 x$

(B) $-\cos^2 x$

(C) 0

(D) $\cos^2 x$

(E) $\cos^3 x$

41. If n is an integer, which of the following is a possible value of $((i-4)(i+4))^n$?

(A) -1

(B) 17

(C) 34

(D) 289

(E) 4913

42. The area of an equilateral triangle, in centimeters squared, is equal to its perimeter, in centimeters. What is the length of each side of this triangle?

(A) 1.00 cm

(B) 3.46 cm

(C) 4.24 cm

(D) 6.93 cm

(E) 9.00 cm

GO ON TO THE NEXT PAGE

43. What is the center of the hyperbola with the equation
$9x^2 - 16y^2 + 3 = 147$?

   (A) $(0, 0)$
   (B) $(3, 4)$
   (C) $(4, 3)$
   (D) $(-3, -4)$
   (E) $(-4, -3)$

44. Scientists found a virus that infects mice at an exponential rate. In the past 10 months, the number of infected mice increased from 200 to 5000. How many mice will be infected in total after 10 more months?

   (A)   10,000
   (B)   125,000
   (C)   178,746
   (D)   250,000
   (E)   3,125,000

45. Point P is the intersection of n distinct lines in a plane, where $n > 1$. Another line L in the same plane does not pass through point P. Which of the following is true about the n lines in the plane?

   (A) Exactly one of them must be perpendicular to L.
   (B) At least $n - 1$ of them intersect line L.
   (C) At most $n - 1$ of them intersect line L.
   (D) They intersect line L in at least n points.
   (E) Exactly one of them must be parallel to L.

GO ON TO THE NEXT PAGE

USE THIS SPACE FOR SCRATCH WORK.

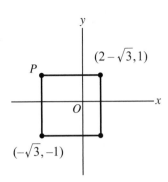

46. The square above is plotted on an *xy*-plane. What is point *P* in polar coordinates?

(A) $\left(\sqrt{3}, \frac{3\pi}{4}\right)$

(B) $\left(-\sqrt{3}, 1\right)$

(C) $\left(\frac{5\pi}{6}, 2\right)$

(D) $\left(-2, \frac{5\pi}{6}\right)$

(E) $\left(2, \frac{5\pi}{6}\right)$

47. $\begin{bmatrix} 8 & -2 \\ 2 & 5 \end{bmatrix} \times \begin{bmatrix} 2 & 1 \\ 1 & 3 \end{bmatrix} =$

(A) $\begin{bmatrix} 16 & -2 \\ 2 & 5 \end{bmatrix}$

(B) $\begin{bmatrix} 10 & -1 \\ 3 & 8 \end{bmatrix}$

(C) $\begin{bmatrix} 14 & 2 \\ 9 & 17 \end{bmatrix}$

(D) $\begin{bmatrix} 18 & 14 \\ 9 & 17 \end{bmatrix}$

(E) $\begin{bmatrix} 18 & 2 \\ -1 & 17 \end{bmatrix}$

GO ON TO THE NEXT PAGE

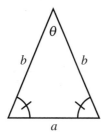

Note: Figure not drawn to scale.

48. An isosceles triangle has one side of length a and two sides of length b. If θ is the angle opposite the side of length a, and $\frac{a}{b} = 0.74$, then cos $\theta =$

(A) 0.2738

(B) 0.4524

(C) 0.5476

(D) 0.7262

(E) 1.3514

49. If n is any integer, which of the following equations represents the locations of the asymptotes of the function $f(x) = \tan\left(2\left(x + \frac{\pi}{2}\right)\right)$?

(A) $x = \frac{\pi n}{2}$

(B) $x = \frac{\pi}{4}(2n - 1)$

(C) $x = \frac{\pi}{2}(2n - 1)$

(D) $x = \frac{\pi n}{4} - 1$

(E) $x = \frac{\pi n}{2} - 1$

USE THIS SPACE FOR SCRATCH WORK.

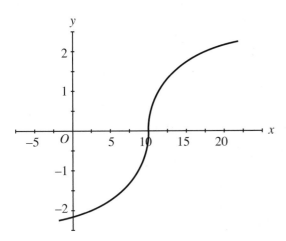

50. Which of the following parametric equations is represented by the graph above?

(A) $x = t$
     $y = t^3 - 10$

(B) $x = t$
     $y = t^3 + 10$

(C) $x = t^3 - 10$
     $y = t$

(D) $x = t^3 + 10$
     $y = t$

(E) $x = -t^3 + 10$
     $y = t$

STOP

**If you complete this test before the end of your allotted time,
you may check your work.**

Answers and Scoring

Scoring Your Test
Part 1

The easiest way to score your test is to use our Cloud scoring tool. The Cloud tool also provides more detailed results by showing you how you performed on specific kinds of questions. To score your test by hand, follow the directions below.

 For more detailed scoring results, please visit **cloud.ivyglobal.com.**

Answers

1. D	11. D	21. B	31. B	41. D
2. A	12. C	22. B	32. B	42. D
3. D	13. E	23. A	33. C	43. A
4. B	14. B	24. D	34. B	44. B
5. E	15. A	25. C	35. A	45. B
6. C	16. A	26. B	36. E	46. E
7. D	17. A	27. E	37. B	47. C
8. C	18. D	28. B	38. C	48. D
9. D	19. B	29. C	39. A	49. B
10. B	20. D	30. A	40. A	50. D

Raw Scores

To score your test, first use the answer key to mark each of your responses as correct or incorrect. Don't mark or count questions you left blank. Then, calculate your raw score for each section by subtracting one fourth the number of incorrect responses from the number of correct responses. Scores should be rounded to the nearest whole number, with .5 and above rounding up. Use the tables below to help you calculate your scores:

Scores		
Number Correct	_____ −	
Number incorrect	_____ / 4 =	_____
Raw Score	= _____	
Scaled Score	_____	

Scaled Scores

Once you have found your raw score for each test, convert it into an approximate scaled test score using the following chart. To find a scaled test score for each section, find the row in the Raw Score column which corresponds to your raw score for that section, then check the column for the section you are scoring in the same row. For example, if you had a raw score of 31, your scaled score would be 580. Keep in mind that these scaled scores are estimates only. Your actual SAT Subject Test in Mathematics Level 2 score will be scaled against the scores of all other students at your grade level taking the test on your test date.

Scaled Score							
Raw Score	Scaled Score	Raw Score	Scaled Score	Raw Score	Scaled Score	Raw Score	Scaled Score
50	800	34	710	18	560	2	440
49	800	33	700	17	560	1	430
48	800	32	690	16	550	0	410
47	800	31	680	15	540	−1	390
46	800	30	670	14	530	−2	370
45	800	29	660	13	530	−3	360
44	800	28	650	12	520	−4	340
43	800	27	640	11	510	−5	340
42	790	26	630	10	500	−6	330
41	790	25	630	9	500	−7	320
40	780	24	620	8	490	−8	320
39	770	23	610	7	480	−9	320
38	750	22	600	6	480	−10	320
37	740	21	590	5	470	−11	310
36	730	20	580	4	460	−12	310
35	720	19	570	3	450		

Explanations
Part 2

1. The correct answer is (D). The only kind of line without an x-intercept is a horizontal line, which takes the form $y = a$, where a is any real number.

    If you chose (E), you may have confused vertical lines with horizontal lines.

2. The correct answer is (A). Subtract 8 from both sides to get $5x < 8$, and divide by 5 to get $x < \frac{8}{5}$.

    If you chose (D), you may have flipped the inequality when you divided by 5, but you should only do this when dividing or multiplying by a negative number.

3. The correct answer is (D). Since $y \neq 0$, divide both sides by y to get $9 = y^{\frac{3}{2}-1} = y^{\frac{1}{2}} = \sqrt{y}$. Finally, square both sides to get $y = 81$.

4. The correct answer is (B). To find the common ratio of a geometric sequence, you can divide any term by the previous term. In this case, the common ratio is equal to $\frac{-10.01}{14.3} = -0.7$.

    If you chose (A), you may have divided one of the terms by the following term. If you chose (C), you may have missed the minus sign.

5. The correct answer is (E). You can calculate the slope of the given line from the x and y intercepts, $(-2, 0)$ and $(0, 8)$, to find that the slope is $\frac{rise}{run} = \frac{8-0}{0-(-2)} = \frac{8}{2} = 4$. Any line parallel to a line with a slope of 4 will also have a slope of 4.

6. The correct answer is (C). The weight limit for transport trucks in Presidio County is 80,000 pounds. The total weight of the given transport truck is cab + trailer + driver = 25,000 + 10,000 + 200 = 35,200 pounds. Therefore, the total weight of cargo that this transport truck can carry before it reaches the limit is 80,000 − 35,200 = 44,800 pounds. Because one garbage bag weighs 20 pounds, this truck can carry $\frac{44,800}{20} = 2,240$ garbage bags.

    If you chose (A) or (B), you may have misinterpreted "must not exceed 80,000 pounds" to mean the weight must be less than 80,000 pounds ($x < 80,000$), when it means the weight can be less than *or equal to* 80,000 pounds ($x \leq 80,000$). If you chose (E), you may have forgotten to include the driver's weight in the total weight of the transport truck.

7. The correct answer is (D). To find the range of the data, find the largest value in the data set and subtract the smallest value in the data set from it. You can tell from the box plot that the largest value in the data set is 14 and the smallest value is 4, so the range is $14 - 4 = 10$.

8. The correct answer is (C). To answer this question, you should plug $x = 0.5$ into the expression for $f(x)$. This gives you $f(0.5) = 3^{0.5-3} + 10(0.5) = 3^{-2.5} + 5 = 0.06 + 5 = 5.06$.

9. The correct answer is (D). The fastest way to answer this question is to remember that $\sin 2x = 2 \sin x \cos x$, so $\sin 100° = 2 \sin 50° \cos 50°$, and therefore $\dfrac{\sin 100°}{\sin 50° \cos 50°} = \dfrac{2(\sin 50° \cos 50°)}{\sin 50° \cos 50°} = \dfrac{2}{1} = 2$. You can also solve this problem by plugging the expression into your calculator.

10. The correct answer is (B). The best way to answer this question is to set up a system of equations where n is "ounces of nuts" and r is "ounces of raisins." First, because there are 16 ounces in a pound and one pound of trail mix is made of nuts and raisins, you know that $n + r = 16$. Second, because this pound of trail mix costs $22.50, you know that $1.25n + 1.5r = 22.5$. To find how many ounces of nuts are in the trail mix, simply isolate "r" in the first equation ($r = 16 - n$) and plug it into the second:

$$1.25n + 1.5r = 22.5$$
$$1.25n + 1.5(16 - n) = 22.5$$
$$1.25n + (24 - 1.5n) = 22.5$$
$$-0.25n = -1.5$$
$$n = 6$$

11. The correct answer is (D). Factor the numbers in (D): $255 = 3 \times 5 \times 17$ and $182 = 2 \times 7 \times 13$. They have no prime factors in common.

You can quickly eliminate choice (A) as any two even integers share at least the prime factor 2. The integers in (B) share the prime factor 7, and the integers in (C) and (E) share the prime factor 3.

12. The correct answer is (C). The function $\cot x = \dfrac{1}{\tan x}$, and the graph shown is the reciprocal of the graph of $\tan x$.

The graphs of sine and cosine look like continuous waves, so you can eliminate (A) and (B). The graphs of secant and cosecant look like U-shapes that alternate between opening up and down, so you can eliminate (D) and (E).

13. The correct answer is (E). The first person to leave the party can be any one of the 10 people, so there are 10 choices. The second person to leave can be any of the remaining 9 people, so there are 9 choices. For the third person to leave, there are 8 choices, and so on. In total, the number of choices is:
$10! = 10 \times 9 \times 8 \times 7 \times 6 \times 5 \times 4 \times 3 \times 2 \times 1 = 3,628,800$.

14. The correct answer is (B). To answer this question, it's helpful to know the formula to find the distance between two points (x_1, y_1, z_1) and (x_2, y_2, z_2): $d = \sqrt{(x_1 - x_2)^2 + (y_1 - y_2)^2 + (z_1 - z_2)^2}$. Plug in the values of the two points to get $\sqrt{(3-1)^2 + (5-2)^2 + (5-(-2))^2} = \sqrt{4 + 9 + 49} \approx 7.9$

15. The correct answer is (A). One way to answer this question is to apply each answer choice to the given graphs—in general and, if necessary, by choosing specific points. (A) is true because if $x \geq 0$, then $x = |x|$, so (A) says that $f(x) = g(x)$, which is true when $x \geq 0$. If $x < 0$, then (A) says that, for example, $g(-1) = f(|-1|) = f(1)$, which is true, as you can see from the graphs. Therefore, for any value of x, $g(x) = f(|x|)$.

(B) is false because $g(x)$ is only greater than $f(x)$ when $x < 0$, and otherwise $g(x) = f(x)$. (C) is false because $g(x)$ is never less than $f(x)$. (D) is false because the function $-f(x)$ would be $f(x)$ reflected across the x-axis. (E) is false because the function $f(-x)$ would be $f(x)$ reflected across the y-axis.

16. The correct answer is (A). The easiest way to answer this question is to remember that $\tan \theta = \dfrac{\sin \theta}{\cos \theta}$ and then use the given information to substitute $-\cos \theta$ for $\sin \theta$: $\dfrac{-\cos \theta}{\cos \theta} = -1$. You could also find a value of θ such that $\sin \theta = -\cos \theta$, for example $\theta = \dfrac{3\pi}{4}$, and then find that $\tan \theta = -1$.

17. The correct answer is (A). Rewrite the expression as $\dfrac{(2x^3)^{\frac{1}{3}}}{x^2}$ by simply adding $x^3 + x^3$ in the numerator. Now, you know that $(2x^3)^{\frac{1}{3}} = 2^{\frac{1}{3}} \times (x^3)^{\frac{1}{3}} = x \cdot \sqrt[3]{2}$, so the entire expression can be simplified: $\dfrac{x \cdot \sqrt[3]{2}}{x^3} = \dfrac{\sqrt[3]{2}}{x^2}$.

18. The correct answer is (D). First, rearrange the first equation so that it is in the form $y = mx + b$:

$$\frac{y - 3}{a} = x$$
$$y - 3 = ax$$
$$y = ax + 3$$

Now, looking at both equations, you may notice that they both have a y-intercept of 3. This means that both lines intersect at the point $(0, 3)$. However, even if you don't notice that, you can set the right sides of the equations equal to each other and solve for x to find the x-value of their intersection point. Doing this gives you $ax + 3 = \dfrac{-1}{a} x + 3$, so $ax + \dfrac{1}{a} x = 0$. Factoring out the x gives you $x(a + \dfrac{1}{a}) = 0$, so either $x = 0$ and a can have any value, or $a + \dfrac{1}{a} = 0$ and x can have any value. It is impossible for $a + \dfrac{1}{a}$ to be equal to 0, so you know that the intersection point must be at $x = 0$. You can plug $x = 0$ into either of the two original equations to find that $y = 3$, so the intersection point of the two lines is at $(0, 3)$.

19. The correct answer is (B). Take the natural logarithm of both sides of the equation: $\ln(15) = \ln(153^z)$, which is the same as $\ln(15) = z \cdot \ln(153)$. Rearrange to get $z = \dfrac{\ln(15)}{\ln(153)}$, then plug the right-hand side into your calculator to arrive at $z \approx 0.54$.

20. The correct answer is (D). This question requires you to synthesize information from the graph and the question. To calculate the total stopping distance (d_t) of a car travelling 20 miles per hour, you must calculate both its reaction distance (d_r) and braking distance (d_b). The d_r of a car travelling at 20 mph is not stated directly on the graph, so you must find the equation of the line. First, you know that the y-intercept is 0. Second, choose two easy-to-find points to calculate the slope of the line — (10, 11) and (0, 0) — so $m = \dfrac{rise}{run} = \dfrac{11-0}{10-0} = \dfrac{11}{10} = 1.1$. Therefore, $d_r = 1.1x$, where x is the speed of the car, so a car travelling 20 mph has a $d_r = 1.1(20) = 22$ feet. The d_b of a car travelling at 20 mph can be found by plugging 20 into the formula given in the questsion: $d_b = 0.05r^2 = 0.05(20)^2 = 0.05(400) = 20$ feet. Plug these values into the final equation: $d_t = d_r + d_b = 22 + 20 = 42$ feet.

21. The correct answer is (B). The sum of two prime numbers is always even, unless one of the primes is 2 (because all other prime numbers are odd). If $p + q$ is prime, then it must be odd (since it can't be as small as 2), and so one of p and q must be equal to 2. Since you know that $p < q$, $p = 2$.

22. The correct answer is (B). The root is the point at which $y = 0$, so plug in and solve as follows: $0 = 12x^3 - 6x^2 + 3 = 3(2x + 1)(2x^2 - 2x + 1)$. You can use either polynomial long division or synthetic division to factor the right-hand side as shown. The quadratic formula tells you that $2x^2 - 2x + 1$ has no roots, so the only root of the original equation must be where $2x + 1 = 0$, which occurs at $x = -\dfrac{1}{2}$.

23. The correct answer is (A). Use the two given pieces of information to write

$$f(0) = 2g(0) + 3 = 2(-2) + 3 = -4 + 3 = -1$$

If you chose (D), you may have thought $g(0) = 0$.

24. The correct answer is (D). First, find the side length of the box. Since it's a cube, its volume is equal to the length of one of its sides cubed: $\sqrt[3]{8} = 2\ ft$. Since 2 feet is equal to 24 inches, and each orange has a diameter of 4 inches, you know that $\dfrac{24}{4} = 6$ oranges can be lined up along any one of the sides. That means that $6 \times 6 \times 6 = 216$ oranges fit in the box.

25. The correct answer is (C). If a right triangle is inscribed in a circle, its hypotenuse must be a diameter of the circle. You can then use the Pythagorean theorem to find the length of the hypotenuse using the lengths of the other two sides: $h^2 = 6^2 + 7^2 = 85$, so $h = 9.22$, which is the diameter of the circle. The radius is half the diameter, so it is $\dfrac{9.22}{2} = 4.61$.

26. The correct answer is (B). Plug in the values of a and b and evaluate the given expression:

$$\frac{a^b - b^a}{a - b} = \frac{3^5 - 5^3}{3 - 5} = \frac{243 - 125}{-2} = \frac{118}{-2} = -59$$

27. The correct answer is (E). To test (I), simply add the populations in each county, which may take some time. Alternatively, look at the cities with the highest populations: in Multnomah county, the population of Portland alone is about 3 times greater than the sum of the three largest cities in Lane County, while the rest of the cities in Lane County have small populations of about 5,000 or less. So, (I) is true. Since you've determined that Multnomah County has a greater total population, and it also has fewer cities, it follows that the average population per city must be greater in Multnomah County than in Lane County, so (II) is true. Finally, the range of a set of data is equal to the difference between the greatest and least value in the set. For Lane County, $156,185 - 253 = 155,932$, and for Multnomah County, $639,863 - 752 = 639,111$, so (III) is true.

28. The correct answer is (B). You know from the chart that the function has two roots: $x = -2$ and $x = 1$. Also, all polynomial functions are continuous, meaning that they are one connected curve. This means that, to go from 5 at $x = -1$ to -5 at $x = 0$, the function must cross the x-axis between -1 and 0, so you know there must be a root in that range as well, for a total of at least 3 roots.

(A) is incorrect because the chart gives you no information about the maximum value of the function (if it has one) outside of the listed points. For example, the function could continue to grow larger than 8 when $x > 2$. (C) is incorrect because two different x-values (-2 and 1) get mapped to the same y-value (0) by f, meaning that the function does not pass the horizontal line test, and so does not have an inverse. (D) is incorrect because all that the table tells you about the function's degree is that it must be at least 3 (since there are 3 roots). The degree of f could be greater than 7, but could also be any integer greater than or equal to 3. (E) is incorrect because you do not know the degree of the polynomial. If the degree is odd, the range of the function will be $\{y \in \mathbb{R}\}$, but if the degree is even, it will not be.

29. The correct answer is (C). There are 8 possible outcomes, all equally likely: HHH, HHT, HTH, HTT, THH, THT, TTH, TTT. Of these, 3 of them have exactly two heads (HHT, HTH, THH). Therefore, the probability of tossing exactly 2 heads is $\frac{3}{8}$.

If you chose (A), you may have just found the probability of one specific outcome (e.g. HHT). If you chose (B), you may have thought it was equally likely to toss 0, 1, 2, or 3 heads. If you chose (D), you may have found the probability of tossing at least 2 heads, not exactly two heads.

30. The correct answer is (A). If $f(x)$ is shifted 2 units to the left, the new graph will be described by the expression $f(x + 2)$. Then, if this graph is shifted 4 units up, the resulting graph will be described by the expression $f(x + 2) + 4$.

If you chose (B), you may have thought that shifting left by 2 units resulted in the function's argument being $x - 2$, not $x + 2$.

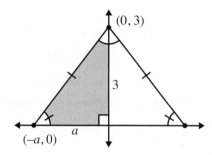

31. The correct answer is (B). To answer this question, it may be useful to draw a quick diagram similar to the one above. Divide the original equilateral triangle to create two equal right triangles in which the base has length a and the height has length 3. You know these new triangles will be 30-60-90 triangles, since all of the angles in an equilateral triangle are 60°, so you can apply the rules of this special triangle to the given triangle. Because the horizontal side has length a, the vertical side must have length $\sqrt{3}\,a$. But you know the vertical side has length 3, which means that $\sqrt{3}\,a = 3$, so $a = \sqrt{3}$.

32. The correct answer is (B). The question tells you that the farm charges a fixed cost, $1.00 admission, and two variable costs, a charge of $2.25 per quart (or part thereof) picked and a discount of $0.15 per quart container returned. The function $\lceil x \rceil$, defined in the question, means that any fractional quart of strawberries picked will count as a full quart of strawberries: $\lceil 4.6 \rceil = 5$. Therefore, the correct coefficient for $\lceil x \rceil$ is 2.25—you can eliminate (A), (D), and (E). You can also eliminate (A) and (E) because they have the wrong fixed costs. Because $0.15 per quart container returned is a discount, this variable should be negative, so you can eliminate (C). Therefore, the correct equation is $2.25\lceil x \rceil - 0.15r + 1.00$.

33. The correct answer is (C). The inverse graph of a function will look like the original function mirrored across the line $y = x$. You can visualize this by drawing it, as seen below:

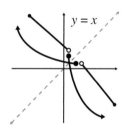

34. The correct answer is (B). You can start by figuring out that the angles in the triangle must be 56°, 56° (because it is isosceles), and 68° (because $180° - 56° - 56° = 68°$). You can use the Sine Law to find that

$$\frac{r}{\sin 56°} = \frac{s}{\sin 68°}, \text{ and so } \frac{r}{s} = \frac{\sin 56°}{\sin 68°} = 0.894.$$

If you chose (A), you may have forgotten to take sines, and just found $\frac{56}{68}$. If you chose (C), you just found sin 68°. If you chose (D), you found $\frac{s}{r}$. If you chose (E), you found $\frac{68}{56}$.

35. The correct answer is (A). This question is asking you to define a line of best fit for the data. Specifically, it is asking you to fine the slope, m, and the y-intercept, b. An estimated line of best fit runs through about $(2010, 30)$ and $(2017, 70)$, so the y-intercept is approximately 30 and and the slope is approximately $\frac{70-30}{2017-2010} = \frac{40}{7} = 5.71$, which is approximately 6.

36. The correct answer is (E). Of the answer choices, (B) and (E) are the only ones that open downward; that is, they go to negative infinity as x gets very large. However, (B) has an x-intercept at $x = 4$ and the graph does not, so you know the correct answer is (E).

If you weren't sure of your answer, you could graph the functions on your calculator and see which one looks like the graph shown.

37. The correct answer is (B). You know that the student has at least one black pen and one blue pen, because the student has at least one of each color. If the student only had one black and one blue pen, then b would equal k and $\frac{r}{b} = \frac{r}{k}$, which is not true since $\frac{r}{b} > \frac{r}{k}$. Therefore, the student must have at least one other pen that is either black or blue.

(A) is incorrect because the student cannot have 11 red pens, since then they would be forced to have one blue and one black pen, which is impossible because of the argument above. (C) is incorrect because the student could have a total of 12 black and blue pens (for example, 7 black, 5 blue, 1 red). (D) and (E) are incorrect because the student must have more black pens than blue pens for the inequality $\frac{r}{b} > \frac{r}{k}$ to be true.

38. The correct answer is (C). There are no vertical asymptotes listed among the answer choices, and you know that there will be no horizontal asymptotes because the numerator has a higher degree than the denominator, so the function will grow to infinity in the positive direction, and to negative infinity in the negative direction. Therefore, you must check whether there are oblique asymptotes.

To find an oblique asymptote, use polynomial long division to divide the numerator by the denominator and get a remainder, as follows:

$$
\begin{array}{r}
5x + 5 \\
x-1\overline{)5x^2 + 0x + 2} \\
\underline{5x^2 - 5x} \\
5x + 2 \\
\underline{5x + 5} \\
7
\end{array}
$$

Rewrite this to show that the function is equal to $5x + 5 + \frac{7}{x-1}$. By looking at this expression, you can tell that as x gets very large, the denominator of $\frac{7}{x-1}$ becomes large, so that expression becomes very small. Therefore, the function is closely approximated by the line $y = 5x + 5$, which means that this line is an asymptote of the function.

39. The correct answer is (A). Call the original cube's side length a, the original cube's volume v, the new side length a_2, and the new volume v_2. You know that $v = a^3$, since the volume of a cube is equal to the length of its side cubed, and that $v_2 = a_2^3$ for the same reason. You also know that $v_2 = 3v$, since the new cube's volume is 3 times the original volume. From here, it's just a matter of getting a_2, the length of the new side, in terms of a. If $v = a^3$, then $v_2 = 3a^3$. If $v_2 = a_2^3$, then $3a^3 = a_2^3$, so $a_2 = \sqrt[3]{3a^3} = a\sqrt[3]{3}$.

40. The correct answer is (A). You can start by removing a common factor of $\cos x$ to get $\cos x\,(\sin^2 x - 1)$. Since $\sin^2 x + \cos^2 x = 1$, you know that $\sin^2 x - 1 = -\cos^2 x$. Therefore, the expression is equivalent to $\cos x\,(-\cos^2 x) = -\cos^3 x$.

41. The correct answer is (D). Simplify the equation as much as possible: $((i-4)(i+4))^n = (-1 + 4i - 4i - 16)^n = (-17)^n$. This makes it easy to eliminate (A), (B), and (C), as no values of n can make the equation true, but $(-17)^2$ is 289, so (D) is correct.

    If you chose (E), you may have forgotten the negative sign, as $(-17)^3 = -4913$.

42. The correct answer is (D). You know the triangle is equilateral, so you can assume that the length of each side is a centimeters. You can find the height of the triangle using the Pythagorean Theorem: $h = \sqrt{a^2 - \left(\frac{a}{2}\right)^2} = \sqrt{\frac{3a^2}{4}} = \frac{\sqrt{3}\,a}{2}$

    The area of the triangle is the product of the base and the height divided by 2, which is $\dfrac{a\left(\frac{\sqrt{3}\,a}{2}\right)}{2} = \dfrac{\sqrt{3}\,a^2}{4}$, and the perimeter of the triangle is $3a$, so if these are equal, then $\dfrac{\sqrt{3}\,a^2}{4} = 3a$, and dividing both sides by a (since you know $a \neq 0$), you get $\dfrac{\sqrt{3}\,a}{4} = 3$, so $a = \dfrac{12}{\sqrt{3}} = 6.93$ cm.

    If you chose (B), you may have forgotten to divide by 2 when calculating the area. If you chose (C), you may have used the expression $a^2 - \frac{a^2}{2}$ instead of $a^2 - \left(\frac{a}{2}\right)^2$ when calculating the height.

43. The correct answer is (A). The general form of the equation of a hyperbola is $\dfrac{(x-h)^2}{a^2} - \dfrac{(y-k)^2}{b^2} = 1$, where the center is at (h, k). In this case, because the only term containing an x is $9x^3$ and the only term containing a y is $16y^2$, you know that $h = 0$ and $k = 0$, which means that the center is at $(0, 0)$. If you're not sure, you can rearrange this equation fully to get $\dfrac{x^2}{16} - \dfrac{y^2}{9} = 1$, so you can be certain that $h = k = 0$.

44. The correct answer is (B). Because the period of growth when the number of infected mice is known is the same as the period of growth when the number is unknown (10 months each), the fastest way to answer this question is *not* to use the formula for an exponentially growing population, but to simply find the rate of change. In the first 10 months, the number of infected mice increased from 200 to 5000. Because $\dfrac{5000}{200} = 25$, the number of infected mice multiplies by 25 over 10 months. In 10 more months, the number of infected mice (5000) will multiply by 25 again: 125,000 mice will be infected after 10 more months.

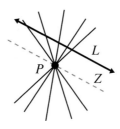

45. The correct answer is (B). Take a look at the diagram above. You can see that every line passing through point P will intersect line L somewhere, with the only exception being the line parallel to line L, which we can call line Z. Line Z may or may not be one of the n lines passing through point P. So, if there are n lines through point P, either they all intersect with line L or all but one do: $(n-1)$. Therefore, at least $(n-1)$ lines intersect line L, so (B) is correct.

(A) is incorrect because it could be that none of the lines are perpendicular to line L. (C) is incorrect because if line Z is not present, every line passing through point P will intersect line L. So, there would be n lines intersecting line L, which is more than $(n-1)$, not "at most $(n-1)$". (D) is incorrect because if line Z is present, there will be $(n-1)$ intersections, which is not "at least n". (E) is incorrect because line Z may or may not exist.

46. The correct answer is (E). Both the x-coordinates and y-coordinates of the two given points have a difference of 2. That means that the sides of the square are parallel to the x- and y-axes and have a length of 2, so P is located at $\left(-\sqrt{3}, 1\right)$. To convert point P into polar coordinates (r, θ), use the two formulas $r = \sqrt{x^2 + y^2}$ and $\theta = \tan^{-1}\frac{y}{x}$. Plugging in, you find that $r = \sqrt{\left(-\sqrt{3}\right)^2 + 1^2} = \sqrt{4} = 2$, and $\theta = \tan^{-1}\dfrac{1}{-\sqrt{3}} = \dfrac{5\pi}{6}$.

47. The correct answer is (C). Multiply the rows of the first matrix by the columns of the second matrix:

$$\begin{bmatrix} 8 & -2 \\ 2 & 5 \end{bmatrix} \times \begin{bmatrix} 2 & 1 \\ 1 & 3 \end{bmatrix} = \begin{bmatrix} (8 \times 2)+(-2 \times 1) & (8 \times 2)+(-2 \times 3) \\ (2 \times 2)+(5 \times 1) & (2 \times 1)+(5 \times 3) \end{bmatrix} = \begin{bmatrix} 14 & 2 \\ 9 & 17 \end{bmatrix}$$

Simplify each element to get (C).

48. The correct answer is (D). The easiest way to answer this question is to use the Cosine Law and rearrange the equation. Start by writing $a^2 = b^2 + b^2 - 2(b)(b)\cos\theta$, and then combining like terms to get $a^2 = 2b^2 - 2b^2\cos\theta$. Factoring out $2b^2$ from the right hand side gives you $a^2 = 2b^2(1 - \cos\theta)$. Divide both sides by $2b^2$ to get $\dfrac{a^2}{2b^2} = 1 - \cos\theta$. However, you know that $\dfrac{a}{b} = 0.74$, and so the left side of this equation is equal to $\dfrac{\left(\frac{a}{b}\right)^2}{2} = \dfrac{0.74^2}{2} = 0.2738$. Rearranging the equation gives you $\cos\theta = 1 - 0.2738 = 0.7262$.

49. The correct answer is (B). The easiest way to answer this question is to graph the function and notice that the asymptotes are at $\frac{\pi}{4}, \frac{3\pi}{4}, \frac{5\pi}{4}$, and so on. In other words, they are at the odd integer multiples of $\frac{\pi}{4}$, which you can write as $\frac{\pi}{4}(2n-1)$, because, if n is any integer, then $2n-1$ is always an odd integer. If you didn't graph it, you could realize that the function $\tan x$ has asymptotes when $\cos x = 0$, so the function $f(x) = \tan\left(2\left(x+\frac{\pi}{2}\right)\right)$ has asymptotes when $\cos\left(2\left(x+\frac{\pi}{2}\right)\right) = \cos\left(2x+\pi\right) = 0$, which is when $2x+\pi$ is an odd multiple of $\frac{\pi}{2}$, which occurs when x is an odd multiple of $\frac{\pi}{4}$.

50. The correct answer is (D). Often, the easiest way to analyze parametric equations is to plug values of t into the equations for x and y, and see what points on the graph result from that. For a given value of t, you can see what point (x, y) arises from it in each answer choice, and then check that point against the provided graph to see if it actually lies on the curve. The easiest value to start with is $t = 0$. Choice (A) gives the point $(0, -10)$, which does not lie on the curve, so you can rule out (A). (B) gives the point $(0, 10)$ and (C) gives the point $(-10, 0)$, neither of which lie on the curve shown, so you can rule out (B) and (C) as well. (D) and (E) both give you the point $(10, 0)$, which does lie on the curve. Next, you can try $t = 1$ to help decide between (D) and (E). (D) gives the point $(11, 1)$ and (E) gives the point $(9, 1)$. It is easy to see that $(9, 1)$ is not on the curve, because when $x = 9$, y is negative. However, $(11, 1)$ does lie on the curve. By process of elimination, the answer must be (D).

Practice Test 5

YOUR NAME (PRINT): _____

LAST   FIRST   MI

Correct ●   Incorrect ⊗ ⊘ ◓   ★ ◯ ◒ ⊕

Make sure you use a No. 2 pencil. Each answer must be marked in the corresponding row on the answer sheet. Each bubble must be filled in completely and darkly within the lines. Extra marks on your answer sheet may be marked as incorrect answers and lower your score.

○ Literature	○ Mathematics Level 1	○ German
○ Biology E	○ Mathematics Level 2	○ Italian
○ Biology M	○ U.S. History	○ Latin
○ Chemistry	○ World History	○ Modern Hebrew
○ Physics	○ French	○ Spanish

1 Ⓐ Ⓑ Ⓒ Ⓓ Ⓔ   21 Ⓐ Ⓑ Ⓒ Ⓓ Ⓔ   41 Ⓐ Ⓑ Ⓒ Ⓓ Ⓔ   61 Ⓐ Ⓑ Ⓒ Ⓓ Ⓔ   81 Ⓐ Ⓑ Ⓒ Ⓓ Ⓔ

2 Ⓐ Ⓑ Ⓒ Ⓓ Ⓔ   22 Ⓐ Ⓑ Ⓒ Ⓓ Ⓔ   42 Ⓐ Ⓑ Ⓒ Ⓓ Ⓔ   62 Ⓐ Ⓑ Ⓒ Ⓓ Ⓔ   82 Ⓐ Ⓑ Ⓒ Ⓓ Ⓔ

3 Ⓐ Ⓑ Ⓒ Ⓓ Ⓔ   23 Ⓐ Ⓑ Ⓒ Ⓓ Ⓔ   43 Ⓐ Ⓑ Ⓒ Ⓓ Ⓔ   63 Ⓐ Ⓑ Ⓒ Ⓓ Ⓔ   83 Ⓐ Ⓑ Ⓒ Ⓓ Ⓔ

4 Ⓐ Ⓑ Ⓒ Ⓓ Ⓔ   24 Ⓐ Ⓑ Ⓒ Ⓓ Ⓔ   44 Ⓐ Ⓑ Ⓒ Ⓓ Ⓔ   64 Ⓐ Ⓑ Ⓒ Ⓓ Ⓔ   84 Ⓐ Ⓑ Ⓒ Ⓓ Ⓔ

5 Ⓐ Ⓑ Ⓒ Ⓓ Ⓔ   25 Ⓐ Ⓑ Ⓒ Ⓓ Ⓔ   45 Ⓐ Ⓑ Ⓒ Ⓓ Ⓔ   65 Ⓐ Ⓑ Ⓒ Ⓓ Ⓔ   85 Ⓐ Ⓑ Ⓒ Ⓓ Ⓔ

6 Ⓐ Ⓑ Ⓒ Ⓓ Ⓔ   26 Ⓐ Ⓑ Ⓒ Ⓓ Ⓔ   46 Ⓐ Ⓑ Ⓒ Ⓓ Ⓔ   66 Ⓐ Ⓑ Ⓒ Ⓓ Ⓔ   86 Ⓐ Ⓑ Ⓒ Ⓓ Ⓔ

7 Ⓐ Ⓑ Ⓒ Ⓓ Ⓔ   27 Ⓐ Ⓑ Ⓒ Ⓓ Ⓔ   47 Ⓐ Ⓑ Ⓒ Ⓓ Ⓔ   67 Ⓐ Ⓑ Ⓒ Ⓓ Ⓔ   87 Ⓐ Ⓑ Ⓒ Ⓓ Ⓔ

8 Ⓐ Ⓑ Ⓒ Ⓓ Ⓔ   28 Ⓐ Ⓑ Ⓒ Ⓓ Ⓔ   48 Ⓐ Ⓑ Ⓒ Ⓓ Ⓔ   68 Ⓐ Ⓑ Ⓒ Ⓓ Ⓔ   88 Ⓐ Ⓑ Ⓒ Ⓓ Ⓔ

9 Ⓐ Ⓑ Ⓒ Ⓓ Ⓔ   29 Ⓐ Ⓑ Ⓒ Ⓓ Ⓔ   49 Ⓐ Ⓑ Ⓒ Ⓓ Ⓔ   69 Ⓐ Ⓑ Ⓒ Ⓓ Ⓔ   89 Ⓐ Ⓑ Ⓒ Ⓓ Ⓔ

10 Ⓐ Ⓑ Ⓒ Ⓓ Ⓔ   30 Ⓐ Ⓑ Ⓒ Ⓓ Ⓔ   50 Ⓐ Ⓑ Ⓒ Ⓓ Ⓔ   70 Ⓐ Ⓑ Ⓒ Ⓓ Ⓔ   90 Ⓐ Ⓑ Ⓒ Ⓓ Ⓔ

11 Ⓐ Ⓑ Ⓒ Ⓓ Ⓔ   31 Ⓐ Ⓑ Ⓒ Ⓓ Ⓔ   51 Ⓐ Ⓑ Ⓒ Ⓓ Ⓔ   71 Ⓐ Ⓑ Ⓒ Ⓓ Ⓔ   81 Ⓐ Ⓑ Ⓒ Ⓓ Ⓔ

12 Ⓐ Ⓑ Ⓒ Ⓓ Ⓔ   32 Ⓐ Ⓑ Ⓒ Ⓓ Ⓔ   52 Ⓐ Ⓑ Ⓒ Ⓓ Ⓔ   72 Ⓐ Ⓑ Ⓒ Ⓓ Ⓔ   92 Ⓐ Ⓑ Ⓒ Ⓓ Ⓔ

13 Ⓐ Ⓑ Ⓒ Ⓓ Ⓔ   33 Ⓐ Ⓑ Ⓒ Ⓓ Ⓔ   53 Ⓐ Ⓑ Ⓒ Ⓓ Ⓔ   73 Ⓐ Ⓑ Ⓒ Ⓓ Ⓔ   93 Ⓐ Ⓑ Ⓒ Ⓓ Ⓔ

14 Ⓐ Ⓑ Ⓒ Ⓓ Ⓔ   34 Ⓐ Ⓑ Ⓒ Ⓓ Ⓔ   54 Ⓐ Ⓑ Ⓒ Ⓓ Ⓔ   74 Ⓐ Ⓑ Ⓒ Ⓓ Ⓔ   94 Ⓐ Ⓑ Ⓒ Ⓓ Ⓔ

15 Ⓐ Ⓑ Ⓒ Ⓓ Ⓔ   35 Ⓐ Ⓑ Ⓒ Ⓓ Ⓔ   55 Ⓐ Ⓑ Ⓒ Ⓓ Ⓔ   75 Ⓐ Ⓑ Ⓒ Ⓓ Ⓔ   95 Ⓐ Ⓑ Ⓒ Ⓓ Ⓔ

16 Ⓐ Ⓑ Ⓒ Ⓓ Ⓔ   36 Ⓐ Ⓑ Ⓒ Ⓓ Ⓔ   56 Ⓐ Ⓑ Ⓒ Ⓓ Ⓔ   76 Ⓐ Ⓑ Ⓒ Ⓓ Ⓔ   96 Ⓐ Ⓑ Ⓒ Ⓓ Ⓔ

17 Ⓐ Ⓑ Ⓒ Ⓓ Ⓔ   37 Ⓐ Ⓑ Ⓒ Ⓓ Ⓔ   57 Ⓐ Ⓑ Ⓒ Ⓓ Ⓔ   77 Ⓐ Ⓑ Ⓒ Ⓓ Ⓔ   97 Ⓐ Ⓑ Ⓒ Ⓓ Ⓔ

18 Ⓐ Ⓑ Ⓒ Ⓓ Ⓔ   38 Ⓐ Ⓑ Ⓒ Ⓓ Ⓔ   58 Ⓐ Ⓑ Ⓒ Ⓓ Ⓔ   78 Ⓐ Ⓑ Ⓒ Ⓓ Ⓔ   98 Ⓐ Ⓑ Ⓒ Ⓓ Ⓔ

19 Ⓐ Ⓑ Ⓒ Ⓓ Ⓔ   39 Ⓐ Ⓑ Ⓒ Ⓓ Ⓔ   59 Ⓐ Ⓑ Ⓒ Ⓓ Ⓔ   79 Ⓐ Ⓑ Ⓒ Ⓓ Ⓔ   99 Ⓐ Ⓑ Ⓒ Ⓓ Ⓔ

20 Ⓐ Ⓑ Ⓒ Ⓓ Ⓔ   40 Ⓐ Ⓑ Ⓒ Ⓓ Ⓔ   60 Ⓐ Ⓑ Ⓒ Ⓓ Ⓔ   80 Ⓐ Ⓑ Ⓒ Ⓓ Ⓔ   100 Ⓐ Ⓑ Ⓒ Ⓓ Ⓔ

 For automatic scoring and scaling, please visit **cloud.ivyglobal.com**.

SAT Math Level 2 Subject Test

Reference Materials

THE FORMULAS BELOW MAY BE USEFUL IN ANSWERING QUESTIONS ON THIS TEST.

$S = 4\pi r^2$ is the formula for the surface area of a sphere with a radius of r.

$V = \frac{1}{3}\pi r^2 h$ is the formula for the volume of a right circular cone with a radius of r and a height of h.

$V = \frac{4}{3}\pi r^3$ is the formula for the volume of a sphere with a radius of r.

$V = \frac{1}{3}Bh$ is the formula for the volume of a pyramid with a base area of B and a height of h.

When choosing an answer, find the CLOSEST answer possible. If the precise numerical value that you have found is not an answer choice, select the choice that is closest to your answer. Use the answer sheet and fill in the bubble corresponding to your choice.

Notes: (1) You ARE permitted the use of a graphing or scientific calculator, which you may use at your own discretion. You will also have to choose between degree or radian mode for some questions, so keep track of what mode your calculator is in.

(2) You may assume that figures are drawn as accurately as possible UNLESS it is explicitly stated that a figure is not drawn to scale. Furthermore, all figures are in a plane UNLESS it is stated otherwise.

(3) For any function f, unless otherwise specified, you may assume that a real number x is in the domain of f if and only if $f(x)$ is a real number. The range of f consists of all and only those real numbers of the form $f(x)$, where x is in the domain of f.

(4) Four formulas are provided in the box above for your reference.

GO ON TO THE NEXT PAGE

USE THIS SPACE FOR SCRATCH WORK.

1. What is $\frac{a}{2} + \frac{a}{3} + \frac{a}{5}$?

    (A) $\frac{a}{30}$

    (B) $\frac{a}{10}$

    (C) $\frac{a}{3}$

    (D) $\frac{31a}{30}$

    (E) $30a$

2. The square root of the expression $a^2 \, b^5 \, c^6$ is

    (A) $a(\frac{5}{2}b)(3c)$

    (B) $ab^{\frac{3}{2}}c^3$

    (C) $ab^{\frac{5}{2}}c^3$

    (D) b^3c^4

    (E) $a^4b^{10}c^{12}$

3. What is the slope of the line that passes through $(-2, -4)$ and $(4, 2)$?

    (A) -2
    (B) -1
    (C) 1
    (D) 2
    (E) 4

4. If $3^a = 9$ and $3^b = 27$, what is the value of $a + b$?

    (A) 2
    (B) 3
    (C) 5
    (D) 6
    (E) 12

GO ON TO THE NEXT PAGE

USE THIS SPACE FOR SCRATCH WORK.

5. If the lines $y = (a + 3)x - 4$ and $y = 2ax - 8$ are parallel, then the value of a is

    (A) -4
    (B) -2
    (C) 0
    (D) 2
    (E) 3

$$41, 80, 62, 33, n$$

6. For which of the following values of n is the range of the list above greater than the median?

    (A) 30
    (B) 47
    (C) 62
    (D) 81
    (E) 95

GO ON TO THE NEXT PAGE

USE THIS SPACE FOR SCRATCH WORK.

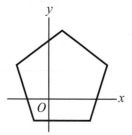

7. A pentagon in the *xy*-plane, shown above, is reflected across the *x*-axis and then across the *y*-axis. Which of the following figures shows the pentagon that results from these reflections?

(A)

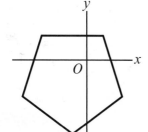

(B)

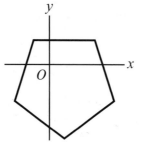

(C)

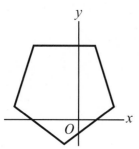

(D)

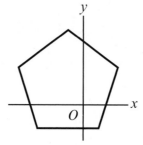

(E)

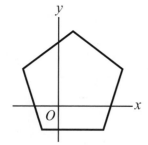

GO ON TO THE NEXT PAGE

USE THIS SPACE FOR SCRATCH WORK.

8. If $3a + 6b < 12$, and a and b are both positive, which of the following is NOT a possible value for a?

(A) 4

(B) 3

(C) 2

(D) 1

(E) $\frac{1}{2}$

9. If $\sin(\pi - \theta) = -0.262$, then $\sin\theta =$

(A) −0.738

(B) −0.262

(C) 0.262

(D) 0.272

(E) 0.965

10. If $y = (2x + 7)^2$, what is the greatest possible value of $|x|$ when $y = 10$?

(A) 0.3377

(B) 1.9189

(C) 5.0811

(D) 6.6623

(E) 46.5000

11. A recipe calls for 7 cups of vegetable stock. If a chef has 2 L of stock, how much stock will be left over after making the recipe?
(1 cup = 237 mL)

(A) 237 mL

(B) 341 mL

(C) 474 mL

(D) 1,185 mL

(E) 1,659 mL

GO ON TO THE NEXT PAGE

12. If $i^2 = -1$, what is $(5i - 12)(3 + i)$?

    (A) $3i$
    (B) $15i - 12$
    (C) $3i - 41$
    (D) $27i + 31$
    (E) $27i - 31$

USE THIS SPACE FOR SCRATCH WORK.

13. The Great Pyramid of Giza is 150 meters high and has a square base with edges 230 meters long. What is the approximate volume of the pyramid?

    (A)   11,500 m³
    (B)   34,500 m³
    (C) 1,725,000 m³
    (D) 2,645,000 m³
    (E) 7,935,000 m³

14. How many x-intercepts does the polynomial $2(x - 3)(x + 5)(3 - x)$ have?

    (A) 0
    (B) 1
    (C) 2
    (D) 3
    (E) 4

15. If Train A is on time, its passengers can catch Train F, as long as it is also on time. If Train A has a 38.1% chance of being on time and Train F has a 32.2% chance of being on time, what is the probability that a passenger can catch both Train A and Train F on time?

    (A)   1.2%
    (B) 12.3%
    (C) 32.2%
    (D) 38.1%
    (E) 70.3%

GO ON TO THE NEXT PAGE

16. If $a = \sqrt[3]{y}$ and $b = \sqrt[3]{x}$, then $x^3 y^3 =$

(A) ab

(B) ab^3

(C) $a^6 b^6$

(D) $a^6 b^9$

(E) $a^9 b^9$

17. What is the y-coordinate of the point of intersection of the lines $3y + 5x + 9 = 0$ and $4y - 7x + 2 = 0$?

(A) -1.78

(B) -0.73

(C) -0.27

(D) 0.75

(E) 53.00

18. Which of the following expressions approaches zero for large values of x ?

(A) $\dfrac{x+1}{2x}$

(B) $\dfrac{2x}{x+1}$

(C) $\dfrac{x}{x^2+1}$

(D) $\dfrac{x^2}{x+1}$

(E) $-\dfrac{x^2}{x+1}$

GO ON TO THE NEXT PAGE

USE THIS SPACE FOR SCRATCH WORK.

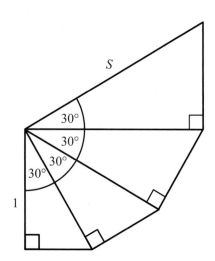

19. In the diagram above, what is the value of S ?

    (A) 1.15
    (B) 1.78
    (C) 5.20
    (D) 9.00
    (E) 16.00

20. A model boat travels along a route modeled by the equation
    $y = 2x^3 + 12$ on the xy-plane. There are checkpoints set up at
    particular (x, y) coordinates. Which of the following checkpoints
    does the model boat pass through?

    (A) $(-3, -66)$
    (B) $(-1, 14)$
    (C) $(2, 28)$
    (D) $(3, 39)$
    (E) $(5, 42)$

GO ON TO THE NEXT PAGE

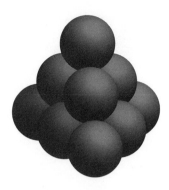

USE THIS SPACE FOR SCRATCH WORK.

21. A two-level tetrahedron can be built with four spheres, three as the base and one at the top. Adding six more spheres to the bottom yields a three-level tetrahedron, as shown above. How many spheres are required for a tetrahedron of seven levels?

    (A)   28
    (B)   56
    (C)   68
    (D)   84
    (E)   120

22. If A and B are different points in 3-space, the set of all points that are closer to A than to B is a region of 3-space

    (A)   on one side of a line
    (B)   bounded by a cube
    (C)   bounded by a sphere
    (D)   on one side of a plane
    (E)   on one side of a paraboloid

GO ON TO THE NEXT PAGE

x	$f(x)$
a	-9
2	3
5	b
10	35

23. If $f(x)$ is a linear function, what is ab?

 (A) -15

 (B) -5

 (C) -4

 (D) 0

 (E) 5

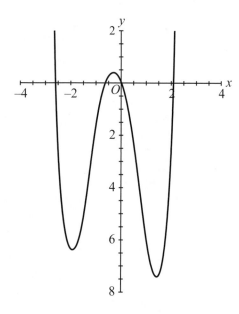

24. Which of the following functions is graphed above?

 (A) $y = x^3 - 2x^2 + 5x$

 (B) $y = -x^3 + 4x^2 - 2x$

 (C) $y = x^4 + x^3 - 5x^2 - 3x$

 (D) $y = -x^4 - x^3 + 3x^2 - x$

 (E) $y = x^4 + 2x^3 - 4x^2 + 3x + 6$

GO ON TO THE NEXT PAGE

USE THIS SPACE FOR SCRATCH WORK.

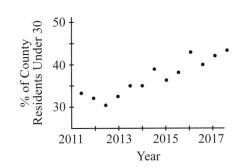

25. The scatterplot above shows the percentage of people living in Griston County under the age of 30 over a period of several years. If there were 35,602 people living in Griston County at the beginning of 2014, approximately how many of those residents were age 30 or older?

(A) 12,461
(B) 14,241
(C) 18,551
(D) 21,361
(E) 23,141

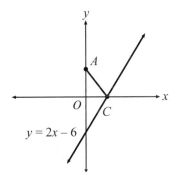

$y = 2x - 6$

26. If point A is $(0, 4)$, what is the length of AC?

(A) 3.00
(B) 4.22
(C) 5.00
(D) 5.62
(E) 7.00

GO ON TO THE NEXT PAGE

USE THIS SPACE FOR SCRATCH WORK.

27. A red car drives for 5 hours at 45 miles per hour, a green car drives for 3 hours at 70 miles per hour, and a blue car drives for 4 hours at 55 miles per hour. What is the average distance travelled by the three cars?

(A)   15 miles
(B)   55 miles
(C)   57 miles
(D) 218 miles
(E) 220 miles

28. The three sides of a triangle are consecutive integers that add to 39. What is the measure of the angle between the shortest sides?

(A)   52°
(B)   59°
(C)   68°
(D)   71°
(E) 112°

29. If ln $a = b$, then ln $2a =$

(A) $2b$
(B) $e^b \ln 2$
(C) $b \ln a$
(D) $be \ln 2$
(E) $b + \ln 2$

30. The point $(p - 6, q - 8)$ lies on a parabola whose vertex is at (p, q). Which of the following points must also lie on the parabola?

(A) $(p - 6, q + 8)$
(B) $(p + 6, q - 8)$
(C) $(p + 6, q + 8)$
(D) $(p - 3, q - 4)$
(E) $(q - 8, p - 6)$

GO ON TO THE NEXT PAGE

USE THIS SPACE FOR SCRATCH WORK.

31. If $(f-g)(x) = 2x^2 + 5x - 7$, for which of the following values of x is $f(x) = g(x)$?

    (A) −1
    (B)   0
    (C)   1
    (D)   2
    (E)   5

32. Which of the following is NOT true of the graph of $\csc x$?

    (A) It has no roots.
    (B) It has a period of 2π.
    (C) It is an odd function.
    (D) It is always positive.
    (E) It has asymptotes at the x-intercepts of $\sin x$.

33. The first term of a geometric series is 1, and the series converges to a value of 1.5. Which of the following could be the common ratio of the series?

    (A) $\frac{1}{3}$

    (B) $\frac{1}{2}$

    (C) $\frac{2}{3}$

    (D) $\frac{3}{4}$

    (E) $\frac{7}{8}$

GO ON TO THE NEXT PAGE

USE THIS SPACE FOR SCRATCH WORK.

34. Function f is a polynomial of degree n. If $g(x) = \dfrac{f(x)}{x^{\frac{n}{2}}}$ is also a polynomial, and $g(x) = g(-x)$, which of the following must be true?

(A) $g(x)$ is of an even degree and $f(x)$ is of an odd degree.

(B) $g(x)$ is of an odd degree and $f(x)$ is of an even degree.

(C) $g(x)$ and $f(x)$ are both of an odd degree.

(D) $g(x)$ and $f(x)$ are both of an even degree.

(E) $g(x)$ and $f(x)$ have the same degree.

35. Which of the following is true for all values of θ ?

(A) $\sin\theta = \cos(\theta + \pi)$

(B) $\sin\theta = \cos(\theta - \pi)$

(C) $\sin\theta = \cos(\theta - \dfrac{\pi}{2})$

(D) $\sin\theta = \cos(\theta + \dfrac{\pi}{2})$

(E) $\sin(\theta + \pi) = \cos\theta$

36. What is the domain of the function $f(x) = \dfrac{5 - x^2}{\sqrt{5x - 4}}$?

(A) $\{x \in \mathbb{R} : x < \sqrt{5}\}$

(B) $\{x \in \mathbb{R} : x \geq \sqrt{5}\}$

(C) $\left\{x \in \mathbb{R} : x > \dfrac{4}{5}\right\}$

(D) $\left\{x \in \mathbb{R} : x < \dfrac{5}{4}\right\}$

(E) $\left\{x \in \mathbb{R} : x \geq \dfrac{4}{5}\right\}$

GO ON TO THE NEXT PAGE

USE THIS SPACE FOR SCRATCH WORK.

$$f(x) = \begin{cases} -x^2 - 4x + 5 & , \ x < -2 \\ 2x + 2 & , \ -2 \le x \le 8 \\ \dfrac{72}{x} & , \ x > 8 \end{cases}$$

37. At how many x-values is $f(x)$ equal to 9?

(A) 0
(B) 1
(C) 2
(D) 3
(E) 4

38. What is the period of $f(x) = \sin x + \sin \dfrac{2x}{3}$?

(A) π

(B) 2π

(C) 3π

(D) 5π

(E) 6π

39. If $f(f(x)) > 0$ for all real numbers x, then f could be

(A) a linear function with a positive slope
(B) a linear function with a negative slope
(C) a quadratic function
(D) a cubic function
(E) a cube root function

GO ON TO THE NEXT PAGE

USE THIS SPACE FOR SCRATCH WORK.

40. A positive integer n has a remainder of 2 when it is divided by 3, and a remainder of 3 when it is divided by 5. What is the remainder when n is divided by 15?

(A) 2
(B) 3
(C) 5
(D) 6
(E) 8

41. Fermium-257 decays at a rate of 0.69% per day. Which of the following expressions is equal to the half-life of Fermium-257 in days?

(A) $\dfrac{\log 2}{\log 0.9931}$

(B) $\dfrac{\log 0.9931}{\log 2}$

(C) $\dfrac{\log 0.5}{\log 0.9931}$

(D) $\dfrac{\log 0.9931}{\log 0.5}$

(E) $\dfrac{\log 1.0069}{\log 0.5}$

42. If $g(x) = x^2 - 1$ and $f(g(x)) = 1 - \dfrac{1}{x^2}$, which of the following could be an expression for $f(x)$?

(A) $\sqrt{x} - x$

(B) $x - \dfrac{1}{x}$

(C) $\dfrac{x}{x+1}$

(D) $\dfrac{x}{x-1}$

(E) $\dfrac{x+1}{x^2}$

GO ON TO THE NEXT PAGE

USE THIS SPACE FOR SCRATCH WORK.

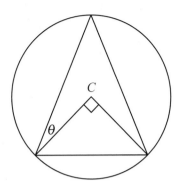

Note: Figure not drawn to scale.

43. If C is the center of the circle above, and both triangles are isosceles, what is the measure of angle θ ?

(A) 15.0°
(B) 22.5°
(C) 27.5°
(D) 30.0°
(E) 67.5°

$$x^2 = z^3$$
$$4z^2 = y^6$$
$$x = 2z$$

44. Given the set of relationships above, what is a possible value of $x + y + z$?

(A)   8
(B) 12
(C) 14
(D) 16
(E) 20

45. If the surface area of a sphere is decreased by 30%, by what percent does the volume of the sphere decrease?

(A)   3%
(B) 34%
(C) 41%
(D) 59%
(E) 84%

GO ON TO THE NEXT PAGE

USE THIS SPACE FOR SCRATCH WORK.

$$\frac{x^2}{49} + \frac{y^2}{16} = 25$$

46. A planet orbits its star in an elliptical motion, according to the equation above, where the planet's position in the plane of its orbit is given by (x, y). Which of the following parametric equations could model the position of the planet after t days?

(A) $x(t) = 1{,}225 \cos t$
    $y(t) = 400 \sin t$

(B) $x(t) = 49 \cos t$
    $y(t) = 16 \sin t$

(C) $x(t) = 7 \cos t$
    $y(t) = 4 \sin t$

(D) $x(t) = 35 \cos t$
    $y(t) = 20 \sin t$

(E) $x(t) = 16 \cos t$
    $y(t) = 49 \sin t$

47. For which of the following matrices X does X^2 exist?

(A) $\begin{bmatrix} -3 & 4 \\ 6 & 0 \end{bmatrix}$

(B) $\begin{bmatrix} 0 \\ -3 \end{bmatrix}$

(C) $\begin{bmatrix} 0 & 4 \\ 9 & 16 \\ 25 & 1 \end{bmatrix}$

(D) $\begin{bmatrix} -2 & 0 & 6 \\ 5 & 5 & 5 \end{bmatrix}$

(E) $\begin{bmatrix} 1 & 1 \end{bmatrix}$

GO ON TO THE NEXT PAGE

USE THIS SPACE FOR SCRATCH WORK.

48. A school's track and field team has 14 members, 7 of whom can run either the 1 km or 5 km race, and 7 of whom can run either the 5 km or 10 km race. If the team needs to enter 4 people into the 1 km race, 6 people into the 5 km race, and 4 people into the 10 km race, how many different ways are there to enter the team members in the races?

(A)   35
(B)   96
(C)   720
(D) 1,225
(E) 3,003

49. If $\sin^2 x \cos^2 x = \frac{1}{4}$, which of the following is a possible value of $\sin x + \cos x$?

(A) $\frac{1}{4}$

(B) $\frac{1}{2}$

(C) $\frac{1}{\sqrt{2}}$

(D) 1

(E) $\sqrt{2}$

50. Which of the following is an asymptote of the hyperbola $\frac{(x-2)^2}{4} - \frac{(y-1)^2}{64} = 1$?

(A) $y = \frac{1}{4}x + \frac{1}{2}$

(B) $y = -\frac{1}{4}x + \frac{3}{2}$

(C) $y = 4x - 2$

(D) $y = 4x + 7$

(E) $y = -4x + 9$

STOP

If you complete this test before the end of your allotted time, you may check your work.

Answers and Scoring

Scoring Your Test
Part 1

The easiest way to score your test is to use our Cloud scoring tool. The Cloud tool also provides more detailed results by showing you how you performed on specific kinds of questions. To score your test by hand, follow the directions below.

 For more detailed scoring results, please visit **cloud.ivyglobal.com.**

Answers

1. D	11. B	21. D	31. C	41. C
2. C	12. C	22. D	32. D	42. C
3. C	13. D	23. A	33. A	43. B
4. C	14. C	24. C	34. D	44. C
5. E	15. B	25. E	35. C	45. C
6. A	16. E	26. C	36. C	46. D
7. A	17. A	27. D	37. B	47. A
8. A	18. C	28. C	38. E	48. D
9. B	19. B	29. E	39. C	49. E
10. C	20. C	30. B	40. E	50. E

Raw Scores

To score your test, first use the answer key to mark each of your responses as correct or incorrect. Don't mark or count questions you left blank. Then, calculate your raw score for each section by subtracting one fourth the number of incorrect responses from the number of correct responses. Scores should be rounded to the nearest whole number, with .5 and above rounding up. Use the tables below to help you calculate your scores:

Scores	
Number Correct	_____ −
Number incorrect	_____ / 4 = _____
Raw Score	= _____
Scaled Score	_____

Scaled Scores

Once you have found your raw score for each test, convert it into an approximate scaled test score using the following chart. To find a scaled test score for each section, find the row in the Raw Score column which corresponds to your raw score for that section, then check the column for the section you are scoring in the same row. For example, if you had a raw score of 31, your scaled score would be 580. Keep in mind that these scaled scores are estimates only. Your actual SAT Subject Test in Mathematics Level 2 score will be scaled against the scores of all other students at your grade level taking the test on your test date.

Scaled Score							
Raw Score	Scaled Score	Raw Score	Scaled Score	Raw Score	Scaled Score	Raw Score	Scaled Score
50	800	34	710	18	560	2	440
49	800	33	700	17	560	1	430
48	800	32	690	16	550	0	410
47	800	31	680	15	540	−1	390
46	800	30	670	14	530	−2	370
45	800	29	660	13	530	−3	360
44	800	28	650	12	520	−4	340
43	800	27	640	11	510	−5	340
42	790	26	630	10	500	−6	330
41	790	25	630	9	500	−7	320
40	780	24	620	8	490	−8	320
39	770	23	610	7	480	−9	320
38	750	22	600	6	480	−10	320
37	740	21	590	5	470	−11	310
36	730	20	580	4	460	−12	310
35	720	19	570	3	450		

Explanations

Part 2

1. The correct answer is (D). To add fractions, you must first find a common denominator. In this case, write all the terms with a denominator of 30: $\frac{15a}{30} + \frac{10a}{30} + \frac{6a}{30} = \frac{31a}{30}$.

2. The correct answer is (C). Taking the square root of an expression is the same as raising the expression to the power of $\frac{1}{2}$. Therefore, the square root of this expression is $(a^2 b^5 c^6)^{\frac{1}{2}} = ab^{\frac{5}{2}}c^3$, since you can multiply each of the exponents by $\frac{1}{2}$.

3. The correct answer is (C). Use the slope formula $\frac{y_1 - y_2}{x_1 - x_2}$ to compute the slope of the line: $\frac{-4-2}{-2-4} = \frac{-6}{-6} = 1$.

4. The correct answer is (C). If $3^a = 9$, then $a = 2$, because $3^2 = 9$. If $3^b = 27$, then $b = 3$. Therefore, $a + b = 2 + 3 = 5$.

5. The correct answer is (E). The first line has a slope of $(a + 3)$ and the second line has a slope of $2a$. Since the lines are parallel, these slopes are equal: $a + 3 = 2a$ so $a = 3$.

6. The correct answer is (A). Trial and error might be the fastest way for you to solve this question, but you could also think about possible values of n and the ranges and medians that they entail. If $n < 33$, then the range will be $80 - n$ and the median will be 41, which means that (A) is correct (the range, 50, is greater than the median, 41).

   If $33 < n < 80$, then the range is $80 - 33 = 47$, and the median could be n or something else: for (B), the median is 47 and equal to the range; for (C), the median is 62 and greater than the range. So, you can eliminate both (B) and (C). If $n > 80$, then the range is $n - 33$ and the median will be 62, which means that you must have $n - 33 > 62$, or $n > 95$, so you can eliminate (D) and (E).

7. The correct answer is (A). It might be helpful to draw a diagram to help you imagine the transformations. Imagine flipping the pentagon over the x-axis, and then flipping the resulting shape over the y-axis, as shown in the figure below.

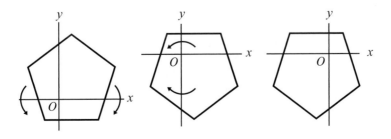

8. The correct answer is (A). If $a = 4$, the left side of the inequality would equal $12 + 6b$, which could only be less than 12 if b was negative. However, you are told in the question that a and b are both positive, so it is not possible for a to equal 4.

Choices (B), (C), (D), and (E) are all possible because they would make $3a$ less than 12, meaning that there would be a possible positive value for b.

9. The correct answer is (B). For any angle θ, $\sin\theta = \sin(\pi - \theta)$. Therefore, if $\sin(\pi - \theta) = -0.262$, then $\sin\theta$ is also equal to -0.262.

10. The correct answer is (C). Since $y = 10$, you know that $10 = (2x + 7)^2$. Take the square root of each side, remembering to account for both the positive and negative roots, to get either $2x + 7 = \sqrt{10}$ or $2x + 7 = -\sqrt{10}$. Solving these equations for x means that either $x = -1.9189$ or $x = -5.0811$. Since you are trying to find the greatest possible value of $|x|$, the solution is $x = -5.0811$, so that $|x| = 5.0811$.

11. The correct answer is (B). The chef needs 7 cups of stock, which is 7×237 mL $= 1,659$ mL. Since the chef started with 2 L, or 2,000 mL of stock, there will be 2,000 mL $-$ 1,659 mL $= 341$ mL left over.

12. The correct answer is (C). Remember that $i^2 = -1$, then expand the parentheses using FOIL to get

$$15i + 5i^2 - 36 - 12i$$
$$= 3i - 36 - 5$$
$$= 3i - 41$$

13. The correct answer is (D). The formula for the volume of a square-based pyramid is given on the first page of the test: $V = \frac{1}{3} Bh$. Because the base is a square, its area, B, is equal to its side length squared, or s^2. Simply plug the given values in to find the answer: $V = \frac{1}{3}(230^2) \times 150 = 2,645,000 \ m^3$.

14. The correct answer is (C). To find the number of x-intercepts, you can find the values of x at which the polynomial is equal to 0. Because this polynomial is already in factored form, you can simply set each factor equal to 0 individually to find the possible values of x. Either $x - 3 = 0$, $x + 5 = 0$, or $3 - x = 0$, meaning that x must equal 3 or -5 (since $x - 3 = 0$ and $3 - x = 0$ lead to the same solution for x). Therefore, this polynomial has two x-intercepts, at $x = 3$ and $x = -5$.

15. The correct answer is (B). The chance that Train A arrives on time does not affect the chance that Train F arrives on time, so Train A arriving and Train F arriving are independent events. Therefore, the probability that both will arrive on time is $P(A \cap F) = P(A) \times P(F) = 0.381 \times 0.322 = 0.122682 \cong 0.123 = 12.3\%$.

If you picked (C) or (D), you might have thought that one of the trains arriving on time guaranteed that the other one would also arrive on time. If you picked (E), you may have added the probabilities instead of multiplying them.

16. The correct answer is (E). If $a = \sqrt[3]{x}$ and $b = \sqrt[3]{y}$, then $a^3 = x$ and $b^3 = y$. Therefore, $x^3 y^3 = (a^3)^3 (b^3)^3 = a^9 b^9$.

17. The correct answer is (A). To find the point of intersection, you must solve the system of equations. Since you want to find the y-coordinate, it is easier to start by eliminating x. You can do this by multiplying the first equation by 7 and the second equation by 5, to get $21y + 35x + 63 = 0$ and $20y - 35x + 10 = 0$. Adding these two equations gives you $41y + 73 = 0$, which you can solve to find $y = -\dfrac{73}{41} = -1.78$.

18. The correct answer is (C). A rational function will approach 0 for large values of x if the denominator grows faster than the numerator, which means that the denominator must have a higher degree than the numerator. In this case, the numerator in option (C) has degree 1 and the denominator has degree 2, so (C) is correct.

In the other options, the degree of the numerator is either greater than or equal to the degree of the denominator, so the function will not approach 0 as x approaches infinity.

19. The correct answer is (B). Each of the triangles is a $30°$–$60°$–$90°$ triangle, so the ratio of the hypotenuse to the longer leg is $\dfrac{2}{\sqrt{3}}$. Since the side length marked in the diagram has length 1, the hypotenuse of the smallest triangle has length $\dfrac{2}{\sqrt{3}}$. The hypotenuse of the second triangle has length $\left(\dfrac{2}{\sqrt{3}}\right)^2$, the hypotenuse of the third triangle has length $\left(\dfrac{2}{\sqrt{3}}\right)^3$, and the hypotenuse of the fourth triangle (the side marked s) has length $\left(\dfrac{2}{\sqrt{3}}\right)^4 = 1.78$.

If you picked (A), you might have found the length of the smallest hypotenuse and stopped there.

20. The correct answer is (C). The fastest way to solve this problem is to use trial and error. Since the boat is traveling along the path given by the equation $y = 2x^3 + 12$, it will pass through every point that satisfies this relationship. If $x = 2$ then $y = 2(2^3) + 12 = 28$, so the boat passes through $(2, 28)$. The other answer options do not satisfy the relationship $y = 2x^3 + 12$.

21. The correct answer is (D). The first level requires 1 sphere, the second requires $1 + 2 = 3$ spheres, and the third requires $1 + 2 + 3 = 6$ spheres. You can model this sequence with the formula $a_n = a_{n-1} + n$, where a is the level of the tetrahedron and n is the number of spheres in that level. Therefore, $a_4 = a_3 + 4 = 6 + 4 = 10$, $a_5 = 15$, $a_6 = 21$, and $a_7 = 28$, which is only the number of spheres in the seventh level. To find the total number of spheres in a tetrahedron of seven levels, sum the spheres in each level: $a_1 + a_2 + a_3 + a_4 + a_5 + a_6 + a_7 = 1 + 3 + 6 + 10 + 15 + 21 + 28 = 84$.

22. The correct answer is (D). To solve this problem, it is helpful to start in two dimensions: if you have two points on a plane, then there is a line that runs exactly between them, dividing the plane into points closer to A and points closer to B. To extend the image to three dimensions, you can imagine two points in space, and imagine a flat plane that lies exactly between them (perhaps using an image, such as a piece of paper).

(A) is incorrect because a line would only separate the A-points from the B-points in two dimensions. (B), (C), and (E) are incorrect because a bounded or semi-bounded shape will necessarily exclude some possible points.

23. The correct answer is (A). You know that f is a linear function, so you can find its slope using the two given points and the slope equation: $(2, 3)$, $(10, 35)$, and $\frac{35-3}{10-2} = \frac{32}{8} - 4$. You can then find the y-intercept by plugging either of these given points into the slope-intercept equation:

$$y = mx + b$$
$$y = 4x + b$$
$$3 = 4(2) + b$$
$$b = 3 - 8 = -5$$

The equation of the line is $y = 4x - 5$. Plug in the given values at $(a, -9)$ and $(5, b)$ to find a and b:

$$-9 = 4(a) - 5 \qquad b = 4(5) - 5$$
$$a = -1 \qquad\qquad b = 15$$

Therefore, $ab = (-1)(15) = -15$.

24. The correct answer is (C). You can tell from the shape of the function that its degree is at least four, since it changes direction three times (or, instead, because it has at least 4 roots). Therefore, you can eliminate (A) and (B). You can eliminate (D) because you know that the coefficient of the x^4 term must be positive, because the function opens upward. Finally, you can eliminate (E) because that function has a y-intercept of 6, but the graphed function has a y-intercept of 0.

25. The correct answer is (E). To determine how many residents were 30 years or older in 2014 in Griston County, you must read the scatterplot, which tells you the percentage of residents aged under 30: 35%. Then you can subtract 0.35 from 1 to get the percentage of residents who were 30 years or older, and multiply it by the 2014 population: $1 - 0.35 = 0.65$, and $0.65 \times 35,602 = 23,141$.

If you chose (A), you may have thought the scatterplot's y-axis told you the percentage of residents who were 30 or older, rather than under 30.

26. The correct answer is (C). To find the distance between A and C, start by finding the coordinates of point C. Since it lies on the x-axis and the line $y = 2x - 6$, set $y = 0$ to solve for x: $0 = 2x - 6$, so $x = 3$ and point C is $(3, 0)$. From there, use the distance formula $d = \sqrt{(x_1 - x_2)^2 + (y_1 - y_2)^2}$ to see that the distance between A and C is $\sqrt{(0-3)^2 + (4-0)^2} = \sqrt{(-3)^2 + 4^2} = \sqrt{9 + 16} = \sqrt{25} = 5$.

27. The correct answer is (D). To find the average distance travelled by the three cars, you must first find the distance travelled by each car: multiply the time travelled by the speed travelled for each car. Then, you can add these and divide by 3 to find the average distance travelled: $\frac{5 \times 45 + 3 \times 70 + 4 \times 55}{3} = 218.3$ miles.

28. The correct answer is (C). Since the triangle's side lengths are consecutive integers that add to 39, you can write them as x, $x + 1$, and $x + 2$. If you set $x + x + 1 + x + 2 = 39$, you can solve to find $x = 12$, and therefore the side lengths must be 12, 13, and 14. To find the angle between the sides of length 12 and 13, you can use the cosine law:

$$14^2 = 12^2 + 13^2 - 2(12)(13) \cos \theta$$
$$196 = 313 - 312 \cos \theta$$
$$\cos \theta = 0.375$$
$$\theta = 68°$$

29. The correct answer is (E). Recall that $\ln ab = \ln a + \ln b$, and rewrite the equation given in the question as $\ln 2a = \ln 2 + \ln a$. Since $\ln a = b$, this is equal to $b + \ln 2$.

30. The correct answer is (B). You might want to draw a diagram to help visualize the scenario, or just imagine what it would look like.

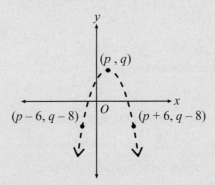

You know that the point $(p - 6, q - 8)$ will be down and to the left of the vertex of the parabola. This means that the parabola must open downwards. Since you know all parabolas are symmetrical around the vertical line that runs through their vertex, you know that each point on the parabola has a twin point on the opposite side of the line of symmetry. So, if one point lies 6 units to the left of the line of symmetry, another point must lie 6 to the right at the same y-value. So, $(p + 6, q - 8)$ is another point on the parabola.

31. The correct answer is (C). You know that $f(x) = g(x)$ when $f(x) - g(x) = 0$, which is the same as writing $(f - g)(x) = 0$. You need to find a value of x for which $(f - g)(x) = 0$, which means $2x^2 + 5x - 7 = 0$. Factor this expression to get $(2x + 7)(x - 1) = 0$, so the two solutions for x are $x = 1$ and $x = -\frac{7}{2}$. Of these, only $x = 1$ is an answer option.

32. The correct answer is (D). Since $\csc x = \frac{1}{\sin x}$, $\csc x$ is negative at any x-value where $\sin x$ is negative, so it is not always positive.

(A) is incorrect; $\csc x$ is never equal to 0 because there is no value of $\sin x$ that you could divide 1 by to get 0. (B) is incorrect; the period of $\csc x$ is 2π, the same as the period of $\sin x$. (C) is incorrect; $\csc x$ is an odd function because $\sin x$ is an odd function, and so $\csc x = -\csc (-x)$ for all values of x where $\csc x$ exists. (E) is incorrect; the asymptotes of $\csc x$ lie where $\sin x = 0$, which is at the x-intercepts of $\sin x$.

33. The correct answer is (A). If a geometric series has a common ratio of r, where $|r| < 1$, and an initial value of a, the formula for its sum is $\frac{a}{1-r}$. In this case, $a = 1$ and the sum is equal to 1.5, so $1.5 = \frac{1}{1-r}$. Taking the reciprocal of both sides gives you $\frac{2}{3} = 1 - r$, so $r = \frac{1}{3}$.

34. The correct answer is (D). Since $g(x)$ is a polynomial and $g(x) = g(-x)$, you know g is an even function and therefore must have an even degree. If $f(x)$ had an odd degree, then $\frac{f(x)}{x^{\frac{n}{2}}}$ would not be a polynomial, since the term with the highest exponent would have an exponent of $\frac{n}{2}$, which is not an integer since n is odd. Therefore, $f(x)$ and $g(x)$ must both have even degrees.

35. The correct answer is (C). This is an identity that you can memorize. If you haven't memorized it, you can think about the graphs of $\sin\theta$ and $\cos\theta$. The graphs are the same, except that the graph of $\cos\theta$ is shifted to the left by $\frac{\pi}{2}$. Therefore, you know that $\sin\theta = \cos\left(\theta - \frac{\pi}{2}\right)$.

Alternatively, you can plug in some values for each of the answer options and find that (C) is the only one which is always true, but this would be more time-consuming.

36. The correct answer is (C). You know that the expression under a square root can never be negative, so $5x - 4 \geq 0$. However, in this case, if $5x - 4 = 0$, the denominator of the function would be equal to 0, which is undefined. Therefore, you know that $5x - 4 > 0$. You can solve this inequality to get $x > \frac{4}{5}$. Therefore, the domain of the function consists of all real numbers x such that $x > \frac{4}{5}$, which is option (C).

If you chose (E), you may not have realized that the expression under the square root could not equal 0 because it is in the denominator.

37. The correct answer is (B). Because this is a piecewise function, you have to look at each piece of it and see how many times the function is equal to 9 on that domain. In the first piece, $f(x) = -x^2 - 4x + 5$. If you set $-x^2 - 4x + 5 = 9$, you can factor it to get $(x + 2)^2 = 0$, so $x = -2$. However, $x = -2$ is not included in the domain $x < -2$, so the function is never equal to 9 in this piece. In the second piece, $f(x) = 2x + 2$. If you set $2x + 2 = 9$, you can solve to find $x = \frac{7}{2}$, which is included in this domain. So far you have found one point at which the function is equal to 9. Finally, in the third piece, $f(x) = \frac{72}{x}$. If you set $\frac{72}{x} = 9$, you can solve to find $x = 8$. However, $x = 8$ is not included in the domain $x > 8$, so the function is never equal to 9 on the domain $x > 8$. Therefore, the only x-value at which $f(x) = 9$ is $x = \frac{7}{2}$.

38. The correct answer is (E). The period of $\sin x$ is 2π and the period of $\sin\frac{2x}{3}$ is $\frac{2\pi}{\frac{2}{3}} = 3\pi$. This means that the period of the sum of the functions will be 6π, since 6π is divisible by both 2π and 3π, and so the function will repeat itself every time x increases by 6π. You could also have graphed the function and found the period visually.

39. The correct answer is (C). If $f(x) = x^2 + 1$, for example, then $f(f(x)) > 0$ for every value of x, simply because $f(x)$ is always positive.

   In general, any function whose range is all real numbers will not satisfy the property in the question, because it will be negative for some value of x. This includes linear, cubic, and cube root functions.

40. The correct answer is (E). You know the remainder when the number n is divided by 15 will be some number k, where $0 \le k \le 14$. That means you can write the number n as $n = 15a + k$, where a is some other positive integer. When you divide n (or $15a + k$) by 3, you know you get a remainder of 2. $15a$ is evenly divisible by 3, because it is a multiple of 15, so dividing k by 3 must also leave a remainder of 2. For the same reason, you know that k must leave a remainder of 3 when divided by 5. The only integer between 0 and 14 that leaves these remainders is 8, so you know $k = 8$.

   Instead, you could simply try out some numbers. For example, you could notice that 23 leaves a remainder of 2 when divided by 3, and 3 when divided by 5. You can then check and see that it leaves a remainder of 8 when divided by 15, so 8 must be correct.

41. The correct answer is (C). If $y(t)$ represents the amount of Fermium-257 remaining after t days, and a represents the initial amount of Fermium-257, then $y(t) = a \times 0.9931^t$, since decaying at a rate of 0.69% per day is equivalent to 99.31% of the sample remaining per day. Since you are trying to find the value of t when $y(t) = \frac{1}{2}a$, set $y(t) = \frac{1}{2}a$ and divide both sides by a to get $\frac{1}{2} = 0.9931^t$. Take the logarithm (to any base!) of both sides to get $\log \frac{1}{2} = \log(0.9931^t) = t \log 0.9931$ by log laws. Solving for t gives you $t = \dfrac{\log 0.5}{\log 0.9931}$.

42. The correct answer is (C). Because you are not given $f(x)$ but only $f(g(x))$, where $g(x) = x^2 - 1$, you must write x in a form that looks like $g(x)$ to find what $f(x)$ is. Let $x = a^2 - 1$. Therefore, $f(x) = f(a^2 - 1) = 1 - \dfrac{1}{a^2}$. Now you can solve your original let-statement for a^2: if $x = a^2 - 1$, then $a^2 = x + 1$. Substitute this into the first equation you derived: $f(x) = 1 - \dfrac{1}{a^2} = 1 - \dfrac{1}{(\sqrt{x+1})^2}$. Finally, find a common denominator to simplify this expression:

$$f(x) = 1 - \frac{1}{(\sqrt{x+1})^2}$$

$$f(x) = 1 - \frac{1}{x+1}$$

$$f(x) = \frac{(x+1) - 1}{x+1} = \frac{x}{x+1}$$

   Alternatively, you could plug the expression for $g(x)$ into the answer options, but this would be time consuming

43. The correct answer is (B). Whenever a circle contains an inscribed angle and a central angle (an angle at the circle's center) that have the same endpoints, the central angle is twice the measure of the inscribed angle. Therefore, since the central angle in this figure is 90°, the angle at the top of the larger triangle is $\frac{90°}{2} = 45°$. Since this triangle is isosceles, each of its other angles measures $\frac{180° - 45°}{2} = 67.5°$. To find the angle marked θ, subtract the measure of the angle in the smaller triangle. Since that triangle is also isosceles and right-angled, each of its other two angles measures 45°. Therefore, $\theta = 67.5° - 45° = 22.5°$.

44. The correct answer is (C). Substitute $x = 2z$ into the first equation to get $(2z)^2 = z^3$, so $4z^2 = z^3$, and $z = 4$. Since $x = 2z$, $x = 8$. Now, substitute $z = 4$ into the second equation to get $4(4^2) = y^6$, or $64 = y^6$, so $y = 2$. Therefore, $x + y + z = 4 + 2 + 8 = 14$.

45. The correct answer is (C). The surface area of a sphere is $A = 4\pi r^2$, and the volume of a sphere is $V = \frac{4}{3}\pi r^3$. The fastest way to solve problems about the relations between measures, areas, and volumes is to know the relations or "proportionalities" between the variables. For spheres, surface area is directly proportional to the square of the radius ($A \propto r^2$ or $\sqrt{A} \propto r$). If the surface area decreases by 30%, that means the new surface area is 70% of the original area, or $0.7A$, and the new radius is $\sqrt{0.7}\,r = 0.837r$. Similarly, for spheres, the volume is directly proportional to the cube of the radius ($V \propto r^3$ or $\sqrt[3]{V} \propto r$). If the new radius is $0.837r$, then the new volume is $(0.837)^3\,V \cong 0.59V$. If the new volume is 59% of the original volume, that means the volume of the sphere has decreased by $1 - 0.59 = 0.41$, or 41%.

If you chose (A) or (B), you may have simply cubed 30% or 70%. If you chose (D), you may have stopped after finding what percent of the original volume the new volume was, rather than by what percent the original volume had decreased. If you chose (E), you may have stopped after finding the new radius.

46. The correct answer is (D). Start by dividing both sides of the ellipse equation by 25 to get $\frac{x^2}{1,225} + \frac{y^2}{400} = 1$. This means that the length of the semimajor axis (in this case, half the horizontal axis) is $\sqrt{1,225} = 35$ and the length of the semiminor axis (in this case, half the vertical axis) is $\sqrt{400} = 20$.

If you don't know how to turn ellipse equations into parametric equations off the top of your head, you can notice that since the maximum value of $\sin t$ is 1 (and the maximum value of $\cos t$ is also 1), then if $x(t) = 35 \cos t$, the maximum value of x that will satisfy this equation will be $x = 35$ (which will occur at any value of t for which $\cos t = 1$). This aligns with the shape that the ellipse has, since its rightmost point will be at $(35, 0)$. Similarly, this equation will produce the leftmost point $(-35, 0)$ for any value of t when $\cos t = -1$. With the equation $y(t) = 20 \sin t$, the greatest and least values of y will be produced when $\sin t = 1$ and $\sin t = -1$, and they will be $y = 20$ and $y = -20$. These values also align with the topmost and bottommost points on the ellipse, which are at $(0, 20)$ and $(0, -20)$.

47. The correct answer is (A). To multiply two matrices together, the horizontal dimension of the first one must equal the vertical dimension of the second one. When the two matrices are identical, as in this question (since $X^2 = X \times X$), this means that the matrix must have the same size for its vertical dimension as its horizontal dimension: in other words, it must be square. The only square matrix among the answer options is (A).

48. The correct answer is (D). Since there are 7 team members who can run the 1 km race, and you need to choose 4 of them to do it, there are $\binom{7}{4} = \dfrac{7!}{4!(7-4)!} = 35$ ways to create a team. The three non-chosen members must then be assigned to run the 5 km race. Of the 7 team members who can run the 10 km race, again, there are 35 ways to choose 4 of them for that race. The remaining 3 of them must then run the 5 km race. Therefore, since there are 35 ways to assign the 1 km-or-5 km runners, and 35 ways to assign the 5 km-and-10 km runners, there are $35 \times 35 = 1{,}225$ total ways to assign all the runners.

If you picked (A), you just found the number of ways to assign one of the groups of 7 runners.

49. The correct answer is (E). Substitute $\cos^2 x = 1 - \sin^2 x$ in the original equation to get $\sin^2 x\,(1 - \sin^2 x) = \dfrac{1}{4}$, and so $\sin^2 x - \sin^4 x = \dfrac{1}{4}$. Replace $\sin^2 x$ with a, multiply the equation by 4 to get the quadratic equation $4a^2 - 4a + 1 = 0$, and factor it to get $(2a - 1)^2 = 0$. The solution to this is $a = \dfrac{1}{2}$; therefore, $\sin^2 x = \dfrac{1}{2}$, so $\sin x = \dfrac{1}{\sqrt{2}}$ or $-\dfrac{1}{\sqrt{2}}$. When $\sin x = \dfrac{1}{\sqrt{2}}$ or $-\dfrac{1}{\sqrt{2}}$, $\cos x$ must also equal either $\dfrac{1}{\sqrt{2}}$ or $-\dfrac{1}{\sqrt{2}}$ because of the identity $\sin^2 x + \cos^2 x = 1$. Therefore, the possibilities for $\sin x + \cos x$ are either $\dfrac{1}{\sqrt{2}} + \dfrac{1}{\sqrt{2}} = \sqrt{2}$, $\dfrac{1}{\sqrt{2}} + \dfrac{-1}{\sqrt{2}} = 0$, or $\dfrac{-1}{\sqrt{2}} + \dfrac{-1}{\sqrt{2}} = -\sqrt{2}$. Of these, only $\sqrt{2}$ is an answer choice.

Instead, you could have taken the square root of both sides of the equation to get either $\sin x\,\cos x = \dfrac{1}{2}$ or $\sin x \cos x = -\dfrac{1}{2}$. In the case where $\sin x\,\cos x = \dfrac{1}{2}$, you can multiply both sides by 2 to get $2 \sin x\,\cos x = 1$. Because of the identity $2 \sin x \cos x = \sin 2x$, you know that $\sin 2x = 1$. Since $\sin \dfrac{\pi}{2} = 1$, then $x = \dfrac{\pi}{4}$ is a solution to the original equation. In this case, $\sin \dfrac{\pi}{4} + \cos \dfrac{\pi}{4} = \dfrac{1}{\sqrt{2}} + \dfrac{1}{\sqrt{2}} = \sqrt{2}$.

This is a faster way to find one possible solution, but it is not as thorough as the method explained first.

50. The correct answer is (E). Given a hyperbola of the form $\dfrac{(x-h)^2}{a^2} - \dfrac{(y-k)^2}{b^2} = 1$, where the transverse axis is horizontal, the asymptotes are defined by $y = \pm \dfrac{b}{a}(x-h) + k$. Since the given hyperbola is already in standard form, pull out each constant and plug them into the formula to get $h = 2$, $k = 1$, $a = 2$, and $b = 8$. So, the asymptotes are at $y = 4(x-2) + 1 = 4x - 7$ and $y = -4(x-2) + 1 = -4x + 9$.

Practice Test 6

YOUR NAME (PRINT): _____

LAST   FIRST   MI

| Correct ● | Incorrect ⊘ ⊗ ⊘ ◓ ✪ ○ ⊜ ✸ | **Make sure you use a No. 2 pencil.** Each answer must be marked in the corresponding row on the answer sheet. Each bubble must be filled in completely and darkly within the lines. Extra marks on your answer sheet may be marked as incorrect answers and lower your score. |

○ Literature   ○ Mathematics Level 1   ○ German
○ Biology E   ○ Mathematics Level 2   ○ Italian
○ Biology M   ○ U.S. History   ○ Latin
○ Chemistry   ○ World History   ○ Modern Hebrew
○ Physics   ○ French   ○ Spanish

1 Ⓐ Ⓑ Ⓒ Ⓓ Ⓔ   21 Ⓐ Ⓑ Ⓒ Ⓓ Ⓔ   41 Ⓐ Ⓑ Ⓒ Ⓓ Ⓔ   61 Ⓐ Ⓑ Ⓒ Ⓓ Ⓔ   81 Ⓐ Ⓑ Ⓒ Ⓓ Ⓔ
2 Ⓐ Ⓑ Ⓒ Ⓓ Ⓔ   22 Ⓐ Ⓑ Ⓒ Ⓓ Ⓔ   42 Ⓐ Ⓑ Ⓒ Ⓓ Ⓔ   62 Ⓐ Ⓑ Ⓒ Ⓓ Ⓔ   82 Ⓐ Ⓑ Ⓒ Ⓓ Ⓔ
3 Ⓐ Ⓑ Ⓒ Ⓓ Ⓔ   23 Ⓐ Ⓑ Ⓒ Ⓓ Ⓔ   43 Ⓐ Ⓑ Ⓒ Ⓓ Ⓔ   63 Ⓐ Ⓑ Ⓒ Ⓓ Ⓔ   83 Ⓐ Ⓑ Ⓒ Ⓓ Ⓔ
4 Ⓐ Ⓑ Ⓒ Ⓓ Ⓔ   24 Ⓐ Ⓑ Ⓒ Ⓓ Ⓔ   44 Ⓐ Ⓑ Ⓒ Ⓓ Ⓔ   64 Ⓐ Ⓑ Ⓒ Ⓓ Ⓔ   84 Ⓐ Ⓑ Ⓒ Ⓓ Ⓔ
5 Ⓐ Ⓑ Ⓒ Ⓓ Ⓔ   25 Ⓐ Ⓑ Ⓒ Ⓓ Ⓔ   45 Ⓐ Ⓑ Ⓒ Ⓓ Ⓔ   65 Ⓐ Ⓑ Ⓒ Ⓓ Ⓔ   85 Ⓐ Ⓑ Ⓒ Ⓓ Ⓔ
6 Ⓐ Ⓑ Ⓒ Ⓓ Ⓔ   26 Ⓐ Ⓑ Ⓒ Ⓓ Ⓔ   46 Ⓐ Ⓑ Ⓒ Ⓓ Ⓔ   66 Ⓐ Ⓑ Ⓒ Ⓓ Ⓔ   86 Ⓐ Ⓑ Ⓒ Ⓓ Ⓔ
7 Ⓐ Ⓑ Ⓒ Ⓓ Ⓔ   27 Ⓐ Ⓑ Ⓒ Ⓓ Ⓔ   47 Ⓐ Ⓑ Ⓒ Ⓓ Ⓔ   67 Ⓐ Ⓑ Ⓒ Ⓓ Ⓔ   87 Ⓐ Ⓑ Ⓒ Ⓓ Ⓔ
8 Ⓐ Ⓑ Ⓒ Ⓓ Ⓔ   28 Ⓐ Ⓑ Ⓒ Ⓓ Ⓔ   48 Ⓐ Ⓑ Ⓒ Ⓓ Ⓔ   68 Ⓐ Ⓑ Ⓒ Ⓓ Ⓔ   88 Ⓐ Ⓑ Ⓒ Ⓓ Ⓔ
9 Ⓐ Ⓑ Ⓒ Ⓓ Ⓔ   29 Ⓐ Ⓑ Ⓒ Ⓓ Ⓔ   49 Ⓐ Ⓑ Ⓒ Ⓓ Ⓔ   69 Ⓐ Ⓑ Ⓒ Ⓓ Ⓔ   89 Ⓐ Ⓑ Ⓒ Ⓓ Ⓔ
10 Ⓐ Ⓑ Ⓒ Ⓓ Ⓔ   30 Ⓐ Ⓑ Ⓒ Ⓓ Ⓔ   50 Ⓐ Ⓑ Ⓒ Ⓓ Ⓔ   70 Ⓐ Ⓑ Ⓒ Ⓓ Ⓔ   90 Ⓐ Ⓑ Ⓒ Ⓓ Ⓔ
11 Ⓐ Ⓑ Ⓒ Ⓓ Ⓔ   31 Ⓐ Ⓑ Ⓒ Ⓓ Ⓔ   51 Ⓐ Ⓑ Ⓒ Ⓓ Ⓔ   71 Ⓐ Ⓑ Ⓒ Ⓓ Ⓔ   81 Ⓐ Ⓑ Ⓒ Ⓓ Ⓔ
12 Ⓐ Ⓑ Ⓒ Ⓓ Ⓔ   32 Ⓐ Ⓑ Ⓒ Ⓓ Ⓔ   52 Ⓐ Ⓑ Ⓒ Ⓓ Ⓔ   72 Ⓐ Ⓑ Ⓒ Ⓓ Ⓔ   92 Ⓐ Ⓑ Ⓒ Ⓓ Ⓔ
13 Ⓐ Ⓑ Ⓒ Ⓓ Ⓔ   33 Ⓐ Ⓑ Ⓒ Ⓓ Ⓔ   53 Ⓐ Ⓑ Ⓒ Ⓓ Ⓔ   73 Ⓐ Ⓑ Ⓒ Ⓓ Ⓔ   93 Ⓐ Ⓑ Ⓒ Ⓓ Ⓔ
14 Ⓐ Ⓑ Ⓒ Ⓓ Ⓔ   34 Ⓐ Ⓑ Ⓒ Ⓓ Ⓔ   54 Ⓐ Ⓑ Ⓒ Ⓓ Ⓔ   74 Ⓐ Ⓑ Ⓒ Ⓓ Ⓔ   94 Ⓐ Ⓑ Ⓒ Ⓓ Ⓔ
15 Ⓐ Ⓑ Ⓒ Ⓓ Ⓔ   35 Ⓐ Ⓑ Ⓒ Ⓓ Ⓔ   55 Ⓐ Ⓑ Ⓒ Ⓓ Ⓔ   75 Ⓐ Ⓑ Ⓒ Ⓓ Ⓔ   95 Ⓐ Ⓑ Ⓒ Ⓓ Ⓔ
16 Ⓐ Ⓑ Ⓒ Ⓓ Ⓔ   36 Ⓐ Ⓑ Ⓒ Ⓓ Ⓔ   56 Ⓐ Ⓑ Ⓒ Ⓓ Ⓔ   76 Ⓐ Ⓑ Ⓒ Ⓓ Ⓔ   96 Ⓐ Ⓑ Ⓒ Ⓓ Ⓔ
17 Ⓐ Ⓑ Ⓒ Ⓓ Ⓔ   37 Ⓐ Ⓑ Ⓒ Ⓓ Ⓔ   57 Ⓐ Ⓑ Ⓒ Ⓓ Ⓔ   77 Ⓐ Ⓑ Ⓒ Ⓓ Ⓔ   97 Ⓐ Ⓑ Ⓒ Ⓓ Ⓔ
18 Ⓐ Ⓑ Ⓒ Ⓓ Ⓔ   38 Ⓐ Ⓑ Ⓒ Ⓓ Ⓔ   58 Ⓐ Ⓑ Ⓒ Ⓓ Ⓔ   78 Ⓐ Ⓑ Ⓒ Ⓓ Ⓔ   98 Ⓐ Ⓑ Ⓒ Ⓓ Ⓔ
19 Ⓐ Ⓑ Ⓒ Ⓓ Ⓔ   39 Ⓐ Ⓑ Ⓒ Ⓓ Ⓔ   59 Ⓐ Ⓑ Ⓒ Ⓓ Ⓔ   79 Ⓐ Ⓑ Ⓒ Ⓓ Ⓔ   99 Ⓐ Ⓑ Ⓒ Ⓓ Ⓔ
20 Ⓐ Ⓑ Ⓒ Ⓓ Ⓔ   40 Ⓐ Ⓑ Ⓒ Ⓓ Ⓔ   60 Ⓐ Ⓑ Ⓒ Ⓓ Ⓔ   80 Ⓐ Ⓑ Ⓒ Ⓓ Ⓔ   100 Ⓐ Ⓑ Ⓒ Ⓓ Ⓔ

For automatic scoring and scaling, please visit **cloud.ivyglobal.com**.

SAT Math Level 2 Subject Test

Reference Materials

THE FORMULAS BELOW MAY BE USEFUL IN ANSWERING QUESTIONS ON THIS TEST.

$S = 4\pi r^2$ is the formula for the surface area of a sphere with a radius of r.

$V = \frac{1}{3}\pi r^2 h$ is the formula for the volume of a right circular cone with a radius of r and a height of h.

$V = \frac{4}{3}\pi r^3$ is the formula for the volume of a sphere with a radius of r.

$V = \frac{1}{3}Bh$ is the formula for the volume of a pyramid with a base area of B and a height of h.

When choosing an answer, find the CLOSEST answer possible. If the precise numerical value that you have found is not an answer choice, select the choice that is closest to your answer. Use the answer sheet and fill in the bubble corresponding to your choice.

Notes: (1) You ARE permitted the use of a graphing or scientific calculator, which you may use at your own discretion. You will also have to choose between degree or radian mode for some questions, so keep track of what mode your calculator is in.

(2) You may assume that figures are drawn as accurately as possible UNLESS it is explicitly stated that a figure is not drawn to scale. Furthermore, all figures are in a plane UNLESS it is stated otherwise.

(3) For any function f, unless otherwise specified, you may assume that a real number x is in the domain of f if and only if $f(x)$ is a real number. The range of f consists of all and only those real numbers of the form $f(x)$, where x is in the domain of f.

(4) Four formulas are provided in the box above for your reference.

GO ON TO THE NEXT PAGE

USE THIS SPACE FOR SCRATCH WORK.

1. If $y = 0.48x + 0.74^x$, then what is the value of y when $x = 4.3$?

(A) 0.75

(B) 1.79

(C) 2.34

(D) 3.39

(E) 5.01

2. What is the y-intercept of a line with an x-intercept at $x = -2$ and a slope of $\frac{5}{4}$?

(A) $\frac{5}{4}$

(B) $\frac{5}{2}$

(C) $\frac{4}{5}$

(D) $\frac{2}{5}$

(E) 2

GO ON TO THE NEXT PAGE

$$y = \frac{1}{2}x + 3$$

3. The line of best fit above above most closely approximates the data in which of the following scatterplots?

(A)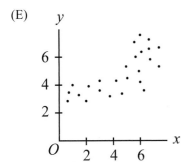

(B)

(C)

(D)

(E)

4. If $f(x) = 3x + 5$ and $g(x) = -x - 1$, what is $f(g(g(7)))$?

(A) −27

(B) −8

(C)   7

(D) 26

(E) 27

GO ON TO THE NEXT PAGE

USE THIS SPACE FOR SCRATCH WORK.

5. Four jars are arranged so that each jar is 1.5 times the volume of the previous one. If the smallest jar has a volume of 4 L, what is the volume of the largest jar?

    (A)   6.00 L
    (B)   8.50 L
    (C)   9.00 L
    (D) 13.50 L
    (E) 20.25 L

6. $m^p + 2m^p + 3m^{pq} =$

    (A) $3m^{pq}$
    (B) $3m^{2p} + 3m^{pq}$
    (C) $3m^{p+q}$
    (D) $3(m^p + m^q)$
    (E) $3(m^p + m^{pq})$

Note: Figure not drawn to scale.

7. A rope runs from the corner of the sail of a ship along its base and up the mast to the top of the sail, as shown in the figure above. If the shortest edge of the sail measures 5 feet and the longest edge of the sail measures 13 feet, how long is the rope?

    (A) 12 feet
    (B) 13 feet
    (C) 17 feet
    (D) 18 feet
    (E) 25 feet

GO ON TO THE NEXT PAGE

8. A plane is described by the equation $2x + 3y + 4z = 6$. Which of the following points is found on the plane?

    (A) $(0, 0, 0)$
    (B) $(1, 0, 1)$
    (C) $(0, 2, 1)$
    (D) $(3, 0, 2)$
    (E) $(3, 2, 0)$

9. Eight honeybees approach a hive. In how many different orders can they enter?

    (A) 8
    (B) 64
    (C) 256
    (D) 40,320
    (E) 16,777,216

10. An ant is standing on a coordinate plane at $(5, 5)$. If the ant walks to pick up food at $(2, 9)$ and then carries it back to the anthill at $(0, 0)$, how far does the ant walk in total?

    (A)   5.00
    (B)   7.07
    (C)   9.22
    (D) 14.22
    (E) 21.29

GO ON TO THE NEXT PAGE

$$P = \frac{150}{V^2}, V > 0$$

USE THIS SPACE FOR SCRATCH WORK.

11. The pressure of a compressed gas, P, is related to its volume, V, according to the equation above. Which of the following graphs models this relationship?

(A)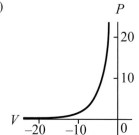

(B)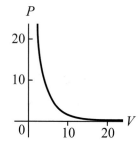

(C)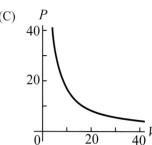

(D)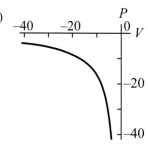

(E)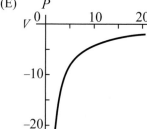

12. If the base of an isosceles triangle has length 40 and its two legs each have length 20.309, then its two congruent angles each measure

(A)   1.0°
(B)   10.0°
(C)   44.6°
(D)   59.9°
(E)   80.0°

GO ON TO THE NEXT PAGE

USE THIS SPACE FOR SCRATCH WORK.

13. Vector $\mathbf{u} = \langle -3,5 \rangle$, $\mathbf{v} = \langle 0,7 \rangle$, and $\mathbf{w} = \langle 8,-2 \rangle$.
    What is $2\mathbf{v} - (\mathbf{w} + 3\mathbf{u})$?

    (A) $\langle 1,1 \rangle$
    (B) $\langle 1,-3 \rangle$
    (C) $\langle -17,1 \rangle$
    (D) $\langle -17,-3 \rangle$
    (E) $\langle -5,11 \rangle$

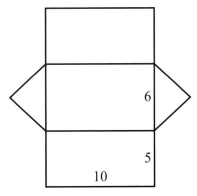

Note: Figure not drawn to scale.

14. The net for a triangular solid is shown in the figure above. When the solid is formed, what is its surface area?

    (A) 160
    (B) 174
    (C) 184
    (D) 204
    (E) 208

15. If $x = \cos^2 29°$ and $y = \sin^2 29°$, then $\dfrac{x^2 - y^2}{x - y} =$

    (A) 0.245
    (B) 0.530
    (C) 0.640
    (D) 0.765
    (E) 1.000

GO ON TO THE NEXT PAGE

USE THIS SPACE FOR SCRATCH WORK.

16. The length, width, and height of a rectangular prism are consecutive integers that add to 12. What is the greatest linear distance between two points on the surface of the prism?

(A)   5.20
(B)   6.93
(C)   7.07
(D)   8.66
(E)   28.78

17. $(3 + 2i)(2 - 5i) =$

(A) -15
(B) 5
(C) $-4 - 11i$
(D) $16 - 11i$
(E) $6 - 21i$

Stem	Leaf
0	1, 1, 2, 2, 3, 4, 4, 5
1	1, 2, 4, 5, 5
2	0, 1, 2, 3, 6, 7
3	3, 4, 5, 5, 8, 9
4	0, 0, 1, 4, 5
5	2, 6, 7, 7
6	1, 2, 4, 4, 4
7	3

Note: 1 | 1 represents 11.

18. The stem-and-leaf plot above shows the ages of family members at a 40-person family reunion. Which of the following statements is true about the mean, median, and mode of the ages of the family members?

(A)   mean > median > mode
(B)   mean > mode > median
(C)   median > mean > mode
(D)   mode > median > mean
(E)   mode > mean > median

GO ON TO THE NEXT PAGE

19. The first round of a data-collection survey records the exact ages of 50 individuals aged 30 to 39. The second round records the exact ages of 25 individuals aged 20 to 29 and 25 individuals aged 40 to 49. Which of the following can be inferred about the collected data?

I. The standard deviation of the data after the first round is less than the standard deviation of the data after the second round.
II. The median of the data after the first round is equal to the median of the data after the second round.
III. The mean of the data after the first round is equal to the mean of the data after the second round.

(A) I only
(B) III only
(C) I and II only
(D) II and III only
(E) I, II, and III

USE THIS SPACE FOR SCRATCH WORK.

20. If θ is in the interval $[-2\pi, 2\pi]$, for how many values of θ is $\sin\theta = 0.321$?

(A) 0
(B) 2
(C) 4
(D) 5
(E) 8

21. The graph of function f has one line of symmetry and a range $\{y \in \mathbb{R} : y \leq 1\}$. Function f could be

(A) linear
(B) quadratic
(C) cubic
(D) exponential
(E) logarithmic

GO ON TO THE NEXT PAGE

USE THIS SPACE FOR SCRATCH WORK.

22. If the function $f(x) = x - b$ is translated 10 units down, which results in the function $g(x) = x - 6b$, what is $f(1)$?

(A) -1

(B) $-\dfrac{2}{3}$

(C) 1

(D) $\dfrac{8}{3}$

(E) 3

23. Which of the following rational functions has a horizontal asymptote at $y = \dfrac{10}{3}$, a vertical asymptote at $x = 5$, and an x-intercept at $x = 0$?

(A) $y = \dfrac{x - 5}{3x - 10}$

(B) $y = \dfrac{3x - 5}{10x}$

(C) $y = \dfrac{5x}{3x - 10}$

(D) $y = \dfrac{10x}{3x - 15}$

(E) $y = \dfrac{10x - 50}{3x}$

24. Which of the following sets contain(s) a maximum element?

I. The set of negative rational numbers
II. The set of positive rational numbers
III. The set of rational numbers r such that $r^3 \leq 8$

(A) None
(B) I only
(C) III only
(D) I and II only
(E) I and III only

GO ON TO THE NEXT PAGE

USE THIS SPACE FOR SCRATCH WORK.

25. If $f(x) = 5x + 3$, then $f(1) - f^{-1}(1) =$

    (A) −7.6
    (B)   0.0
    (C)   7.6
    (D)   8.4
    (E) 20.0

26. A triangle has angles measuring 41°, 53°, and 86°. If the two shortest sides of the triangle are 2.3 and 2.8 cm long, how long is the triangle's longest side?

    (A) 2.9 cm
    (B) 3.5 cm
    (C) 4.3 cm
    (D) 4.5 cm
    (E) 4.8 cm

27. Which of the following is true about the graph of the function $f(x) = \dfrac{x^3 - 5}{2x^2 + 8}$?

    (A) It has at least one vertical asymptote.
    (B) It has at least one horizontal asymptote.
    (C) It has at least one removable discontinuity.
    (D) It has a root at $x = -2$.
    (E) It has a negative y-intercept.

28. If $x_n = 1 + (-1)^n \, 2n$, where n is a positive integer, which of the following statements is true?

    (A) For all n, x_n is an odd integer.
    (B) For all n, x_n is an even integer.
    (C) x_n alternates between being odd and even.
    (D) As n increases, x_n always increases.
    (E) As n increases, x_n always decreases.

GO ON TO THE NEXT PAGE

USE THIS SPACE FOR SCRATCH WORK.

29. To make a molecule of carbon dioxide, two oxygen atoms bond with one carbon atom. In a certain experiment, many carbon and oxygen atoms combine to make carbon dioxide molecules, using up all of the oxygen atoms but leaving some carbon atoms left over. If c represents the starting number of carbon atoms, and x represents the starting number of oxygen atoms, which of the following inequalities must be true?

(A) $x < 2c$

(B) $2x < c$

(C) $c < 2x$

(D) $2c < x$

(E) $c < x$

30. If $f(x) = a(x - h)^2 + 1$, which of the following values of a and h satisfy $f(1) < 1$?

(A) $a = -1, h = 1$

(B) $a = -1, h = 0$

(C) $a = 1, h = 1$

(D) $a = 1, h = -1$

(E) $a = 1, h = 0$

31. The function $c(t) = 54e^{-0.24t}$ models the value, c, of a cryptocurrency t years after the introduction of the cryptocurrency. In how many years after the introduction of the cryptocurrency will the value of the cryptocurrency halve?

(A) 1.64

(B) 2.89

(C) 3.28

(D) 6.87

(E) The value of the cryptocurrency will never halve.

32. If $y = x^4 - 81$, what is $\dfrac{y}{x - 3}$?

(A) $x^3 + 3x^2 + 9x + 27$

(B) $x^3 - 3x^2 + 9x - 27$

(C) $x^3 + 3x^2 - 9x - 27$

(D) $x^3 - 3x^2 - 9x - 27$

(E) $x^3 + 27$

GO ON TO THE NEXT PAGE

USE THIS SPACE FOR SCRATCH WORK.

33. Let a, b, x, and y represent real numbers greater than 1. If $a\log_b y = x$, which of the following must be true?

(A) $b^y = x^a$

(B) $b^x = y^a$

(C) $b^{ax} = y$

(D) $b^{a+x} = y$

(E) $ab^x = y$

$$f(x) = \begin{cases} x^2 + 3x, & x \le 2 \\ 7x - 9, & x > 2 \end{cases}$$

$$g(x) = \begin{cases} 1 + 2^x, & x \le 3 \\ \sqrt{x-1}, & x > 3 \end{cases}$$

34. The functions f and g are defined above. What is the value of $f(g(5))$?

(A)   5

(B)   10

(C)   222

(D)   754

(E) 1,188

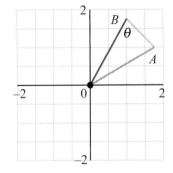

35. In the diagram above, $A = (2, 30°)$ and $B = (2, 60°)$ in polar coordinates. What is the measure of angle θ?

(A) 30°

(B) 45°

(C) 60°

(D) 75°

(E) 90°

GO ON TO THE NEXT PAGE

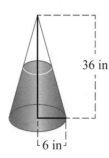

36 in

6 in

Note: Figure not drawn to scale.

36. In the figure shown above, what is the volume of the shaded region if it is $\frac{2}{3}$ the height of the entire cone?

(A)　　50 in³
(B)　　955 in³
(C)　1,156 in³
(D)　1,307 in³
(E)　1,357 in³

Year	Value
1987	$35.00
1995	$3.00
2005	$53.00

37. The value of a lunchbox over several years is shown in the table above. If the value of the lunchbox can be described quadratically and it reached its lowest value in 1995, what is the value of the lunchbox in 2018?

(A)　$83.00
(B)　$98.50
(C)　$143.50
(D)　$267.50
(E)　$310.00

GO ON TO THE NEXT PAGE

USE THIS SPACE FOR SCRATCH WORK.

38. Which of the following is true about the function
    $f(x) = \sqrt{(x-3)(x+5)}$?

    (A) $f(x)$ is never equal to 0.
    (B) $f(x)$ has an inverse function.
    (C) The range of $f(x)$ is $\{x: x \leq -5 \text{ or } x \geq 3\}$.
    (D) The domain of $f(x)$ is $\{x: x \leq -5 \text{ or } x \geq 3\}$.
    (E) $f(x)$ has a negative y-intercept.

39. If $\cos a + \sin a = 0.52$ and $\cos a - \sin a = 1.32$, what is $\cos 2a$?

    (A) 0.39
    (B) 0.69
    (C) 0.80
    (D) 0.84
    (E) 1.84

40. If n is any integer, and n^2 has k positive integer divisors, which of the
    following could be k?

    (A) 2
    (B) 4
    (C) 8
    (D) 9
    (E) 12

41. If $\log_b x = 2$ and the value of b is twice the value of x, then $x =$

    (A) $\frac{1}{4}$

    (B) $\frac{1}{2}$

    (C) 1

    (D) 2

    (E) 4

GO ON TO THE NEXT PAGE

USE THIS SPACE FOR SCRATCH WORK.

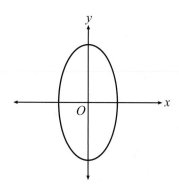

42. The relation $x^2 - ky^2 = 1$ is graphed above. Which of the following is a possible value of k ?

    (A) -2

    (B) $-\dfrac{1}{2}$

    (C) 0

    (D) $\dfrac{1}{2}$

    (E) 2

43. If $f(x) = \dfrac{3}{x-2}$ and $g(x) = \dfrac{2x}{3}$, what is the domain of $f(g(x))$?

    (A) $\left\{ x \in \mathbb{R} : x \neq \dfrac{2}{3} \right\}$

    (B) $\{ x \in \mathbb{R} : x \neq 2 \}$

    (C) $\{ x \in \mathbb{R} : x \neq 3 \}$

    (D) $\{ x \in \mathbb{R} : x \neq 2 \text{ and } x \neq 3 \}$

    (E) $\{ x \in \mathbb{R} \}$

GO ON TO THE NEXT PAGE

USE THIS SPACE FOR SCRATCH WORK.

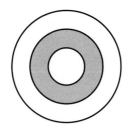

44. The target shown in the figure above consists of three concentric circles with radii of 30 cm, 20 cm, and 10 cm. If a dart is randomly thrown at the target, what is the probability that it will hit the shaded ring?

(A) 17%
(B) 25%
(C) 33%
(D) 50%
(E) 67%

$$dB = 10\log\left(\frac{I}{10^{-12}}\right)$$

45. The loudness of sound, in dB, is modeled by the equation above, where I is sound intensity in Wm^{-2}. If human ear damage occurs above 90 dB, what is the highest intensity sound a human can hear without damage?

(A) $10^{97}\ Wm^{-2}$
(B) $10^{73}\ Wm^{-2}$
(C) $10^{20}\ Wm^{-2}$
(D) $10^{8}\ Wm^{-2}$
(E) $10^{-3}\ Wm^{-2}$

GO ON TO THE NEXT PAGE

USE THIS SPACE FOR SCRATCH WORK.

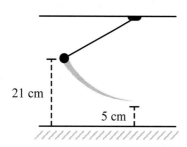

21 cm

5 cm

Note: Figure not drawn to scale.

46. A weight on the end of a pendulum starts at a height of 21 cm above a desk, as shown in the figure above. It takes 4 seconds to reach its minimum height of 5 cm before returning to a height of 21 cm. What trigonometric function models the height of the pendulum in centimeters, h, over time in seconds, t?

    (A) $h = 8 \cos t + 5$

    (B) $h = 8 \cos \dfrac{\pi}{4}t + 5$

    (C) $h = 8 \cos \dfrac{\pi}{4}t + 13$

    (D) $h = 16 \cos t + 13$

    (E) $h = 16 \cos \dfrac{\pi}{4}t + 5$

47. A circle C is described by the equation $x^2 + y^2 = 25$. What is the length of the part of the line $y = 7x - 25$ that passes through the inside of C?

    (A)   5.00
    (B)   7.07
    (C)   8.94
    (D)   9.90
    (E)   10.00

GO ON TO THE NEXT PAGE

USE THIS SPACE FOR SCRATCH WORK.

48. If a function, f, has vertical asymptotes at $x = \frac{n\pi}{3}$ for every natural number n, which of the following could be the function?

(A) $f(x) = 3\tan 2x$

(B) $f(x) = 2\tan 3x$

(C) $f(x) = \tan(2x + \frac{\pi}{3})$

(D) $f(x) = \tan(3x + \frac{\pi}{2})$

(E) $f(x) = \tan(x + \frac{\pi}{2})$

49. Triangle ABC is located on the xy-plane at points A $(-2, 0)$, B $(0, -2)$, and C $(2, 2)$. If A is shifted along a line so that the area of ABC remains constant, then the equation of the line is

(A) $x = -2$

(B) $y = -x - 2$

(C) $y = \frac{1}{2}x + 1$

(D) $y = x + 2$

(E) $y = 2x + 4$

50. A "polite number" is a number that can be written as the sum of two or more consecutive positive integers. Which of the following is NOT a polite number?

(A)   510

(B)   960

(C) 1,023

(D) 4,096

(E) 8,195

STOP

**If you complete this test before the end of your allotted time,
you may check your work.**

Answers and Scoring

Scoring Your Test
Part 1

The easiest way to score your test is to use our Cloud scoring tool. The Cloud tool also provides more detailed results by showing you how you performed on specific kinds of questions. To score your test by hand, follow the directions below.

 For more detailed scoring results, please visit **cloud.ivyglobal.com.**

Answers

1. C	11. B	21. B	31. B	41. A
2. B	12. B	22. A	32. A	42. B
3. B	13. A	23. D	33. B	43. C
4. D	14. C	24. C	34. B	44. C
5. D	15. E	25. D	35. D	45. E
6. E	16. C	26. B	36. D	46. C
7. C	17. D	27. E	37. D	47. B
8. B	18. D	28. A	38. D	48. D
9. D	19. C	29. A	39. B	49. E
10. D	20. C	30. B	40. D	50. D

Raw Scores

To score your test, first use the answer key to mark each of your responses as correct or incorrect. Don't mark or count questions you left blank. Then, calculate your raw score for each section by subtracting one fourth the number of incorrect responses from the number of correct responses. Scores should be rounded to the nearest whole number, with .5 and above rounding up. Use the tables below to help you calculate your scores:

Scores	
Number Correct	_____ −
Number incorrect	_____ / 4 = _____
Raw Score	= _____
Scaled Score	_____

Scaled Scores

Once you have found your raw score for each test, convert it into an approximate scaled test score using the following chart. To find a scaled test score for each section, find the row in the Raw Score column which corresponds to your raw score for that section, then check the column for the section you are scoring in the same row. For example, if you had a raw score of 31, your scaled score would be 580. Keep in mind that these scaled scores are estimates only. Your actual SAT Subject Test in Mathematics Level 2 score will be scaled against the scores of all other students at your grade level taking the test on your test date.

Scaled Score							
Raw Score	Scaled Score	Raw Score	Scaled Score	Raw Score	Scaled Score	Raw Score	Scaled Score
50	800	34	710	18	560	2	440
49	800	33	700	17	560	1	430
48	800	32	690	16	550	0	410
47	800	31	680	15	540	−1	390
46	800	30	670	14	530	−2	370
45	800	29	660	13	530	−3	360
44	800	28	650	12	520	−4	340
43	800	27	640	11	510	−5	340
42	790	26	630	10	500	−6	330
41	790	25	630	9	500	−7	320
40	780	24	620	8	490	−8	320
39	770	23	610	7	480	−9	320
38	750	22	600	6	480	−10	320
37	740	21	590	5	470	−11	310
36	730	20	580	4	460	−12	310
35	720	19	570	3	450		

Explanations

Part 2

1. The correct answer is (C). Plug in 4.3 wherever x appears in the equation:
$y = 0.48(4.3) + 0.74^{4.3} = 2.064 + 0.274 = 2.34$.

2. The correct answer is (B). Since you know the slope of the line, you know the equation of the line is $y = \frac{5}{4}x + b$, where b is the y-intercept. Because you also know that when $y = 0$, $x = -2$, you can plug those values in and solve for b: $0 = \frac{5}{4}(-2) + b$, so $b = \frac{5}{2}$.

3. The correct answer is (B). The given line of best fit is linear, has a positive slope of $\frac{1}{2}$, and has a y-intercept at $y = 3$. The only graph matching these three criteria is (B).

   (E) is incorrect because the data on this graph would be best approximated by an exponential curve of best fit.

4. The correct answer is (D). Although the function may look intimidating, it is straightforward if you work from the inside out. Start by evaluating $g(7)$ and then plug that into the next function:

$$g(7) = -7 - 1 = -8$$
$$g(g(7)) = g(-8) = -(-8) - 1 = 8 - 1 = 7$$
$$f(g(g(7))) = f(7) = 3(7) + 5 = 26$$

5. The correct answer is (D). Since the first jar has a volume of 4 L, the second jar will have a volume of $4 \times 1.5 = 6$ L, the third will have a volume of $6 \times 1.5 = 9$ L, and the fourth will have a volume of $9 \times 1.5 = 13.5$ L.

6. The correct answer is (E). Add the first two terms together to get $3m^p + 3m^{pq}$, and then factor out 3 to get $3(m^p + m^{pq})$.

7. The correct answer is (C). The question tells you that the rope runs along the bottom and left edges of the sail. Since the bottom edge is 5 feet long, you can use the Pythagorean Theorem to calculate the length of the vertical edge: $\sqrt{13^2 - 5^2} = \sqrt{144} = 12$ feet. Therefore, since the rope runs along the edges of length 5 and 12 feet, its total length is $5 + 12 = 17$ feet.

   If you picked (D), you may have thought that the vertical edge of the sail was 13 feet long or used the hypotenuse.

8. The correct answer is (B). The easiest way to solve this problem is to test each option to see whether plugging in the given point makes the equation true. In the case of $(1, 0, 1)$, you can see that $2(1) + 3(0) + 4(1) = 6$.

9. The correct answer is (D). There are 8 bees that could enter the hive first. After the first bee has entered, there are 7 bees that could enter the hive second, 6 that could enter third, and so on. Multiplying these numbers gives you $8 \times 7 \times 6 \times 5 \times 4 \times 3 \times 2 \times 1 = 8! = 40{,}320$.

10. The correct answer is (D). You can use the distance formula $d = \sqrt{(x_1 - x_2)^2 + (y_1 - y_2)^2}$ to determine the total distance travelled by the ant. It travels from $(5, 5)$ to $(2, 9)$ first: $d = \sqrt{(5-2)^2 + (5-9)^2} = \sqrt{25} = 5$. Then, it travels from $(2, 9)$ to $(0, 0)$: $d = \sqrt{(2-0)^2 + (9-0)^2} = \sqrt{85} \approx 9.22$. The total distance travelled by the ant is the sum of the two parts of the journey: $5 + 9.22 = 14.22$.

11. The correct answer is (B). Because $V > 0$, you can eliminate (A) and (D). You can see from the equation that P must also be positive, because V^2 is always positive, so you can also eliminate (E). To choose between (B) and (C), you can plug in a value for V, for example, $V = 10$, since it is easy to square and appears on both graphs. This gives $P = 1.5$, so answer (B) is correct because it passes through the point $(10, 1.5)$.

12. The correct answer is (B). The easiest way to solve this question is to draw the triangle and then add a vertical line dividing it into two right-angled triangles. Now, you know each base of these right-angled triangles has length 20, and each hypotenuse has length 20.309. If θ is the measure of the small angle in each right-angled triangle (which is the angle you are trying to find), then $\cos\theta = \dfrac{20}{20.309} = 0.985$, so $\theta = \cos^{-1} 0.985 = 10°$.

13. The correct answer is (A). To multiply a vector by a constant, multiply both coordinates of the vector by that constant. To add two vectors, add the first coordinates and add the second coordinates:

$$2v - (w + 3u)$$
$$= 2\langle 0, 7 \rangle - \langle 8, -2 \rangle - 3\langle -3, 5 \rangle$$
$$= \langle 0, 14 \rangle - \langle 8, -2 \rangle - \langle -9, 15 \rangle$$
$$= \langle 0 - 8 + 9, 14 + 2 - 15 \rangle$$
$$= \langle 1, 1 \rangle$$

14. The correct answer is (C). The surface area of a solid is the sum of the areas of each of its faces. The sum of the areas of the two outside rectangles is $(5 \times 10) + (5 \times 10) = 100$. The area of the inner rectangle is $6 \times 10 = 60$. The triangles are isosceles with a base of 6 and legs of length 5, which means that you can divide them into two 3-4-5 right-angled triangles to get their height, 4. Since the isosceles triangles have a base of 6 and a height of 4, they each have an area of $\frac{1}{2} bh = \frac{1}{2} (6)(4) = 12$, and so together the two triangular faces have an area of 24. Therefore, the surface area is $100 + 60 + 24 = 184$.

If you picked (A), you might have forgotten to account for the triangular faces. If you picked (B), you may have thought all the rectangular faces had an area of 50, and if you picked (D), you might have thought they all had an area of 60. If you picked (E), you may have forgotten to divide by 2 when calculating the areas of the triangles.

15. The correct answer is (E). Although you can simply plug in the given values to find the answer, it is much easier to first factor the numerator of the fraction to get $\dfrac{(x - y)(x + y)}{x - y} = x + y = \sin^2 29° + \cos^2 29° = 1$, since $\sin^2 a + \cos^2 a = 1$ for any value of a.

16. The correct answer is (C). First, since the dimensions of the prism are three consecutive integers that add up to 12, they must be 3, 4, and 5. The greatest linear distance between two points on the surface of the prism will be the distance between two opposite corners. This can be found using the formula for distance in 3 dimensions: $d = \sqrt{3^2 + 4^2 + 5^2} = \sqrt{50} = 7.07$.

17. The correct answer is (D). Remember that $i^2 = -1$ and use FOIL to expand the parentheses:

$$(3 + 2i)(2 - 5i)$$
$$= 6 - 15i + 4i - 10i^2$$
$$= 6 - 11i + 10$$
$$= 16 - 11i$$

If you picked (C), you might have thought that $i^2 = 1$.

18. The correct answer is (D). The mean will take a while to calculate, so it might be faster to try to solve this problem by first finding only the median and mode. There are 40 family members, which means that the median age is the average of the ages of the 20th and 21st family members: $\frac{33 + 34}{2} = 33.5$. The mode is the most frequently occurring age: 64. Because 64 is the second-highest age in the family, you can guess that the mean will be less than 64, so you can eliminate (A), (B), and (C). To distinguish between (D) and (E), you can guess that the mean will be less than the median, because there are more of the lowest ages than of the highest, but you should calculate it to be sure: $\frac{\Sigma}{n} = 31.55$. Therefore, (D) is correct: $64 > 33.5 > 31.55$.

19. The correct answer is (C). You can infer (I) because after the first round of data collection, there are 50 data points within a range of 9, and after the second round, there are 100 data points within a range of 29. This means that the data is more spread out after the second round, so the data set will have a higher standard deviation. You can infer (II) because the second round of data collection adds an equal number of data points above and below what the original median would have been, so the median won't change. You can't infer (III) because you don't know exactly what the data points are, only what range they fall within, so the mean could move up, move down, or stay the same.

20. The correct answer is (C). The period of the function $\sin \theta$ is 2π, which means that the function completes one wave over 2π units along the x-axis. Within each complete wave, it passes through every positive and negative value twice (once on the way up and once on the way down), except for 1 and -1. Therefore, over the period $[-2\pi, 2\pi]$, which has length 4π, the function will reach each value between -1 and 1 four times. In this case, $\sin \theta = 0.321$ at $\theta = -5.956, -3.468, 0.327,$ and 2.815.

21. The correct answer is (B). Because the question states that all y-values are less than or equal to 1, the graph cannot be cubic, logarithmic, or linear with a nonzero slope, since all these functions have a range equal to all real numbers. It could not be linear with a slope of 0 because lines have infinitely many lines of symmetry, not just 1. Therefore, you can eliminate (A), (C), and (E). It could not be exponential because exponential functions have no lines of symmetry, so you can eliminate (D). However, quadratic functions have one line of symmetry, and in this case the function could be $f(x) = -x^2 + 1$, for example. Therefore, (B) is correct.

22. The correct answer is (A). Translating the function $f(x) = x - b$ down 10 units results in the function $x - b - 10$. Since you know this is equal to $g(x) = x - 6b$, you can set these equal and solve for b:

$$x - b - 10 = x - 6b$$
$$-10 = -5b$$
$$b = 2$$

Therefore, you know that $f(x) = x - 2$, so $f(1) = 1 - 2 = -1$.

23. The correct answer is (D). A horizontal asymptote is found by dividing the coefficient of the highest-degree term of the numerator by the coeffcient of the highest-degree term of the demominator. In this case, since you know the function has a horizontal asymptote at $y = \frac{10}{3}$, the answer must be (D) or (E). Rational functions have a vertical asymptote when their denominator is equal to 0. (D) has a vertical asymptote at $x = 5$ while (E) has one at $x = 0$, so (D) is correct.

24. The correct answer is (C). The set of negative rational numbers, (I), does not contain a maximum element. This is because if any number q belongs to this set (i.e. q is a negative rational number), then $\frac{q}{2}$ (for example) will also be a negative rational number, and will be greater than q. The set of positive rational numbers, (II), also does not have a maximum element, because these numbers continue to infinity. However, the set of rational numbers r such that $r^3 \le 8$ has a maximum element of 2. Any rational number greater than 2 will not satisfy $r^3 \le 8$, so 2 is the maximum element of this set. Therefore, the only set with a maximum element is (III).

25. The correct answer is (D). Solving for $f(1)$ is straightforward: $f(1) = 5(1) + 3 = 8$. To solve for $f^{-1}(1)$, you need to find a value of x such that $f(x) = 1$. Set up the equation $1 = 5x + 3$ and solve for x to get $x = -\frac{2}{5} = -0.4$. Finally, $f(1) - f^{-1}(1) = 8 - (-0.4) = 8.4$.

26. The correct answer is (B). The shortest side of a triangle is always opposite from its smallest angle, and the longest side is opposite from the largest angle. Therefore, the longest side of the triangle is opposite from the 86° angle, and the shortest side, which is 2.3 cm long, is opposite from the 41° angle. Use Sine Law to find x, the length of the longest side: $\frac{x}{\sin 86°} = \frac{2.3}{\sin 41°}$. Solving for x gives you $x = 3.5$ cm.

27. The correct answer is (E). The y-intercept occurs when $x = 0$, and plugging in $x = 0$ shows you that $f(0) = -\frac{5}{8}$, which is negative.

(A) and (C) are incorrect because the denominator of the function, $2x^2 + 8$, can never equal 0, so the function has no vertical asymptotes or removable discontinuities. (B) is incorrect because the polynomial in the numerator is of a higher degree than that in the denominator, so the function has no horizontal asymptote. When $x = -2$, $f(x) = \frac{-8 - 5}{2(4) + 8} = -\frac{13}{16} \ne 0$, so -2 is not a root of this function and therefore (D) is incorrect.

28. The correct answer is (A). Since n is a positive integer, $2n$ is an even integer, so $(-1)^n\ 2n$ will always be an even integer, although it could be positive or negative depending on whether n is even or odd. Since x_n is this term plus 1, it will always be an even integer plus 1, and therefore will always be an odd integer.

If you picked (B), you might have forgotten the "1 +" at the beginning of the expression for x_n. (D) and (E) are incorrect because the sign of the term $(-1)^n\ 2n$ alternatives between positive and negative, so the sequence is neither increasing nor decreasing.

29. The correct answer is (A). To make carbon dioxide, for every carbon atom, you need two oxygen atoms (so, for c carbon atoms, you need $2c$ oxygen atoms). Let x represent the number of available oxygen atoms in a given experiment. In this experiment, if no atoms were left over when making carbon dioxide out of c carbon atoms and x oxygen atoms, then $2c$ would equal x, because the number of available oxygen atoms (x) would be exactly equal to the number of oxygen atoms needed to combine with the carbon ($2c$). However, some carbon atoms *are* left over, which means the number of available oxygen atoms (x) must be less than what is needed to combine with all the carbon atoms ($2c$), so $x < 2c$.

If you chose (B), (C), or (D), you may have confused the relationship between the atoms and their variables, for instance by using $2x$ instead of x to represent the number of oxygen atoms.

30. The correct answer is (B). You need to find when $a(1 - h)^2 + 1 < 1$, which is the same as finding when $a(1 - h)^2 < 0$. Since $(1 - h)^2$ is always either positive or 0, you need to find values of a and h such that a is negative and $(1 - h)^2$ is positive. Now that you know that a must be negative, you can eliminate options (C), (D), and (E). If $h = 1$ then $(1 - h)^2 = 0$, so you can eliminate option (A) as well. However, if $h = 0$ and $a = -1$, then $f(1) = -1^2 + 1 = 0 < 1$, so (B) is correct.

31. The correct answer is (B). At its introduction ($t = 0$), the value of the cryptocurrency is $c(0) = 54$. To find the value of t when $c(t) = 27$, you can solve for t:

$$27 = 54e^{-0.24t}$$
$$\frac{1}{2} = e^{-0.24t}$$
$$\ln\frac{1}{2} = -0.24t$$
$$-0.693 = -0.24t$$
$$t = 2.89$$

Therefore, the value of the cryptocurrency will halve after 2.89 years.

32. The correct answer is (A). Factor $y = x^4 - 81 = (x^2 - 9)(x^2 + 9) = (x - 3)(x + 3)(x^2 + 9)$. Next, divide this expression by $x - 3$ to get $\frac{y}{x-3} = (x + 3)(x^2 + 9) = x^3 + 3x^2 + 9x + 27$.

33. The correct answer is (B). Rewrite the equation as $\log_b y = \frac{x}{a}$. From the definition of a logarithm, this is the same as $b^{\frac{x}{a}} = y$. Raising both sides to the power of a gives you $b^x = y^a$.

34. The correct answer is (B). Since $x > 3$, use the second equation for $g(x)$: $g(5) = \sqrt{5-1} = 2$. Then $f(2) = 2^2 + 3(2) = 10$.

If you chose (A), you may have chosen the correct equation for $g(x)$, but the incorrect equation for $f(x)$ based on its domain. If you chose (C) or (E), you might have chosen the wrong equation for $g(x)$ based on its domain.

35. The correct answer is (D). The polar coordinates tell you that the angle between the positive x-axis and the line segment leading to point A is $30°$, and the angle between the positive x-axis and the line segment leading to point B is $60°$, which means that the internal angle at the bottom of the triangle is $60° - 30° = 30°$. Since both line segments have length 2, you know that the triangle is isosceles, and the remaining two angles are equal to one another. Therefore, since the sum of all the angles is equal to $180°$, angle B is equal to $180° - 30° = 150°$, and $\frac{150°}{2} = 75°$.

36. The correct answer is (D). First, calculate the volume of the entire cone, then subtract the volume of the small, unshaded cone from it. The volume of the entire cone is $V = \frac{1}{3}\pi r^2 h = \frac{1}{3}\pi(6)^2(36) = 1357.17\,\text{in}^3$. If the height of the shaded region is $\frac{2}{3}$ the height of the entire cone, then the height of the unshaded cone is $\frac{1}{3}$ the entire height, or 12 inches. By similar triangles, the radius of the base of the unshaded cone is $\frac{1}{3}$ the radius of the full cone's base, or 2 inches. Therefore, the volume of the unshaded cone is $V = \frac{1}{3}\pi r^2 h = \frac{1}{3}\pi(2)^2(12) = 50.27\,\text{in}^3$. The volume of the shaded region is $1357.17 - 50.27 = 1306.9 \cong 1307\,\text{in}^3$.

If you chose (A), you found the volume of the unshaded cone. If you chose (B), you may have thought the shaded region was $\frac{1}{3}$ rather than $\frac{2}{3}$ the total cone. If you chose (C), you may have made a mistake calculating similar triangles, and found the radius of the base of the unshaded cone to be 4 in. If you chose (E), you found the volume of the entire cone.

37. The correct answer is (D). You are given the vertex of the parabola, (1995, 3), and several points. Find the corresponding quadratic function by plugging the vertex, (h, k), and one other point, for example (1987, 35), into the vertex form of a quadratic function:

$$f(x) = a(x - h)^2 + k$$
$$f(x) = a(x - 1995)^2 + 3$$
$$35 = a(1987 - 1995)^2 + 3$$
$$32 = 64a$$
$$a = 0.5$$

Therefore, the function is $f(x) = 0.5(x - 1995) + 3$. Simply plug $x = 2018$ into this function to find the value of the lunchbox in the year 2018: $f(2018) = 0.5(2018 - 1995)^2 + 3 = 267.50$.

38. The correct answer is (D). Since the expression under the square root must be nonnegative, you know that $(x-3)$ and $(x+5)$ must not have opposite signs (because if one was positive and the other was negative, their product would be negative). Since $x+5 > x-3$, you know that if $x+5$ is negative then $x-3$ must also be negative, and if $x-3$ is positive then $x+5$ must also be positive. Therefore, you need to require that either $x+5 \leq 0$ or $x-3 \geq 0$, which means that either $x \leq -5$ or $x \geq 3$.

(A) is incorrect because $f(x)$ is equal to 0 at $x = -5$ and $x = 3$. (B) is incorrect because f is not one-to-one, so it does not have an inverse function. (C) is incorrect; the range of f is $\{y: y \geq 0\}$. (E) is incorrect because when $x = 0$ the function is undefined, so it does not have a y-intercept.

39. The correct answer is (B). The fastest way to solve this question is to remember the identity
$\cos 2\alpha = \cos^2 \alpha - \sin^2 \alpha = (\cos \alpha + \sin \alpha)(\cos \alpha - \sin \alpha) = 0.52 \times 1.32 = 0.69$.

If you didn't remember this identity, you could add the two equations to get $2\cos \alpha = 1.84$, so $\cos \alpha = 0.92$. You could then solve for $\alpha = 23.07°$, and then $\cos 2\alpha = \cos 46.14° = 0.69$. However, this method is much more time-consuming.

40. The correct answer is (D). For any positive integer, positive integer divisors come in pairs. If a is a factor of b, then $\frac{b}{a}$ is also a factor of b, since $a \times \frac{b}{a} = b$. Therefore, most positive integers have an even number of divisors. However, perfect squares have an odd number of divisors, because their square root is only counted once instead of twice (for example, the divisors of 16 are 1, 2, 4, 8, and 16). Therefore, since n^2 is a perfect square, it must have an odd number of divisors. The only odd number among the answer choices is 9.

41. The correct answer is (A). If $\log_b x = 2$, then $b^2 = x$. Since the question also tells you that $b = 2x$, you know that $(2x)^2 = 4x^2 = x$, or $4x^2 - x = 0$, which you can factor as $x(4x - 1) = 0$. The two solutions for x are $x = 0$ and $x = \frac{1}{4}$, but since logarithms are not defined at $x = 0$, you know that x must equal $\frac{1}{4}$.

42. The correct answer is (B). You can see that the graph is an ellipse. This means that both the x^2 and y^2 terms must be positive, so you can eliminate options (C), (D), and (E). Then, since the ellipse has a vertical major axis, you know that the denominator of the y^2 term must be greater than the denominator of the x^2 term, so you can also eliminate option (A).

43. The correct answer is (C). The domain of $f(g(x))$ will be all numbers that do not make the denominator of $f(x)$ zero. Keep in mind, however, that those numbers must first "pass through" $g(x)$. Therefore, any value of x that makes $g(x) = 2$ will not be included, because then the denominator of $f(x)$ would be 0. The only number that makes $g(x) = 2$ is $x = 3$, and so (C) is correct.

44. The correct answer is (C). The probability that a randomly thrown dart will hit the shaded ring is equal to the area of the shaded ring divided by the total area of the target. The total area of the target is $\pi r^2 = \pi (30)^2 = 2827.43 \text{cm}^2$. The area of the shaded ring is $\pi (20)^2 - \pi (10)^2 = 942.48$. Therefore, the probability that the dart hits the shaded ring is $\frac{942.48}{2827.43} \cong 0.33$, which is 33%.

45. The correct answer is (E). Plug in 90 for *dB*. The right side of the equation can be rewritten as $10 \log(10^{12} \times I)$, and dividing both sides by 10 gives $9 = \log(10^{12} \times I)$. Raising 10 to the power of each side gives you $10^9 = 10^{12} \times I$, so $I = 10^{-3}$.

46. The correct answer is (C). Read the question's description of the pendulum to find out its amplitude, period, and vertical shift. The pendulum ranges from a height of 5 cm to 21 cm, so its amplitude is $\frac{21-5}{2} = 8$ and its vertical shift is $\frac{21+5}{2} = 13$. Just from these pieces of information, you can already tell that (C) is correct, because it is the only answer option that has a vertical shift of 13 and an amplitude of 8.

The problem also tells you that the pendulum completes a full cycle (from greatest height to lowest height and back) in 8 seconds (4 to go down and 4 to come back up), so you know its period is 8. The period of a trigonometric function is found by dividing 2π by the constant in the bracket in front of the *t*, so you can check that option (C) has a period of $\frac{2\pi}{\frac{\pi}{4}} = 8$.

47. The correct answer is (B). To answer this question, first find the two points at which the line intersects the circle, and then find the distance between those points. Substitute $y = 7x - 25$ into the equation for the circle:

$$x^2 + (7x - 25)^2 = 25$$
$$50x^2 - 350x + 600 = 0$$
$$x^2 - 7x + 12 = 0$$
$$(x - 3)(x - 4) = 0$$
$$x = 3 \text{ or } x = 4$$

Find the two points of intersection by plugging $x = 3$ and $x = 4$ into the equation of the line. If $x = 3$, then $y = -4$. If $x = 4$, then $y = 3$. The distance between the points $(3, -4)$ and $(4, 3)$ is $\sqrt{(3-4)^2 + (-4-3)^2} = \sqrt{50} = 7.07$.

48. The correct answer is (D). The graph of $f(x) = \tan x$ has vertical asymptotes at $\frac{\pi}{2}$, $\frac{3\pi}{2}$, $\frac{5\pi}{2}$, and so on — in other words, at numbers of the form $n\pi - \frac{\pi}{2}$, where *n* is an integer. Since the question tells you that this function has vertical asymptotes at numbers of the form $\frac{n\pi}{3}$, you can conclude that the function you're trying to find must be a transformation in which the function $\tan x$ is shifted left (or right) by $\frac{\pi}{2}$, and also compressed horizontally by a factor of 3 (because it has asymptotes that occur 3 times as often, and that are not offset by $\frac{\pi}{2}$). Therefore, you are looking for a function with a horizontal shift of $\frac{\pi}{2}$ or $-\frac{\pi}{2}$ and a horizontal compression factor of 3. The function in (D) demonstrates both these transformations.

49. The correct answer is (E). Drawing a diagram may help you solve this problem. The area of a triangle is equal to half the base times the height. It will be easiest to think of BC as the base of this triangle, and the perpendicular distance from BC to A as the height. Since moving A along a straight line does not change the area of the triangle, and also does not change the length of the base (since B and C do not move), then you know moving A must not change the height either. This means that A must be moving along a line that is parallel to BC, since that is the only way that the height of the triangle (i.e. the distance from A to the line passing through BC) would not change.

Now, find the slope of the line passing through BC: $\frac{2-(-2)}{2-0} = \frac{4}{2} = 2$. The line along which A is moving is parallel to the line passing through BC, so it must also have a slope of 2. To find the equation, plug the point A into the slope-intercept form of the linear equation, $y = mx + b$: $0 = 2(-2) + b$, so $b = 4$, and the equation of the line is $y = 2x + 4$.

Once you found that the slope was 2, you could have picked (E) right away, since it is the only answer choice with a slope of 2.

50. The correct answer is (D). The easiest way to solve this problem is by process of elimination. All odd numbers are polite, since the number $2m + 1$ can be written as $m + (m + 1)$. Therefore, you can eliminate (C) and (E). Also, all multiples of 3 are polite, since the number $3m$ can be written as $(m - 1) + m + (m + 1)$, and so you can eliminate (A) and (B), since both are multiples of 3. Therefore, the answer must be (D).

To be more thorough, you could prove to yourself that all positive integers are polite except for powers of 2, which are not polite—but this fact takes some time and effort to realise. Here is a proof of the fact that powers of 2 are not polite.

If a number n can be written as a sum of consecutive positive integers, there are two cases to consider. Either it will be the sum of an odd number of numbers, in which case it will look something like this:

$$n = (k - a) + (k - a + 1) + \cdots + k + \cdots + (k + a - 1) + (k + a) = (2a + 1)k$$

where the second equality comes from simply combining like terms and factoring. The other case is when n is the sum of an even number of numbers, which will look something like this:

$$n = (k - a + 1) + \cdots + k + \cdots + (k + a - 1) + (k + a) = k(2a) + a = (2k + 1)a$$

In the first case, $(2a + 1)$ is an odd number because a is an integer, so $(2a + 1)k$ cannot be a power of 2 because it has an odd factor. In the second case, $(2k + 1)$ is an odd number because k is an integer, so by the exact same reasoning, $(2k + 1)a$ cannot be a power of 2. Therefore, if a number is polite, it cannot be a power of 2. Since 4096 is a power of 2, it is not a polite number.

Ivy Global

EDUCATION

Premium College Application Consulting Service

The college application process is more competitive than ever. Make your application stand out with Ivy Global's Premium College Application Consulting Service! Ivy Global has helped hundreds of students gain acceptance to the schools of their choice.

FOR A <u>FREE</u> HALF HOUR initial consultation with an experienced education consultant email us at: **<u>info@ivyglobal.com</u>**.

Consultations may be conducted in person or online via Skype, depending on your location.

OUR SERVICE PROVIDES:

- Academic and extracurricular assessments
- College fit assessment
- Help with essays, resumes, and personal statements
- Interview coaching
- Strategies for early decision/deferral/waitlist
- Test prep strategy (SAT/ACT)

Ivy Global

The World's Most
Comprehensive Test Prep

Order on ivy.gl/books

SAT Guide

The most comprehensive SAT Guide on the market. It includes helpful strategies, extensive up-to-date practice material, and free online scoring with detailed analytics to maximize improvement.

SAT - 6 Practice Tests

This book includes a detailed overview of the test, six full-length SAT practice tests, and free online scoring.

ACT Guide

All the content you need to succeed on the ACT with 3 full-length practice tests, extensive topic reviews, and free online scoring.

SAT Subject Tests - Literature

This is the most up-to-date guide, complete with a review of the essential content, extensive practice, and proven strategies to help you ace the test.

Notes

Notes

Notes

Notes

Notes

Notes

Fill out your answers on **cloud.ivyglobal.com**
to get a detailed score report.

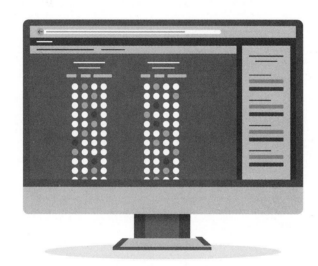